STUDIES IN HIGHER EDUCATION

DISSERTATION SERIES

T0383724

Edited by
PHILIP G. ALTBACH

Monan Professor of Higher Education
Lynch School of Education, Boston College

A ROUTLEDGEFALMER SERIES

SCHOLARSHIP UNBOUND
Assessing Service as Scholarship for Promotion and Tenure

KerryAnn O'Meara

Routledge
Taylor & Francis Group

LONDON AND NEW YORK

Published in 2002 by
RoutledgeFalmer
711 Third Avenue
New York, NY 10017

Published in Great Britain by
RoutledgeFalmer
2 Park Square, Milton Park
Abingdon, Oxfordshire
OX14 4RN

First issued in paperback 2014

Routledge is an imprint of the Taylor & Francis Group, an informa business

Library of Congress Cataloging-in-Publication Data

O'Meara, KerryAnn, 1971–
    Scholarship unbound : assessing service as scholarship for promotion and tenure / KerryAnn O'Meara.
        p. cm. — (Studies in higher education, dissertation series)
    Includes bibliographical references and index.
    ISBN 978-0-415-93223-3 (hbk)
    ISBN 978-0-415-76229-8 (pbk)

    1. College teachers—Promotions—United States. 2. College teachers—Tenure—United States. 3. Teachers and community—United States. I. Title. II Series.

LB2334 .O64 2001
378.1'21—dc21

2001034999

This book is dedicated to three generations: to my parents who were first to believe in me; to Dan, my husband, who always made me feel this was possible; and to our daughters Molly Adair and Emma Grace, who make me strive to be the best kind of person I can be. Thank you for encouraging and sustaining me in this work that I love.

TABLE OF CONTENTS

PREFACE

The original research from which this book derives was conducted under the direction of Dr. Robert Birnbaum, Professor Emeritus, University of Maryland College Park. I have always chosen teachers and mentors who I knew would challenge me, Bob did that and much more. I would like to thank Bob for his patience, careful reading and critique of my work, career advice, and for pushing me to be better than I ever imagined I could be. It is because I had the privilege of working with Bob that I am proud of this research.

I would also like to thank Dr. Cathy Burack from the New England Resource Center for Higher Education (NERCHE), who acted as a constant support, reader, coach, and friend. Cathy thank you for your help with my work, your encouragement during the moments when my spirit was most "tired," and most of all, for your friendship. Also, thank you to Cathy and Dr. Deborah Hirsch for continuing to find small consulting projects or NERCHE faculty professional service events for me to participate in to keep me interested in my topic and to help me to fund my site visits along the way.

Furthermore, thanks are due to Dr. Zee Gamson and the late Dr. Ernest Lynton who both served on my dissertation committee at different times and were kind enough to offer guidance on the direction of my study. Both Zee and Ernest's scholarship contributed in critical ways to my conceptual framework.

I am grateful to my dissertation committee members, Dr.(s) Barbara Finkelstein, James Greenberg, Katherine McAdams and Steven Selden, whose expertise helped to shape my methodology and contributed to my final product. Thank you for your time, interest, careful reading, and support.

During the last year of my dissertation writing I joined the Project on Faculty Appointments at Harvard University and my colleagues Dr.

Richard Chait and Dr. Cathy Trower. Thank you to Cathy Trower who carefully read and edited several of my chapters and rarely receives credit for all of the mentoring she has done for young women scholars. Dick Chait's thinking on tenure and organizational change enlightened my own thinking as I considered the implications of my findings. In addition, the HPFA team provided a warm, supportive nest to "gestate" in as I completed my dissertation and two other more spectacular creations.

SCHOLARSHIP
UNBOUND

CHAPTER ONE

Answering the Call

INTRODUCTION

Dr. Molly Hourihan, professor of education, was asked by a women's shelter to help design a "free university curriculum." The shelter was looking for guidance in how to structure the classes, design the curriculum, and evaluate its success. The innovative aspects of the project involved curriculum development, the design of interview protocols to assess student interests and faculty expertise, and assessment of outcomes for a unique population of students. Professor Hourihan's work required conceptualizing and drawing on understandings of adult student development, women's development, college teaching, and the research on transformative learning in nontraditional educational settings.

After designing the "free university curriculum," for the women's shelter Professor Hourihan began to reflect on the project and what she had learned. As she tried to relate this work back to her career as a scholar in the College of Education she had many questions. How can I link this service with my research and teaching? What is it about this work that makes it scholarship? How is this scholarship similar and different to my other research and teaching activities? Will my department chair and the promotion and tenure committee be able to assess my work as scholarship? What responsibility does my institution have to support me in this work?

The vignette above describes a special kind of faculty work called faculty professional service. The work was done by a faculty member within a college of education, a discipline with its own history, culture, traditions, policies, and criteria for evaluating faculty work. When properly documented, this work may be considered a form of scholarship. Around the country, colleges and universities struggle to determine how they can encourage faculty professional service and the important role faculty can play in sharing their expertise with communities and schools. Most academic reward systems prioritize scholarship over teaching and service. This book considers how faculty professional service can be assessed as scholarship and integrated into the reward system of higher education. More specifically, this book examines how faculty professional service was integrated into four college of education promotion and tenure policies and processes. Findings from case study research in this book suggest that implementing promotion and tenure policies that assess service as scholarship can increase consistency between an institution's service mission, faculty workload and reward system; expand faculty views of scholarship; boost faculty satisfaction, and strengthen the quality of an institution's service culture.

Studying academic reward systems and how faculty professional service might be assessed and rewarded as scholarship is not unlike a person entering an intricate maze of interconnected rooms. In the smaller rooms, there are procedural questions about how to make connections with communities, how to find other faculty and collaborate on projects and how to apply knowledge to these diverse settings and problems. As you walk into the next room there are issues of faculty workload, reward systems, and still further inside a room widens into questions related to the discipline and what constitutes professional practice in the community. Beyond this lies the largest rooms filled with questions about assessment of faculty work, the characteristics of scholarship, and finally the values that are embedded in academic culture.

Consequently, amending academic reward systems to include a broader definition of scholarship is a "messy business" that throws together issues of institutional mission, leadership, external forces, faculty socialization, and the nature of faculty professional service and scholarship into one complex puzzle. For this reason, I chose case study as my method of inquiry. Case study method allows a researcher to explore the contextual conditions within which people, policies, and decisions fall together (Yin, 1994; Guba & Lincoln, 1989; Merriam, 1988).

This book begins with an overview of the broader issues surrounding faculty professional service and academic reward systems, and a brief description of the methodology employed in this research. The second chapter provides context for the study by further describing why reforming faculty roles and rewards is salient today, why colleges are attempting to assess faculty service as scholarship, and why this study chose to narrow its investigation to College of Education. The third through sixth chapters are the real meat of this book. In these chapters the four descriptive case studies of PSU, MWSU, St. Tims, and Erin College are provided. The seventh chapter presents common themes and differences across the four cases. Finally, in the eigth chapter the findings are analyzed and implications drawn for academic leaders and scholars of organizational change and academic culture.

In the opening vignette, we read about Dr. Molly Hourihan considering how to use her expertise to help the women's shelter develop its free university curriculum. She considers this work part of her role as a faculty member in a university with a service mission, and a member of a discipline with a history of applied scholarship. At the end of this book, we will read about Dr. Hourihan's university, and their struggle to meet the challenge her work has put before them. Can Dr. Hourihan's institution live up to the rhetoric of their service mission, transform their academic reward system, and truly assess and reward her service as scholarship?

OVERVIEW

Community service has been integral to the overall mission of U.S. higher education since the later nineteenth century and the development of land grant and city colleges (Checkoway, 2001; Kennedy, 1997; O'Meara, 1995; Rudolph, 1962; Adamay, 1994). However, recent commentators both within and outside of higher education have criticized colleges and universities for neglecting the community service part of their mission, especially as it relates to helping partner cities develop effective solutions to the multiple crises they face (Gamson, 1997; Harkavy & Puckett, 1991; Bok, 1990; Levine, 1994). As a result of their lack of attention to the service mission of higher education, colleges and universities have missed opportunities to improve teaching, research, and service (Harkavy & Puckett, 1991; 1994; Taylor, 1997). Higher education institutions continue to represent potential resources for developing solutions to many of the complex problems of urban life currently facing cities (Checkoway, 2001; Levine, 1994; Boyer, 1990; 1995; Gamson, 1997). The increasing number of university-community partnerships, faculty service and outreach programs, and student volunteers represent a growing recognition on the part of colleges and universities that they should play a more significant role in confronting unmet social needs of their local communities. Concomitantly, mandates for colleges and universities to redirect their academic, physical, and human resources to aid their communities have come from internal and external constituencies.

Outside the academy, a growing dissatisfaction with the ivory tower along with mounting problems in education, public safety, health, and the environment are urging faculty to respond in applied, socially useful ways (Hirsch, 1996; Taylor, 1997). Ernest Boyer (1995) wrote in "The New American College," "a commitment to service as well as teaching and research was never more needed than now.... Higher education has more intellectual talent than any other institution in our culture. Today's colleges and universities surely must respond to the challenges that confront society" (p. A48).

Inside the academy, Boyer's (1990) *Scholarship Reconsidered,* which challenged the academy to work toward a seamless view of scholarship which cuts across teaching, research and service, has become one of the most widely read and utilized documents for universities redesigning their promotion and tenure documents. The recognized importance of this document, along with the movement toward action research (Ansley & Gaventa, 1997; Schön, 1983), the service-learning movement (Bringle & Hatcher, 2000; Gamson, 1995), some of the changes in promotion and tenure (Chait, 2001), and university engagement (AAHE, 2001) make this a particularly generative time for developing the outreach mission of the university. Each of these movements has made higher education take a hard look at the relationship between theory and practice in teaching, research, and service. These external and internal pressures have caused much debate in the higher education community about faculty work and the nature of scholarship (Lynton, 1995; Driscoll & Lynton, 1999; Walshok, 1995; Sandmann et al, 2000; Glassick, Huber, & Maeroff, 1997; Schon, 1995). While the focus for some time has been encouraging greater attention to teaching, scholars are now turning their attention to the role of professional service in higher education.

However, this trend within some colleges and universities to reexamine scholarship and reward faculty professional service as scholarship is working against a dominant professional culture that elevates research over all other kinds of professional work. Schein (1985) defines culture as "a pattern of basic assumptions- invented, discovered, or developed by a given group as it learns to cope with its problems of external adaptation and integration that has worked well enough to be considered valid and therefore has been taught to new members as the correct way to perceive, think, and feel in relation to their problems." Within graduate schools, within professional associations, within faculty reward systems, faculty are socialized into what Gamson and Finnegan (1996) have called a "cultural schema of scholarship" or research paradigm. This research paradigm is based on national rather than local allegiances, values research over teaching and service, and prizes pure over applied research (Gamson & Finnegan, 1996). According to Sewell (1992) this research paradigm operates through cultural schema and is reinforced and perpetuated through resources such as travel funds, released time, equipment, personnel lines, reputation and standing in an academic hierarchy. Research has shown that faculty who engage in a great deal of research make higher salaries than those who do not (Fairweather, 1991, 1993). However, it is not just individual universities that engage in self-perpetuation of a research paradigm. Research on institutional isomorphism suggests that there are social pressures that cause universities to compete against each other for resources (Jencks & Reisman, 1968; Milem, Berger, & Dey, 2000). For example, universities compete against each other for faculty with high publication productivity

(Milem, Berger, & Dey, 2000). In order to gain prestige each university becomes increasingly more focused on research. The conflicting forces of a public call for more faculty outreach and the internal reliance on a research paradigm have created a strong disconnect between internal reviews of faculty work and external expectations of universities (Checkoway, 1997; Gamson, 1997; Sandmann et al, 2000; Lynton & Elman, 1987).

If most universities and faculty members are caught in the web of a research paradigm, then why is it that some universities have acted contrary to this culture and rewarded service as scholarship? A question, which framed this research was: how were four campuses whose faculty had been socialized within a research paradigm able to change or amend their institutional culture, to think of scholarship in new ways, and to reward service as scholarship? The question of how universities were able to do this is a question of both culture and implementation. Defining, documenting, and assessing professional service within the university is perhaps just as challenging as overcoming or transforming institutional culture. While rewarding service as scholarship does not require total abandonment of research culture, or a wholesale rejection of research, it does require significant changes to academic culture. This study examined the process by which academic culture was amended and/or transformed to include service as scholarship.

CONCEPTUAL FRAMEWORK

The colleges and universities that are the subject of this study are organizations with long histories and complex cultures. Organizational theorists such as Birnbaum (1988), Bolman and Deal (1991), Schein (1985; 1992), and Senge (1990) have all studied how organizational culture impacts what people in an organization perceive and how they behave. Culture often takes the form of symbols, myths, rituals and "perceptions of reality that allow participants to establish consensus on appropriate behavior" (Birnbaum, 1988, p. 80). By providing "central tendencies" (Birnbaum, 1988, p.73), higher education culture is the stuff that brings faculty together to support such long held traditions as academic freedom, and intellectual honesty (Birnbaum, 1988). Senge (1990) discusses how mental models or "deeply ingrained assumptions, generalizations influence how we understand the world and how we take action," (Senge, 1990, p.8) and how individual actors come to act collectively and make decisions.

Colleges and universities are made up of many subcultures that interact and influence each other. One of these subcultures is the culture of the academic profession, where faculty work and make policy. Another subculture is the culture of specific disciplines, like colleges of education. In order for faculty professional service to be integrated into the reward system of a university, it must be accepted and integrated into the culture of the faculty. One assumption of this study was that the colleges and universities who had begun to integrate faculty professional service into their promotion and tenure systems and evaluate faculty service as a potential form of scholarship were doing something that most universities were not doing. In a 1996 Carnegie survey less than 20% of Provosts reported that applied scholarship was even being documented, much less assessed as scholarship (Glassick, Maeroff, & Huber, 1997). In a study of over 400 promotion and tenure guidelines, only about 6% had policies that reflected an effort in this direction (O'Meara, 1997). Yet evidence also suggested that faculty were reporting that they were doing professional service and there was a federal, state, and local mandate for it (Hollander, & Hartley, 2000). In addition, the dominant vision of scholarship on most universities had begun to expand to include teaching and professional service (Glassick, Huber, & Maeroff, 1997). Yet few campuses had taken the leap from encouraging this work to rewarding it through assessment as potential scholarship. The question became: Why is it so difficult for faculty members making promotion and tenure decisions to think of service as scholarship? What are the cultural assumptions, biases, myths, or central tendencies embedded in faculty training and academic culture that have kept faculty professional service from being considered scholarship?

PURPOSE OF THE STUDY

The purpose of this case study research was to understand how colleges and universities with exemplary programs for assessing service, assessed faculty professional service as scholarship within a college of education. The study described how these colleges defined scholarship and assessed faculty professional service as scholarship. The procedures through which faculty professional service was assessed for promotion and tenure and the outcomes of these procedures were analyzed. This study was concerned with how faculty within a single discipline assessed service as scholarship within their discipline. However, because this study explored promotion and tenure in four different types of universities, there were four different types of structures for promotion and tenure committees. Therefore, the study explored the assessment of service as scholarship in both college of education promotion and tenure committees and university-wide committees.

METHODOLOGY

A revelatory multiple case study method was adopted (Yin, 1994) in order to explore the process, procedures, outcomes, and culture of exemplary programs for assessing service. The case study method was particularly suited to this study of organizational culture because it was important to understand the contextual conditions within which people, policies, and decisions fell together (Yin, 1994; Guba & Lincoln, 1989; Merriam, 1988).

Case studies are well suited for exploring cultural issues in higher education and to examining university governance structures and processes (Kuh & Whitt, 1988; Tierney, 1988; Rice & Austin, 1988).

Four institutions were chosen because they had revised their promotion policies to include an expanded definition of scholarship, consistent with Boyer's (1990) framework. Each of the institutions claimed that they assessed and rewarded multiple forms of scholarship for promotion and tenure, including service as scholarship. The term promotion and tenure process is intentionally broad to encompass the decisions made by promotion and tenure committees and external factors such as voiced opinions and behavior of senior faculty, department chairs, deans, and candidates who influenced promotion decisions.

The Carnegie classification system was used as a tool to distinguish between university types in order to understand the values at play in four different types of institutions. A research, doctoral, master, and baccalaureate institution were chosen. The pseudonymous institutions-MidWest State University (MWSU), Patrick State University (PSU), Erin College, and St. Timothy (St. Tims)— were recommended by the New England Resource Center for Higher Education (NERCHE) and by the American Association for Higher Education's (AAHE) Forum on Faculty Roles and Rewards as exemplary for their attempts to assess multiple forms of scholarship for promotion and/or tenure.

Between 12 and 15 individuals from each institution were interviewed using semi-structured, open-ended question protocols. Participants included faculty members in the college/unit of education who were currently on the promotion and tenure committee and/ or had been within the last two years, education faculty involved in service as scholarship and those who were not (tenured and untenured), and the dean, department chairs, provost and other academic leaders involved in policy decisions around this issue. In addition to interviews, promotion and tenure guidelines, applicant portfolios and materials, policy documents, institutional reports and memorandum, meeting minutes, descriptions of service projects, guidelines for preparing promotion and tenure applications, and both on and off-campus accounts (Yin, 1994; Merriam, 1988) were reviewed. The documents were obtained through primary informants, through meetings with campus archivists, and from searches of electronic databases.

From the collected data, case reports were drafted that included all of the relevant material from multiple sources (Yin, 1994). From each larger case report, a narrative describing the process to assess service as scholarship at each college was crafted. Yin's (1989) explanation building process guided data analysis—pattern coding, memoing, and the development of shared and divergent theme statements, —first within each case and then across the four cases.

DEFINITION OF TERMS

Faculty professional service was defined for the purposes of this study as work by faculty members based on their scholarly expertise and contributing to the mission of the institution (Elman & Smock, 1985). NERCHE (1995) identified three key components of faculty professional service. Faculty professional service includes work that benefits an entity outside the institution. In engaging in professional service, faculty must use their capacities as experts in their fields. The products resulting from professional service are not proprietary, but are public, available, and shared.

Many scholars have referred to faculty professional service using different but largely synonymous terms. While Elman and Smock (1985) were the first to refer to professional service, "exclusively as work that draws upon one's professional expertise, and is an outgrowth of an academic discipline (p.43)," Rice (1991) refers to the same activity as the "scholarship of practice" or "the application of knowledge to the problems of society (p.125)." Schomberg and Farmer (1993) include "ultimate purpose for the public or common good," (p.16) within their definition. Most recently, the terms "engagement" and "civic renewal" have been used to describe the university and faculty role in public service (Checkoway, 2001; AAHE, 2001).

In this book, the term faculty professional service was used because it most accurately describes an individual faculty member's role (as opposed to institution's role) in trying to connect their service and scholarship. Faculty professional service may take the form of technical assistance, policy analysis, program evaluation, organizational development, community development, program development, or professional development. Faculty may conduct applied research and evaluation, disseminate knowledge, develop new products, practices or clinical procedures, participate in partnerships with other agencies or perform clinical service as part of their involvement in professional service (Schomberg & Farmer, 1993). In the field of education the clients of professional service are generally students, teachers, parents, community schools, community colleges, other colleges, state or federal departments of education, community development organizations, or institutions vested in education in non-traditional settings.

This study acknowledged as service activities which were both paid and unpaid. Just as faculty receive book or monograph payments and still include their book in their promotion and tenure review as scholarship, or teach classes at other institutions and include them in their teaching portfolios, whether service was paid or unpaid was unrelated to its inclusion as scholarship.

Scholarship is defined as work done by faculty discovering, integrating, applying, and teaching knowledge (Boyer, 1990). Scholarship is the "antithesis of rote and routine" (Lynton, 1995). Instead, the scholar (1) has work which includes discovery and originality (2) learns from the activity

(3) identifies and responds to the singular aspects of a situation (4) makes a reasoned choice of goals (5) chooses methods that fit objectives and are consistent with available resources (6) reflects on outcomes and (7) shares what was learned with colleagues (Lynton, 1995).

Faculty professional service versus scholarship. Not all faculty professional service is scholarship. Similarly, not all research and not all teaching activities meet Boyer (1990), Lynton (1995), and Glassick, Maeroff, & Huber's (1997) criteria for scholarship. For example, if Dr. Molly Hourihan had worked for the same shelter as a mentor, or had even done a similar project but had not connected it with her curriculum, teaching, and other research or if she had not documented how she had applied her academic expertise to the project, or if the project used methods and approaches that were not original or which did not create any new knowledge, her service would likely not be considered scholarship.

Exemplary colleges of education Colleges of education in universities that were identified with the help of AAHE and NERCHE as having made significant strides toward assessing service as scholarship in their promotion and tenure system were identified in this study as exemplary colleges.

SIGNIFICANCE

Although increasingly important, faculty professional service has received little research attention (Driscoll, 2000). By describing the criteria and procedures used by colleges with exemplary programs for assessing service as scholarship, the research may provide a guide for promotion and tenure committees making decisions about candidates with service experience in a college of education. It may also provide a useful analysis of how promotion and tenure decisions are made within colleges of education. Since colleges of education are one area of the university most involved in this kind of work (Kirshstein, 1997), it was appropriate to begin to study the reward system for service as scholarship there.

This study may contribute in concrete ways to encouraging high quality service and to illuminating or capturing the scholarship in service. The case study approach allowed a rich description of the faculty member's work that not only served those who evaluated the work, but was also useful in collegial discussions concerning professional service.

The next chapter further contextualizes the significance of this topic by briefly situating it within the history of faculty roles and rewards, the service mission of higher education, and colleges of education.

CHAPTER TWO
Unwrapping Service as Scholarship

After explaining this research on faculty service and reward systems to a colleague, I would expect three follow-up questions that address the, "So what" question. I can imagine my colleague wanting to know why this topic is timely and significant now, given the historic involvement of faculty in outreach. My colleague would likely want to know why I chose to study rewards in colleges of education, instead of other disciplines. Also, he/she might wonder why the attempt is being made to assess faculty service as scholarship, instead of simply rewarding it. This chapter attempts to answer each of these questions, and in doing so, makes an argument for the significance of this topic.

WHY ASSESS AND REWARD SERVICE AS SCHOLARSHIP?

In a 1983 article in *Change* magazine entitled, "A Crisis of Purpose: Reexamining the Role of the University," Lynton wrote:

> Acceleration of change requires faster and more effective dissemination of information and research to potential users-industry, governmental and legislative agencies, public and private sector bodies, and the public at large. Ours is a knowledge intensive society, and there is enormous and growing need not only for data but even more for analysis and synthesis, for explication, technical assistance, and public information...It is the increasing responsibility of the university not merely to be a principal source of new knowledge, but also to be instrumental in analyzing and applying this knowledge and in making it rapidly useful to all societal sectors (pp. 23, 53).

Because this responsibility falls upon the faculty, their involvement in this outreach should be recognized and rewarded as part of a spectrum of scholarship (Lynton, 1983; Driscoll & Lynton, 1999; Glassick; Maeroff, &

Huber, 1997). While community service has always been integral to the overall mission of U.S. higher education, rarely was it assessed and rewarded (Rudolph, 1962; Adamay, 1994). Ernest Lynton, Ernest Boyer, and Gene Rice were among the first academic leaders to suggest service should be assessed and rewarded as scholarship. A part of the reason professional service has not traditionally been rewarded as scholarship is the difficulty of assessing this kind of work.

The territory of assessing service as scholarship has been described as "soft and mushy ground" (Edgerton, 1995). Professional service is often confused with what Lynton (1995) has defined as "institutional citizenship" such as student advising, committee work, or other involvement in institutional operation, or "disciplinary citizenship" such as contributions to a disciplinary or professional association. Professional service does not occur in "standardized units that lend themselves easily to evaluation" (Edgerton, 1995, p. V). Faculty professional service frequently occurs through ad hoc projects and ongoing relationships, rather than discrete units with beginnings, endings and beneficiaries that are easy to define (Edgerton, 1995). In addition, the outcomes of professional service work may not be assessed through student evaluations, or in the form of articles in refereed journals. The artifacts of professional service may include revised curriculum or published results, but are more often community products that come in a variety of forms not previously evaluated for promotion and tenure.

For this and many other reasons, scholars who study higher education have long recognized that existing reward systems and structures in academic communities do not reward faculty professional service as they do teaching and research (Crosson, 1983; Fairweather, 1996; Rice, 1996; Ward, 1998). Crosson, (1983) Boyer (1990), and Lynton (1995) have all called for more sustained analysis of "the service mission in higher education as well as a more careful examination of the structures, policies and practices for delivering service" (Crosson, 1983, p.112).

Elman and Smock (1985) were the first to take on the issue of professional service in their National Association of State Universities and Land Grant Colleges, (N.A.S.U.L.G.C.) report, "Professional Service and Faculty Rewards." They argued that in order to encourage faculty professional service institutions must understand it as a form of scholarship and have ways to define, document, and evaluate it as scholarship for promotion and tenure. In his groundbreaking work, *Making the Case for Professional Service* Lynton (1995) called for each discipline to explore measures of quality for professional service. In a working paper for NERCHE, I described definitions, documentation, and criteria for faculty professional service that might be used by colleges and universities to redesign their promotion and tenure documents to better reward service. In 1997, Glassick, Huber and Maeroff, continued the work started by Ernest Boyer by outlining criteria to assess all forms of scholarly excellence (discovery, teaching, integration and application). In 1999, Driscoll and Lynton extended the faculty professional service frontier in their work, *Making Outreach Visible*, where they used case studies from different disciplines to illuminate how faculty might document their own service as scholarship for promotion and tenure.

This study will respond to the call for more analysis of faculty professional service (Crosson, 1983; Boyer, 1990; Lynton, 1995; Giles & Eyler, 1998) by examining a critical issue: the assessment of service as scholarship for promotion and tenure. The study will also respond to Lynton (1995) and Diamond's (1995) call for each discipline to develop measures of quality for professional service by focusing the examination within colleges of education.

The next section describes how the movement to assess service as scholarship fits within the larger national movement to reform faculty roles and rewards.

WHY REFORM FACULTY ROLES AND REWARDS?

While institutions have historically had unique features and cultures depending on their missions, histories and goals, increasingly they have responded to pressures to emphasize their similarities (Birnbaum, 1988). Recent studies confirm that faculty at all types of four year colleges and universities are spending more time engaged in activities associated with publication and research (Milem, Berger & Dey, 2000). Studies demonstrate that this "institutional drift" also known as "institutional isomorphism" where faculty in less prestigious institutions emulate the work characteristics of their peers at research universities and institutions (DiMaggio & Powell, 1983; Scott, 1995) and less prestigious institutions model their research standards after the most prestigious universities in order to increase their national standing (Reisman, 1956; Jencks & Reisman, 1968; DiMaggio & Powell, 1991; Jacobson, 1992; Dey, Milem, & Berger, 1997, 2000) has taken hold of higher education. In part a symptom and in part a cause of the increase in isomorphism is the nature of the academic reward structure that is becoming increasingly homogenized across institutional and disciplinary type (Massy & Zemsky, 1994; Fairweather, 1993).

Many commentators have noted the considerable changes in faculty roles and rewards over the last hundred years (Rice, 1996; Boyer, 1990, Jencks & Reisman, 1968). As American higher education shifted from colonial colleges to land grant research universities, the American professorate shifted from a "local orientation and campus community loyalty to disciplinary and departmental loyalty (Antonio, Astin & Cress, 2000, p. 375)." Although to different degrees depending on institutional type, a gradual shift or in some cases metamorphosis occurred in which faculty became more influenced by invisible colleges or networks of colleagues at other institutions than by local institutional or community priorities such as teaching and service (Rice, 1996; 2000).

While some argue that the adoption of research culture was the result of expansion, broadening of missions, and a corresponding need for legitimacy and direction (Gamson & Finnegan, 1996) others point to the simultaneous "rise to power of the academic profession" (Jencks & Reisman, 1968). Transformed by the "academic revolution" and forced to compete for resources, institutions were pulled, especially during the 1960s and 1970s, to emulate research culture (Dimaggio & Powell, 1983; Gamson & Finnegan, 1996).

By the late 1980s and early 1990s colleges and universities that had attempted to imitate traditional research culture in their faculty evaluation (by prioritizing research over teaching and service) experienced a fragmentation of sorts where faculty became dissatisfied with the disconnection between institutional mission, faculty interests, faculty workload and faculty rewards (Tierney & Bensimon, 1996; Ansley & Gaventa, 1997; Gamson, 1999). The term "scholarship" was synonymous with traditional research at most four year colleges and universities and did not describe the diversity of faculty work (Boyer, 1990).

Also by the 1980s and early 1990s pressures from within and outside higher education criticized colleges and universities for neglecting the teaching and service aspects of their missions (Bok, 1990; Harkavy & Puckett, 1991; Levine, 1994). Outside the academy, the public, boards of trustees, and state legislatures urged institutions and their faculty to become more intimately involved in the concerns of the day. Faculty were asked to become as involved in knowledge *dissemination* as they were in knowledge *discovery*. Lynton (1983) wrote, "It is the increasing responsibility of the university not merely to be a principal source of new knowledge, but also to be instrumental in analyzing and applying this knowledge and in making it rapidly useful to all societal sectors (pp. 23, 53). Ernest Boyer (1997) wrote, "The academy must become a more vigorous partner in the search for answers to our most pressing social, civic, economic, and moral problems and must reaffirm its historic commitment to what I call the scholarship of engagement (Boyer, 1997, p. 11). Consequently academic leaders found themselves in a quandary—how to maintain high standards for faculty scholarship (thereby continuing to increase their national standing) but also fulfill their teaching and service missions and align societal expectations with faculty workload and rewards.

At this point the national reexamination of faculty roles and rewards lead by AAHE (Rice, 2000), and the seminal work of Ernest Boyer in *Scholarship Reconsidered* (1990) offered colleges and universities an attractive solution. By redefining scholarship—as teaching, discovering, integrating and applying new knowledge—to include not only traditional research but also teaching and service activities, institutions might regain some balance between their teaching, research, and service missions. An assumption was made by academic leaders that if promotion and tenure-the foundation of faculty rewards—acknowledged multiple forms of scholarship, faculty would engage in work that most closely resembled their own strengths and talents and each unit within the university would contribute a more diverse portfolio to its constituencies.

Just four years after Boyer's (1990) *Scholarship Reconsidered* was published, 62% of Chief Academic Officers stated in a Carnegie survey that this work had influenced discussions about, and reforms of, faculty roles and rewards. Since then a great deal of work has been done by Edgerton (1995) Shulman (1983) and others to increase the status of teaching as a form of scholarship. This research is one of the first to take an empirical look at the outcomes of integrating an expanded definition of scholarship into academic cultures. While Boyer suggested academic reward systems be amended to assess and reward teaching, discovery, application and integration as scholarship, this study focused on the integration of service as scholarship in academic reward systems.

The next section describes the historic and current role education faculty play in regards to professional service and why this study focused on college of education reward systems.

WHY STUDY COLLEGES OF EDUCATION?

Of all of the disciplines, education faculty report engaging in the greatest amount of external service (Kirshstein, 1997). Antonio, Astin, and Cress (2000) found that faculty trained in education, along with social work and health education (considered other or service-directed disciplines) were the most committed personally and professionally to community service. There is a long history in education of university faculty engaging in action research, consulting, and professional development activities with schools.

Consequently, colleges of education in universities have an intrinsic stake in making sure faculty professional service is rewarded. However, the history of the development of colleges of education and more specifically the discipline of education has involved an up hill battle on the part of teacher educators for professional status, and this effort has not necessarily been strengthened by elevating the status of service.

Finkelstein and Efthimiou (1995) write about the development of the education profession from colonial days until today. Finkelstein maps the history of this profession in fifty-year increments, noting the following changes and developments. Between 1790 and 1840 the first concept of professionalism began to emerge as republican reformers like Catherine Beecher and Emma Willard defined teaching as a domestic enterprise and as a form of character education (Finkelstein & Efthimiou, 1995). Between 1840 and 1890 the precursor to the college of education or the normal school was built. These were vocational preparation centers where teachers learned not liberal learning but technical skills and had apprenticeship opportunities (Finkelstein & Efthimiou, 1995). During the span of time between 1890 and 1950, teacher educators shifted their emphasis on professional status based on moral or character education to an emphasis on expert skills in the measurement of intelligence, school evaluation, and educational planning (Finkelstein & Efthimoiu, 1995). Colleges of education were born within universities, and education faculty acquired new status as experts with research agendas, graduate programs, and professional associations (Finkelstein & Efthimiou, 1995). Finkelstein argues that by attempting to secure status for the profession of education by making a place for themselves as specialists the educational leaders created new and more elaborate hierarchies, which differentiated teachers from education faculty. Johnson wrote "university schools of education have tended to distance themselves from the training and concerns of classroom teachers (p.16)." In this drift toward educational authority through specialized research, colleges of education lacked a direct, intentional service relationship with schools, teachers, and communities. Finally, from the 1950s through to 1986, the new technocrats emphasized political and management issues in education such as merit pay, national curriculum standards, and stronger assessment procedures. (Finklestein & Efthimiou, 1995). However, more recently "architects of reflective practice and of cooperative learning communities have advocated for more integration of theory and practice in teacher education, more practice-based research, a reconceptualization of concepts of expert knowledge, and acceptance of more qualitative methods (Finklestein & Efthimiou, 1995)."

Just like the status of service within a university is linked to higher education history and culture, the status of professional service within colleges of education is linked to education's peculiar culture and development of what we now call colleges of education. For example, the history of colleges of education suggest that although colleges of education may be in a better place today to reward service then they have been before, those who wish to be rewarded for professional work within schools are still working against a culture which in many ways is designed to reward research over service. Because of the constant need of colleges of education to justify to universities that they are deserving of respect for their "scientific" work, for work that is not "moral" in nature, but rather "intellectual," the effort to reward service seems like a cultural shift backward toward a lower professional status of educators as "moral workers," instead of "scholars."

That having been said, faculty in colleges of education have historically, and currently, act as consultants on special educational issues. For example, Campoy (1996) states that 302 schools and universities have embraced school/university partnerships. Viechnicki, Yanity, and Olinski, (1997) claim that partnerships where faculty work closely with teachers, students, parents and administration can decrease, "the long lag time between research conducted at the university and the implementation of its findings in school settings, the lack of relevance to classroom concerns and realities and the artificial features of experimental procedures imposed on practitioners (p.3)." Despite the history of innovative applied research and service between faculty and educational organizations, little research describes ways to reward faculty for this work or assess it as scholarship (Ward, 1998; Giles & Eyler, 1998). Similar to the rest of the university, few colleges of education have made the leap from encouraging service among its faculty to actually rewarding service as scholarship for promotion and tenure.

Education professional associations have begun to consider the importance of rewarding faculty for their professional service as demonstrated by a statement made by the National Education Association on Faculty Reward Structures. "Institutions whose mission is community outreach should reward service. Service is a major... but often misunderstood and underrated component of the triad of research, teaching, and service. Higher education faculty impact their communities, states and the nation through their service activities" (Diamond, 1995, p.157).

CONCLUSION

In summary, this study is timely for three reasons. First, because now more than ever faculty are being called upon to share their expertise with communities, and without reward systems that support this work it is unlikely university faculty will be able to meet this demand. Second, in recent years reward systems have become increasingly homogenized across institutional type, rewarding mostly research activity. Little to no research has explored how modifications to traditional tenure systems-such as Boyer's expanded definition of scholarship- may impact this trend and its effects on faculty work life. Third, faculty in colleges of education have the most to loose from being considered "nontraditional scholars." Reward systems that truly assess service as scholarship have the potential to greatly impact the status of education faculty within colleges and universities.

The next four chapters describe what happened when four colleges of education attempted to change their cultures and reward service as scholarship.

CHAPTER THREE

Patrick State University

On June 12, 1996, Patrick State University's Faculty Senate adopted an amended set of promotion and tenure guidelines that expanded the definition of scholarship, differentiated between community service and service as scholarship, and instituted a set of criteria to assess and reward service as scholarship. The new guidelines were the result of deliberations by the College of Liberal Arts and Sciences (CLAS), a university-wide committee, and 20 faculty discussion groups. After PSU confirmed the new 1996 guidelines, each college within the university was given the task of revising its promotion and tenure guidelines in accordance with the new university guidelines. The School of Education began implementing their new guidelines in fall 1996. This case describes the process by which PSU, and specifically its School of Education, changed its promotion and tenure guidelines to assess and reward service as scholarship.

The Culture of Patrick State University

Patrick State University (PSU) is a public metropolitan university located in a northwestern city with a population of over one million. The campus is nonresidential, with parks, green spaces, cafes, and galleries positioned throughout so that visitors feel as if they are on a college campus and visiting part of the city at the same time. No clear boundaries separate the campus from the city.

Just over 6,000 full-time and 5,000 part-time undergraduate students and 3,000 full- and part-time graduate students attend PSU. Extensive evening and summer session courses accommodate nontraditional students. Most students live in or near the city and work while they attend the university. Because students tend to be career-oriented, there is a strong emphasis on professional school preparation in both the undergraduate and graduate schools. Over 70 percent of degrees granted by Patrick State

University are in business and marketing, engineering, education and other career-oriented programs.

PSU's 1,000 faculty, 750 of whom are full-time, are organized into eight colleges. Faculty responsibilities include teaching three courses each semester in addition to extensive advising, research, and committee assignments. Historically, most university-wide decisions are made through faculty governance or by the president or provost, rather than by the deans. The faculty senate represents all faculty and colleges and plays an important role in approving major curriculum and policy decisions.

PSU lives in the shadow of the state's flagship land grant campus, which receives greater visibility and funding from the state legislature. Whatever resources PSU is able to garner come through difficult political struggles with the state legislature. In fact, their state is one of the worst in the country for funding of higher education. From the mid 1980s through the early 1990s, the percentage of the state budget that went toward higher education steadily declined, causing PSU to operate in a perpetual budget crisis.

PSU is a young institution, founded in 1946. One administrator said the institution did not have as much to lose from risk-taking as other institutions because PSU is already "a wart on the back of higher education." By this, he meant that both research universities and liberal arts colleges would look down on PSU for its professional focus (as opposed to research and teaching), no matter what it did. Therefore, there was no reason for the university not to "be itself."

Historically, the university responded rapidly to change and evolved to fit the changing needs of students, faculty, and the city. Whether the result of strong academic leadership, a need to respond to fiscal problems, the youth of the institution, or being in the shadow of the land grant university, there is a tendency on this campus to innovate.

PSU's motto, "Let Knowledge Serve the City," is written on the side of a large bridge at the campus entrance. There has always been a strong identification among faculty, students, and staff with PSU's urban service mission. Part of this mission is understood as a commitment to educating a diverse student body for professions throughout the city and state. Another part involves conducting research on social problems and then applying that knowledge to mitigate city education, business, environmental, and social problems. The institution's reputation for this kind of applied research attracts many graduate students and faculty members to the institution.

The School of Education

The School of Education exemplifies PSU's commitment to urban education and service, ability to adapt to change, and strong connections with the practitioner community. The School of Education is a medium-sized college of 60 full-time and 20 part-time faculty, housed in a five-story building on the corner of a major avenue that cuts through the middle of campus. The faculty are organized into three departments, each of which has a department chair: Special Education and Counseling, Curriculum and Instruction, and Educational Administration. Prior to 1989, the School of Education was described by some as having a "normal school" orientation, meaning that the focus was on undergraduate teaching degrees. In 1989, however, the School of Education hired a new dean, who formed an advisory committee of education faculty that recommended a change in the school's focus from undergraduate to graduate education.

At this time, rather than choosing to strengthen the research mission, which is most often associated with graduate schools, the dean made a conscious decision to encourage the School of Education to become a leader in the area in which it had the most resources—service to the profession through exemplary teaching and service. The dean and other administrators wanted the School of Education to become a place that helped professionals apply research to educational problems.

Beginning in the early 1990s, in order to stabilize its graduate student enrollment, make its programs more competitive, and strengthen its service mission, the School of Education made efforts to establish partnerships with local schools. These partnerships were vehicles through which the College could develop new field-based masters cohort programs, engage faculty and students in action research projects, and improve the relationship between the College of Education and nearby urban schools. By 1991, it was clear that in order to move the school toward its goal of exemplary teaching and service, the reward system for faculty would need to change.

The predominant reward system at PSU is promotion and tenure. Historically, PSU's procedures for promotion and tenure were very similar to those at other universities. Faculty submitted portfolios of their teaching, research, and service to a department or college-wide committee of six to eight faculty. The committee discussed the candidate's portfolio for two to five meetings, then took a majority vote by secret ballot. They submitted their decision to the dean of the college, who most often confirmed but could, in fact, overturn their decision; the dean in turn submitted the decision to the provost and Board of Trustees, who ultimately granted or denied tenure and/or promotion. Since there was no university-wide committee, the candidate's fate lay in the hands of their department (or college) colleagues and the dean.

Before the 1990s, the School of Education promotion and tenure process operated on fairly traditional lines, and research and publications were the keys to success. According to faculty in the School of Education and academic administrators, because junior faculty often self-selected out of the process prior to standing for tenure, or were asked to leave if they did not have a strong record of publication, there was a high rate of success among those who actually applied for tenure. Despite the fact that the School of

Education was traditionally very concerned with the quality of research in tenure decisions, it had always been willing to accept less traditional forms of academic writing (e.g. grant applications, articles in practitioner journals, curriculum designs) as evidence of the quality of a faculty member's work. This provided some flexibility in the promotion and tenure system, but by 1991 education faculty, along with others in the university community, were expressing concern that the reward system did not reflect actual workload. The term "scholarship" was synonymous with "research" in PSU's promotion and tenure guidelines and a number of faculty felt this definition of scholarship was too narrow for a place like PSU. Consequently, momentum was building toward change.

In the next section, the steps taken by the PSU and the School of Education to realign the urban service mission and actual faculty workload with the reward system are described.

Moving Toward Change

As early as 1989, PSU's provost, associate provosts, and faculty began conversations to clarify PSU's mission as part of a strategic planning process. There was consensus that PSU had a distinct place in the state system as an urban institution and a special responsibility to connect its research and teaching with the life of the city. In the late 1980s, the strategic plan committee discussed ways to weave the "let knowledge serve the city" motto into how faculty, department chairs, and board members constructed their work. Those who worked on the strategic plan made connections with other urban and metropolitan universities and began to see that PSU had the potential to be a leader among metropolitan universities connecting knowledge resources with city issues. The provost wanted to make changes to the reward system to reflect a stronger emphasis on service and teaching as potential forms of scholarship. However, it was not until 1991 that the university began to draft a formal strategic plan and mission reflecting the idea of service as scholarship.

Between 1991 and 1995 five changes occurred that led Patrick State University to embark on a new course that, in turn, led it to redefine "scholarship" and amend its promotion and tenure system. These changes included 1) a new President who reaffirmed the university's urban service mission; 2) internal restructuring to align the university's structure with the mission; 3) budget cuts that forced a curriculum transformation; 4) increased emphasis on service learning nationally and within the university community; and 5) faculty involvement in the national movement to redefine scholarship. While each of these events is described individually, they were seamlessly connected. These elements created the impetus for, vision behind, and success of subsequent changes to the reward system in the years between 1991 and 1995.

A New President with a Vision

In 1991 PSU hired a new president, Dr. Cathy Hall, a biologist by training who was recruited to be an agent of change. The new president and the provost were kindred spirits; they easily agreed on what needed to be done to move the university toward its urban mission. Almost immediately, Dr. Hall introduced her goal that PSU could be an exemplar for other institutions as an "urban grant university." She was interested in the service mission of the institution and, more specifically, in transforming the PSU reward system to reflect a commitment to service as scholarship

Faculty reported that this vision "dramatically opened people up." There were faculty and administrators who had always been interested in PSU's reinvesting in the service mission but were afraid that they might be accused of pushing a "nonacademic" or "softer" PSU. After the new president discussed PSU's potential to engage in service as scholarship, faculty started talking to each other about the service mission, using the excuse that "this is the direction our president wants us to go." Clearly, Dr. Hall's speeches and conversations with faculty and department chairs sent a powerful message that encouraged the campus community to move forward with the idea of service as scholarship.

Internal Restructuring

During 1991 and 1992, with the support of the president, the provost's office worked with a committee of faculty and administrators to rewrite the mission and strategic plan to be more explicit about PSU's commitment to service scholarship. In fall 1992, the provost began the process of internal restructuring to align the structure of the university with the new mission and strategic plan. Of particular importance to the provost was putting administrative and faculty resources to work on the "let knowledge serve the city" mission. Realizing that no structures or supports were in place to carry out the strategic plan (which emphasized service as scholarship, service-learning, community partnerships, and faculty service projects) the Provost's office decided to combine alumni publications and public relations into an Office of Community Relations that in turn developed partnerships with city organizations.

A task force established to explore the issue of community and university partnerships and how to support them wrote a report recommending the formation of a community outreach office, headed by a new director of outreach. An education faculty member took this position and began connecting faculty with community projects. A federal grant to stimulate involvement in service-learning and an anonymous gift to the university at about the same time provided funding for sustaining faculty partnerships with community agencies, state offices, and schools. The community relations office merged into the new community outreach office. Thus, after the mission and strategic plan were rewritten to reflect the stronger service emphasis, more internal resources were leveraged to sustain the new commitment. Additional staff was hired and human and financial resources were provided to faculty who wanted to integrate service-learning into their coursework or transform their service into scholarship.

Budget Cuts Spur a Curriculum Transformation

At about the same time the university rewrote its strategic plan to strengthen its service mission, PSU was faced with budget cuts. The state legislature put PSU on notice that for the next six years their state funding would be reduced, a decision that resulted in hard choices for PSU. Past budget cuts had already trimmed so much of the university that PSU was now faced with the prospect of cutting entire undergraduate programs. However, the provost decided entire programs could not be eliminated without harming the long-term health of the institution and significantly lowering morale. This meant that PSU's administrators and faculty needed to consider ways to totally restructure its academic spending, which forced the university to examine what it wanted its general education program to accomplish and how that goal could be integrated with PSU's mission.

The committee assigned to restructuring the general education program asked themselves, "how can we integrate our urban mission and general education program, even as we attempt savings?" The Provost recalled that discussions among committee members invoked interest in, and support for, student and faculty service. The committee experimented with different options, such as team teaching, integrating technology into course structures, and introducing service-learning into the curriculum. Departments across campus became involved in these innovations, leading faculty to see opportunities to link their own scholarship with community activities. Most importantly, service learning became a new focus for academic work throughout the undergraduate program. Some, but not all of these innovations eventually saved the university money through reduced course offerings, increased student enrollment, and for-credit internships. Faculty and staff agreed that both the curriculum and faculty morale were enriched by the curriculum transformation process.

The Service-Learning Movement

Because the newly revised undergraduate curriculum required that every PSU student have at least one capstone service-learning experience and most of the general education courses added a service-learning component, most PSU faculty were involved in service-learning in some way by 1993–94. A national service-learning movement in higher education also contributed to faculty in all disciplines becoming more involved in service learning. Faculty from PSU attended national conferences and joined national associations dedicated to service-learning.

Since teaching service-learning courses required additional work that had not previously been a part of faculty workload, the increase in the number of PSU faculty teaching service-learning courses created a strong interest in changing the reward structure. Faculty said to their department chairs, provost, and president, "if we're going to teach this way and it's going to have implications for our scholarly agenda, then we need to look at the promotion and tenure process."

National Redefining Scholarship Movement

During this same period, the provost sent faculty, department chairs, and associate provosts to the American Association of Higher Education's (AAHE) National Forum on Faculty Roles and Rewards conference to discuss with other campuses the service mission of higher education and ways to redefine scholarship. The provost encouraged involvement in national conversations in order to inspire faculty leadership and bring ideas back to campus. He distributed publications on redefining scholarship to faculty leaders and invested significant resources in faculty attending events that would help them to see PSU's effort to redefine scholarship as part of a larger movement within higher education. This interaction with other universities and the national movement toward redefining scholarship clearly had a significant influence on the climate and impetus for change at PSU.

All of these factors coalesced to spark the first steps toward a permanent change to promotion and tenure policies and practice. The first change came in the School of Education.

School of Education Changes: Weighting System for Tenure and Promotion

In 1991 and 1992, as the university moved toward a more service orientation, an increasing number of education faculty became involved in service with the State Department of Education, schools, and communities. Faculty interest in professional development schools—a national model for working with K–12 teachers on innovative teaching techniques, applications of research, and new approaches to educational problems—increased. Changes in the culture at PSU, outside pressures from the city and the State Department of Education for the school to become more intimately involved in service, and an accreditation evaluation that recommended that the school create more School of Education-K–12 partnerships, dovetailed to propel the School toward more outreach.

While the promotion and tenure system throughout the university heavily favored research, most faculty were more involved in teaching and service than research, leaving little relationship between what was required of faculty and the reward system. In addition, many education faculty felt that their teaching and service was a form of scholarship, but there was no formal way to present it as such for promotion and tenure. The dean formed a committee to discuss how the School of Education could align its reward system with the work faculty were actually doing.

The committee suggested a weighting system solution along with a reflective narrative requirement called the "scholarly profile." The School of Education's new weighting system for promotion and tenure allowed faculty to indicate how much time they spent on teaching, research, and service by assigning a minimum weight of 20 percent and a maximum weight of 50 percent to each of the three areas. Faculty were expected to provide evidence in scholarly profiles that substantiated their weighting choices. The scholarly profile, which was limited to 2,500 words, gave the context for the portfolio, indicated a scholarly agenda, guided the reader through the portfolio, and explained plans for future scholarship. Although these changes did not specifically describe teaching and service as potential forms of scholarship, the scholarly profile became a vehicle through which education faculty could make their case for why their service was scholarship.

In 1993, the dean hired an assistant professor whose main focus was the development and implementation of professional development schools. Almost immediately, this person involved at least 12 other faculty in service projects with professional development schools. Therefore, between 1991 and 1993 the School of Education made significant changes both in terms of its new weighting system for tenure and promotion and in providing significant resources to professional development schools.

Redefining Scholarship at Patrick State University

The CLAS Report

Many of the faculty involved in the undergraduate curriculum transformation, service-learning, and service as scholarship were from the College of Liberal Arts and Sciences (CLAS). Therefore, it was no surprise that CLAS was the first to officially suggest a change to the reward system. By December 30, 1994, a committee of faculty in the CLAS prepared and published the *CLAS Report on Redefining Scholarship*. This report stated, "The mission of CLAS requires a definition of scholarship that values teaching, research, and service. This document contains our definition of scholarship and its application to teaching and service" (p. 3). The conclusion included a charge to CLAS departments to begin discussions of how they could redefine scholarship in ways specific to their fields and encouraged faculty to consider how to redefine scholarship for promotion and tenure.

The Provost Appoints a Committee

In fall 1995, the provost appointed a university-wide committee of ten faculty, two deans, the provost, and associate provost to suggest revisions to PSU's existing promotion and tenure guidelines and charged it with reviewing PSU's existing promotion and tenure criteria to ensure that the criteria rewarded activities that supported PSU's mission. The committee was instructed to focus on criteria for tenure and promotion to associate and full professor and not to address merit-raise issues.

Committee: Literature Review and Deliberation

The CLAS task force report, Boyer's *Scholarship Reconsidered* (1995) and an early draft of *Scholarship Assessed* (1998) were assigned as required reading for the committee. In addition to this intellectual and scholarly foundation, several committee members visited other campuses that had revised promotion and tenure processes to assess and reward multiple forms of scholarship. Ernest Boyer and Ernest Lynton visited the campus and held "how-to" workshops, and the committee followed the work of twelve other metropolitan universities that were on a similar journey.

The university committee met over two semesters and produced a draft report. Since most of the committee members were predisposed to rewarding service and teaching as scholarship, there was little debate about whether or not to amend the promotion and tenure guidelines. This allowed the committee to spend most of its time discussing *how* to amend the guidelines. It was more difficult to agree on what documentation, evidence, and criteria should be used to document and assess teaching and service as scholarship than that it should occur. Since these faculty had the most experience assessing research for promotion and tenure, they struggled with how to assess the quality of scholarship outside of a peer-reviewed journal system. The committee relied on the CLAS report and Boyer's *Scholarship Reconsidered* (1995) in its deliberations and, in some cases, excerpted entire sections from these texts for its draft report, including criteria to assess multiple forms of scholarship.

The Campus Reacts

The draft of suggested revisions was sent to all faculty on April 27, 1995, and in May, the committee held over 20 small-group discussions to discuss proposed changes. The committee also met with and received feedback from every department. There were "town hall" meetings at which anyone in the university could discuss the changes to promotion and tenure policies and processes. Supported by the provost, the committee created as many opportunities for feedback as possible, trying to ensure that no faculty member or administrator could say later that they did not have a voice in the process. Correspondence describing these meetings suggested, and faculty and administrators recalled, that few faculty in these discussion groups and town hall meetings disagreed with the idea that teaching and service could be scholarship. However, faculty convinced the committee to revise the draft to say that while all faculty would be expected to engage in teaching, research, and service, no faculty member would be expected to excel in every area.

New drafts were circulated around the university. Committee representatives consulted with the faculty senate and the faculty union, showed them amendments to the draft, and kept them abreast of progress.

Academic administrators from the president and provost's office played a critical role in helping the committee and small-group discussion process move along. Some served as advocates for this new form of scholarship and appeared to work with others to "convince" them that certain kinds of service could be scholarship. Others simply listened to faculty and collected feedback. In addition, academic administrators listened to the national conversation on redefining scholarship and brought information to the committee about how other campuses were dealing with similar issues.

Although the dean of the School of Education was on the university committee that created the changes, the deans as a group did not play a major role in this process. An academic administrator described this phenomenon.

> The deans are a big void in this whole strategy. You will observe that I'm talking about departments and faculty and about the infrastructure units that were created to support these new strategies and about task force and faculty governance. The deans were not there. The deans pretty much reserved the right to be reviewers and distant critics of the process and the outcomes. They have not been active participants in the change conversations or the implementation efforts. A lot varies across the deans, to one degree or another. But in large part this has been an interesting partnership of executive administration and regular faculty.

While the president inspired the change to the promotion and tenure guidelines, she was not visibly involved in committee decision making or the town hall meetings. She signaled her support but left the actual decision making with the provost and faculty senate.

In summary, academic administrators and faculty agreed that the process to develop new promotion and tenure guidelines was an interesting alliance between administration and faculty. There were a few faculty from every college who were very involved in the process, and all faculty became aware of the process. The disadvantage of PSU's process was that three groups of stakeholders who would later have the most important roles in implementing the new policies-Deans, department chairs, and senior faculty on the promotion and tenure committee- (at least in education) were only moderately involved. Deans, department chairs, and senior faculty who sat on promotion and tenure committees, were later given the task of implementing a policy which most of them had not personally developed, even if they eagerly or vaguely approved. The new policies passed with little resistance because they seemed to offer something for everyone. The details of implementation would become more controversial than the process to develop the policies.

Revisions to PSU Promotion and Tenure Guidelines

After a year of discussion across the campus, PSU's Faculty Senate adopted a revised set of guidelines on June 12, 1996. They were approved within a month of having been submitted, a quick turn-around time compared to how long it had taken the faculty senate to make other major decisions. The minority of faculty who disagreed with the changes had many opportunities to discuss, argue, and negotiate, so that their perspectives were incorporated into the new document. Generally, there was widespread approval of the revised promotion and tenure guidelines. Those who were not satisfied were resigned to the changes.

The criteria to evaluate scholarship in the revised guidelines were identical to that presented in the earlier CLAS report. In fact, both the CLAS report and 1991–92 School of Education revisions to tenure and promotion evaluations contained the idea of the "scholarly agenda," which became part of the new amended university-wide promotion and tenure guidelines.

The major changes had to do with defining, documenting, and then assessing multiple forms of scholarship. Since this case study focused on service as scholarship, changes in this area are described below.

Service as Scholarship: New Criteria

For the first time, service was defined as a potential form of scholarship. Scholarship was described as having four expressions: discovery, integration, interpretation, and application. Certain kinds of service were the scholarship of application. The committee changed the categories of faculty activities from "instruction, faculty research and other creative activities, and service," to "teaching and curricular activities, research and creative activities, service as scholarship, professionally related service, and governance." The 1996 guidelines recognized that the first three categories could be performed in scholarly ways.

The new criteria distinguished "service tied directly to one's special field of knowledge and that engages a person's scholarship," from governance and professionally related service. The following passage in the 1996 guidelines further defined service as scholarship.

> Such activities may involve a cohesive series of activities contributing to the definition of problems or issues in society. Not all external activities are service as scholarship in the sense intended here. For example, faculty members who serve as jurors, as youth leaders or coaches, or on the PTA do so in their role as community citizens. In contrast, service as scholarship activities that support promotion and tenure advancement fulfill the mission of the department and of the University and utilize faculty members academic or professional expertise.

The changes not only defined service as scholarship, but also advocated faculty participation more clearly. A statement was added that said, "PSU highly values service scholarship as a part of faculty roles and responsibilities."

The new policies gave greater guidance on how to document service as scholarship. They strongly recommended that evaluation of service as scholarship consider publications, honors, awards, and recognition; adoption of models to solve problems; substantial contributions to public policy; models that enrich the life of the community; and evaluative statements from clients and peers. The new guidelines also stated that, "scholars engaged in service as scholarship should disseminate innovations to audiences." A sample curriculum vitae addendum to the promotion and tenure policies included an example of how to list service as scholarship activities.

Faculty were now expected to form a scholarly agenda, using departmental and university missions as guides. Scholarly agendas were reflective essays intended to "articulate intellectual, creative questions or problems, describe a proposal to contribute toward knowledge, clarify how research, teaching, service, and governance activities flow together, and articulate a relationship between a faculty member's work and the departmental mission and goals." Candidates were told that their scholarly agendas should be developed proactively to articulate their individual focus and contributions to knowledge through varying weights and emphasizes on each of the scholarly responsibilities of research and creative activities, teaching and curricular activities, and service as scholarship. The new guidelines also stated that not only academic colleagues but also community partners and professionals could assess the quality of candidate's scholarship.

Institutional Support for Change

After the faculty senate confirmed the new guidelines, they were widely disseminated throughout the university. Directly following this dissemination and throughout the next two years, the provost's office provided institutional support to the implementation of the guidelines and tried to ensure widespread understanding of the new definition of scholarship. The Center for Academic Outreach set up multiple workshops for deans, department chairs, and promotion and tenure committees, including those in the School of Education, to practice applying the new criteria, using case studies of faculty involved in service as scholarship. The center also provided small faculty grants for service-learning and service as scholarship projects. The director helped faculty publish their writing about teaching and service as scholarship and sent out articles related to assessing multiple forms of scholarship across campus.

The School of Education

Each of PSU's colleges was involved in the university-wide process of redefining scholarship and rewriting the tenure and promotion guidelines to different degrees. The dean of the School of Education sat on the university committee. A few education faculty participated in the small-group discussions and town hall meetings. All education faculty remembered the process occurring, and all but a few remembered supporting it, according to education faculty, department chairs, and the dean. Several academic administrators felt the School of Education was not as involved in the university-wide process as they should have been. Education faculty, however, did not feel that they were uninvolved in the process; in fact, they felt their weighting system was a model for the rest of the university to follow. The disconnection between central academic administration and School of Education faculty perceptions of this process was symptomatic of a chronic lack of communication between the two. The lack of widespread involvement by senior education faculty in the design of the policies and definition of scholarship would later make the implementation more difficult.

Once the university-wide guidelines had been approved, the dean of the School of Education was ready to take on the task of revising their own tenure and promotion procedures to align with the new university guidelines. In this section, the School of Education's effort to amend its guidelines is more closely examined.

Reaction to Promotion and Tenure Changes

Since the dean of the School of Education was involved in the university-wide committee and had a history of wanting faculty workload and rewards to be consistent, he was very supportive of the 1996 changes and began "behind the scenes" work to shepherd the School of Education through implementation. Most faculty in the School of Education saw the obvious benefits to their field of rewarding multiple forms of scholarship and welcomed the changes to promotion and tenure. In fact, the School of Education was firmly convinced that the rest of the university was really following their lead. "We were already doing it," "I don't understand what all the fuss is about, all education faculty work with communities," and "It's about time" were common reactions to the 1996 university-wide promotion and tenure changes. Education faculty and administrators were proud to have been "on board," by including service in faculty roles and rewards before other colleges. Some faculty, however, seemed to use the idea that the School of Education was "already doing this" as a subtle form of resistance to the idea that the guidelines meant anything significant in changing how the School of Education "did business" in relation to promotion and tenure. This subtle resistance to change would make it more difficult for the new definition of scholarship and promotion and tenure guidelines to be interpreted in the spirit in which they were intended.

Amending Policies in the School of Education

During the 1996–1997 academic year, the School of Education promotion and tenure committee deferred to the new 1996 university guidelines and the dean formed a small committee to adapt current promotion and tenure guidelines to reflect the 1996 changes and to educate faculty about these changes.

Faculty on this committee reported that they simply adapted the language and format of the education school guidelines to parallel the university guidelines. Examples of excellence in teaching and service as scholarship in education were added to the School of Education promotion and tenure guidelines. Some of the changes involved differentiating between service as scholarship and other forms of service. A few faculty worried that making these changes would make service as scholarship more important than institutional service. To address these concerns, a statement was put into the guidelines stating that faculty still needed to provide institutional service to be considered for promotion and tenure. This small committee made the appropriate changes and the new policies were approved at a School of Education faculty meeting on April 15, 1997.

About the same time that the School of Education was revising its tenure and promotion guidelines, it went from having three department promotion and tenure committees to one school-wide committee. Two faculty representatives from each of the three departments formed the new committee. This was done in an effort to bring the three education departments closer together and to make the standards for promotion and tenure for each department more consistent. Many of the people on the promotion and tenure committee in 1996–97 reported that it was a difficult year since both changes were made at once.

Promotion and Tenure Decisions

By April 1998, the School of Education had been operating for two years under the new policies. The policy stated that promotion and tenure committees were supposed to use the following criteria to assess service as scholarship: clarity and relevance of goals, mastery of existing knowledge, appropriate use of methodology and resources, effectiveness of communication, significance and impact of results, and consistently ethical behavior. This section describes the actual criteria used by the 1997–1998 School of Education promotion and tenure committee to assess service as scholarship.

Criteria to Assess Service as Scholarship

Promotion and Tenure committee members reported that they agreed with the new 1996 promotion and tenure policies definition of and criteria for scholarship and felt comfortable referring to the policy as they assessed service as scholarship. Several committee members were involved in the Center for Academic Outreach workshops on documenting and assessing service as scholarship and referred to a model developed specifically for assessing service as scholarship in education. The center was well respected and the committee welcomed a visit by the director to consult as the 1996 guidelines were being interpreted.

Overall, PSU's 1997–1998 School of Education promotion and tenure committee used the following criteria to assess service as scholarship: systematic inquiry, outcomes, dissemination, peer review, professional expertise, the candidate's conceptualization of their work, links with teaching and research, ethics, innovation, influence and prestige. Most of the committee's actual criteria were very similar to the 1996 policy criteria, but used slightly different language. The committee stressed the link with teaching and research, influence and prestige, and peer review to a greater degree than the new policy criteria.

Systematic inquiry constituted a major criterion for assessing service as scholarship. The committee evaluated the methods and tools used to address a particular educational problem and looked to see if the strategy or methodology was grounded in the faculty member's discipline or set of disciplines. Committee members noted that scholarship required bringing a discipline's specific framework to a problem and they looked for this framework in the construction of service projects. They examined the service to see if the investigation was ongoing, logical, systematic, and rigorous.

Another important criterion for service as scholarship was outcomes, which in education projects usually consisted of increases in teacher satisfaction, improvement in student test scores, evidence of increased leadership, or products like new curriculum guides, programs, or methods of delivering service. The committee felt that service as scholarship must show evidence of demonstrable outcomes.

Promotion and tenure committee members agreed that service that was scholarship needed to be disseminated for critique to academic peers and/or community partners. Committee members accepted conference presentations, videos, how-to manuals, conference proceedings, grant proposals, articles, newsletters, evaluations, workbooks, and curriculum designs as legitimate forms of disseminating service scholarship, though some members had distinct preferences. While the committee members varied on whether or not they expected that the service be disseminated to all three audiences, all agreed that service work needed to be shared beyond the local school or educational organization where it took place for it to be considered scholarship (according to an interview conducted with the promotion and tenure committee as a group). While faculty applying for promotion from assistant to associate professor were expected to have disseminated to a local or state audience, faculty applying for promotion from associate to full professor were expected to have their service disseminated to a national audience. Committee members who were least supportive of the new guidelines were the most emphatic that for faculty to be promoted, especially to full professor, the quality of the dissemination and written products had to be "at a tremendous, mastery level, something of great magnitude that people can really bite their teeth into." As with all decisions, the majority opinion on a candidate's work prevailed.

The committee evaluated service as scholarship based on the degree of professional and/or academic knowledge and expertise brought to bear. For example, the committee was interested in whether or not the faculty member had included perspectives from the latest educational research and theory. Service as scholarship followed the traditions of its discipline and used agreed-upon definitions of educational problems and appropriate methodology, according to the committee. They wanted to see a "high level of scholarly soundness," professional skills, and understanding of how the service fit into their field.

The committee was influenced by the candidate's own conceptualization of his/her work and how and why the candidate felt his or her service was scholarship. Faculty in the School of Education submitted a scholarly agenda with their portfolio to tie together their work and discuss the scholarly questions that guided their teaching, research, and service. Promotion and tenure committee members reported that the scholarly agenda was perhaps most important for service as scholarship. Since the committee often found the evidence of dissemination for service as scholarship lacking, the scholarly agenda provided an important opportunity for the faculty member to show the inter-relatedness of service to state and national research and educational initiatives and to describe why he or she took a particular approach to an educational problem. The candidate's own conceptual framework for their service often was the key factor to convince the committee that service was, indeed, scholarship.

To be considered scholarship, service needed to be linked to the candidate's teaching, research, and other professional and/or scholarly work. For example, one committee member explained that it would not be considered scholarship if a candidate merely helped to shape a state policy that had an influence on practice. However, if the candidate could demonstrate that the state policy was linked to his/her teaching, research, or professional writing, it was more likely to be considered scholarship.

The committee believed that it was important to consider ethics when assessing service as scholarship. Therefore, they examined the relationship and degree of reciprocity between the candidate and community partner. They wanted to make sure resources were shared, and community partners, research subjects, and students were treated in appropriate ways. However, they did not want to evaluate service as scholarship purely based on the relationship building aspect of the candidate's work. They did not want to know how many meetings the candidate attended but what the ultimate impact of his/her project had been. Committee members disagreed about how much "credit" for service as scholarship a faculty member could receive for ethical behavior. Most committee members felt this criterion was not as important as other criteria because the majority of candidates were ethical in all aspects of their work and ethical behavior did not set candidates apart. A few committee members disagreed and held up the candidate's attempt to develop reciprocal relationships as unique and worthy of merit as service as scholarship.

The creation of new knowledge or innovative use of "old" knowledge in service was another criterion for scholarship. The committee felt that scholarship involved doing something original, even if it was an original synthesis of old material. For example, it would not be considered scholarship if a faculty member administered a standard evaluation tool at a state department meeting. However, if the faculty member collected a variety of old tools to design a new one for the state department, the faculty member would be contributing something new to the field. The committee looked for innovation and new contributions to theory or practice.

Another characteristic of scholarship was influence and prestige. Promotion and tenure committee members felt that after scholarship has been disseminated, it significantly influences those it comes into contact with, and changes the activities, ideas, or behaviors of people. Scholarship makes people see educational issues differently and they act accordingly. The committee wanted to see an influence on the participants, the organization, and the activity itself.

The influence the faculty member's work has had on a community, school, state or national movement reverberates and prestige comes back to the university where the faculty member works. For example, the committee said that they could often tell if service was scholarship because it was replicated around the country or internationally. The promotion and tenure committee considered this characteristic important because if they were going to guarantee the candidate a permanent place on their faculty or improve their rank they wanted assurance that the candidate's scholarship would bring prestige back to their department.

The criteria the College of Education used to assess service as scholarship were characteristic of the conflict senior education faculty felt in accepting and embracing the new policy criteria. On the one hand, committee members were very aware of the new policy criteria and did their best to apply them in decision-making. In some cases committee members were very sensitive to issues related to developing partnerships with schools and more accepting of the nontraditional products of service as scholarship because their own careers had involved similar work. On the other hand, they were often preoccupied with how the candidate's work would reflect back nationally on them, on the academic reputation of written published documents, and on the authority necessary for peer review. Each of these issues were not strongly emphasized in the new policy, but were closely tied to the committee's experience assessing traditional research.

Problems in Assessing Service as Scholarship

The School of Education's promotion and tenure committee faced significant problems in assessing service as scholarship. The committee described this process as "hard to tie down" because they were dealing with "softer data." While most of the tenure cases during the 1997–98 academic year were ultimately successful, promotion and tenure committee members often expressed disapproval of the cases faculty were making for their service as scholarship. They blamed most of the problems associated with this process on the candidates themselves, although many of the problems were inherent in the process of assessment. The reason for this blame seemed to be a mild and unconscious suspicion of the candidate for having chosen an "alternative track" to the research track they had been promoted on, and a reluctance to fully embrace the idea of service as scholarship if it had not resulted in publications.

The committee expressed preferences for certain types of documentation, especially the status of journal articles, and conference presentations. If these were not available, they liked to see reports generated for an agency or through grants. The committee preferred formal academic writing and project reports because they usually contained a literature review, data on the impact of the project, a conceptual framework, methods used, and outcomes attained. Other preferred forms of documentation included curriculum guides, handbooks, or other program descriptions.

The committee felt that the service portfolios they reviewed did not provide this kind of documentation; there was either not enough information or the wrong kind of information. In some cases, faculty submitted an inordinate amount of documentation of their activity, but they documented meetings and relationships, not scholarly approaches taken to problems. While the guidelines did not specify that the candidate had to submit written work (other than the scholarly agenda) to document service as scholarship, the committee found that the more documentation deviated from written products, the more likely it was that they lacked peer review or demonstrated outcomes. The committee felt that in every other form of scholarship there were written products. Teaching had written evaluations and research had peer-reviewed journal articles. Unpublished service projects came up short in their eyes, although they did not want to require all service products to look like research. They stressed that it was not important that service writing be in a peer-reviewed journal as much as simply published. One committee member explained that in order to convince the committee that service was scholarship the candidate needed to tell a story about what they did and how they did it. Few candidates were able to tell that story successfully without significant writing products.

Committee members also believed that the service as scholarship that came before them was often not properly disseminated. The lack of dissemination often convinced the committee that the candidate did community service but "did not take it to that next step" to scholarship. Often candidates did not understand the importance of dissemination.

A related concern was to whom the products of service as scholarship should be sent. Some of the external reviewers included area superintendents, teachers, administrators, State Department of Education officials, and academics from other universities who worked with professional development schools. The committee preferred academics from other universities or educational professionals who had earned their doctoral degrees from PSU's School of Education. While the PSU policy stated that teachers, principals, or other community partners could be external reviewers, the committee felt that, if a reviewer did not have a Ph.D., it was unlikely that he or she could make an educated judgment about the scholarly characteristics of the service. Therefore, the committee said publicly that they followed the university policies but in practice had what they considered a "higher standard" for external reviewers.

Even when the portfolio weighting was 50 percent service as scholarship, some committee members focused more on the research aspects of the candidate's portfolio. One candidate described such a situation where a colleague on the promotion and tenure committee said to her, "Oh, well now maybe I'll really have to listen to you" after she published an article in a well known journal, even though she had recently been promoted based on her service as scholarship.

In the same vein, one or two committee members simply looked for a minimum number of refereed publications. If the candidate had them, the members voted "yes" and if not, voted "no" without really evaluating the candidate's service as scholarship.

Another problem the committee dealt with were committee members feeling that they needed to "save face" with their colleagues. A few committee members worried that by promoting a portfolio that was 50 percent service as scholarship they might appear to their colleagues as if they were not doing a rigorous job but rather were being frivolous or abandoning standards. One senior faculty member described the tenure and promotion process as "culture building," because it would influence what was important to the School of Education. Faculty watched test cases very carefully. Committee members' reputations went with them into the promotion and tenure room. This made these decisions more political than they otherwise might have been.

In conclusion, even among those promotion and tenure committee members who felt positively about the policy changes, there was ambivalence and disagreements on how to assess service as scholarship because of lingering beliefs in and experiences with the traditional research model. It would take time and perhaps a new generation of faculty to make the shift completely. The important thing was that the committee was willing and able to adapt as they conducted their assessment of service as scholarship. Because of that willingness to learn from the new policies and their process, there were several positive outcomes for the College of Education.

Outcomes

Two years after the implementation of the 1996 revised promotion and tenure guidelines, education faculty were well aware of the new promotion and tenure policies. Interviews with education faculty, department chairs, the dean, and numerous documents and events suggested that the widespread dissemination of the policies throughout the School of Education resulted in the emergence of a new culture. The new reward system contributed toward more favorable promotion and tenure decisions, increased involvement by the faculty in service as scholarship, the incorporation of this new orientation into recruitment practices, a more satisfied faculty, greater communication across departments, an improved learning environment for students, better relationships with community partners, and an increase in external grant funding. Despite the positive outcomes, there continued to be a small group of faculty opposed to the changes, resulting in "mixed messages" reported by those considering going up for promotion and tenure. The College of Education faced many barriers to implementation of the 1996–1997 policy, not the least of which were unspoken assumptions about scholarship. Despite this, change was occurring as a result of the new policies.

More Favorable Promotion and Tenure Decisions for Service Scholars

The 1996 university promotion and tenure guidelines gave the weighting system implemented in 1991–92 in the School of Education greater legitimacy and power. In other words, the two systems worked together to ensure that those faculty who wished to be evaluated based on their service as scholarship had a process to formalize and legitimate that decision and a way to document that work as scholarship.

Most importantly, the 1996 guidelines changed the meaning of the word "scholarship" and provided a sound conceptual framework for when and how service could be defined as scholarship. Candidates now had a guide to document their service as scholarship and organize their portfolios for promotion and tenure. One faculty member who was later successful in "making the case" said she organized every piece of evidence by the criteria listed in the new guidelines. The examples of different kinds of service activities in the guidelines helped candidates to weed out citizenship and governance related service from service as scholarship in their portfolios, which strengthened their cases. The guidelines also provided language to discuss how they applied knowledge in service settings and advice on how to present service outcomes and reflections. The new guidelines led candidates to consider what service as scholarship meant and how it differed from the scholarship of teaching and discovery. Candidates developed a more sophisticated understanding of the concept, which resulted in stronger faculty documentation of service as scholarship.

The new guidelines had another benefit as well. They acted as an "official reminder" to reluctant promotion and tenure committee members, reinforcing for them the new policy: if candidates presented appropriate evidence, service had to be rewarded as scholarship. In this way, the new guidelines provided additional cultural support to each candidate's documentation. This additional cultural support provided the "benefit of the doubt" when committee members reverted to old assumptions about scholarship and were an important component of test cases.

The School of Education increased the number of candidates who were awarded tenure and promotion primarily because of service as scholarship. At the time of this case study, four faculty had acted as self-proclaimed "test cases" for the 1996 guidelines in 1996–1997 and 1997–1998, submitting portfolios that gave 50 percent weight to service as scholarship (according to interviews with these faculty, department chairs, promotion and tenure committee members and the dean, as well as documents supporting their cases). Most faculty thought that these candidates would not have been promoted without the guideline changes. These cases were touted by committee members, the candidates themselves, and other faculty in the School of Education as "proof" that the guidelines were working.

School of Education faculty were proud that unlike other colleges on campus, they had really begun to implement the guideline changes. Academic administrators agreed.

> The one place where there have been some really good successful cases is the School of Education. It is not the only place, but they have had a number of people that would never have been promoted and tenured if those new guidelines were not in place. I know for sure that they would not have made it because their emphasis was service as scholarship.

One example of the success of the guidelines was an education faculty member who was very involved in service with professional development schools. After the 1996 guideline changes were in place, she applied for tenure and promotion from assistant to associate professor with 50 percent of her portfolio as service, 25 percent teaching, and 25 percent research. She made the argument that there was scholarship in all three activities. She felt certain that the new guidelines and their implementation influenced her tenure and promotion. This candidate did not have the number of publications that would have been expected during the years preceding her application. However, she designed a portfolio that demonstrated scholarship in her service activities and she was tenured and promoted.

At least five other faculty who were considering applying for tenure or promotion with an emphasis on service as scholarship waited to see the outcomes of these four test cases (according to interviews with these faculty and their department chairs). Once the test cases were successful, they contributed to a culture that expected the 1996 policies to be followed.

The dean was a critical factor in the success of the first few test cases. The dean negotiated among committee members when the process of assessing those first few cases became difficult and was an advocate for faculty with strong service as scholarship portfolios. Consequently, there was some concern that the dean was retiring and the new dean's position on rewarding multiple forms of scholarship was unknown.

A few faculty in the School of Education reported that the guidelines had not as yet had any effect on tenure and promotion outcomes. Since tenure was more often than not granted at PSU, these faculty believed the candidates would have gotten tenure even if the changes in the guidelines had not been in place. Moreover, they argued that all of the successful test cases were applications from assistant professor to associate professor and occurred under the same dean. There were no test cases of the guidelines from associate to full professor, and a few faculty suspected that the committee would revert to a more traditional orientation in judging the scholarship of associate professors applying for promotion to full professor.

Because of the high promotion and tenure rate and the secrecy of the process, it was not possible to definitively conclude that the four test cases were "proof" that the policies were working. However, there was enough evidence from within and outside the College of Education to suggest with confidence that the new policy had had a significant and positive effect on these decisions.

The future application of the guidelines to tenure and promotion decisions, thus, looked positive, but remained uncertain at the time of this research. Since the implementation of the 1996 guideline changes in the School of Education only two classes of promotion and tenure candidates had been reviewed. In the third year, a new promotion and tenure committee would try to make sense of the guidelines all over again. The 1998 committee felt it was a "comfortable struggle," but they recognized that what was comfortable for them still caused faculty candidates for promotion and tenure "personal vulnerabilities amidst this time of changes."

Safer Environment Leads to Increase in Service as Scholarship
Faculty involved in service as scholarship reported that the climate in the School of Education became "safer" for them after 1995. One junior faculty member said that the new 1996 definition of scholarship gave her and other faculty "a little breathing room to do their service a little fuller." Faculty involved in service as scholarship now felt that their work would "count" for promotion and tenure, were less "scared" and "nervous" about proving the legitimacy of their work to other faculty, and were convinced that they could now devote more time toward service as scholarship. Consequently, the School of Education saw a small increase in faculty involvement in service as scholarship.

For the most part, individual faculty members newfound sense of security was grounded in reality. The dean, promotion and tenure committee, and most faculty agreed that there was now a safer environment for junior faculty to be promoted based primarily on their service as scholarship. While this safer environment grew out of the 1996 policy changes and results of the test cases, the most important ingredient in the emergence of a safer climate was the fact that the dean actively supported the policy changes, according to interviews with junior faculty. The dean's support was a key factor in faculty confidence that the new policies would be implemented.

According to the dean, department chairs, and faculty, several factors came together to make the environment "safer" for service a scholarship. The discussions that surrounded the 1996 policy changes, the actual application of the new guidelines to promotion and tenure decisions, and the increased involvement in professional development schools all came together to transform the place of service in the School of Education. Consequently, more faculty transformed their own service into scholarship.

However, academic administrators pointed out that at least half of the education faculty involved in service before the policy changes did not transform their service into scholarship. Part of the reason for this was that some maintained that the service they had always done was scholarship, even though it was not defined as such by the new PSU definition. However, the new tenure and promotion guidelines had only been in existence for two years, and would likely influence other faculty to engage in service as scholarship in the next few years.

In conclusion, the resistance to change, especially on the part of some of the older faculty was significant. On the other hand, the fact that a lone policy was beginning to change the way associate and full professors (who had no plans to apply for promotion) were thinking about and engaging in service as scholarship demonstrated the powerful effect the policy had had on the College of Education.

Recruitment for Service Scholars

The development and implementation of the policy to assess and reward service as scholarship resulted in a stronger commitment by administrators, faculty, and staff to PSU's urban service mission. The clarification and affirmation of the new definition of scholarship and the urban service mission translated into more faculty being recruited to work in a service as scholarship context. While faculty had always been attracted to PSU's urban mission, job searches before the 1996 changes had never intentionally emphasized the urban service mission or PSU's commitment to multiple form of scholarship. The director of outreach conducted interviews with new faculty across the university, including faculty in the School of Education, and found that after the 1996 policy changes, the service as scholarship commitment had started to become institutionalized in the recruitment process. She found that 67 percent of new faculty reported that among other roles, they were hired specifically to engage in service as scholarship projects. New faculty said that they came to the institution because service as scholarship and community partnerships were valued and rewarded.

After the 1996 policy changes, the urban service mission appeared in education faculty position descriptions, prior experience with service as scholarship became part of interview discussions, and capacity for an interest in service as scholarship became criteria for education faculty search decisions. More faculty applied and accepted education faculty positions because of the School's emphasis on and reward system for service as scholarship.

Increase in Faculty Satisfaction

As a result of the 1996 policy, and successful "test cases," there was an increase in faculty satisfaction with work and with PSU among those faculty involved in service as scholarship (according to interviews with service scholars). The "safer" environment made faculty feel more comfortable about engaging in service as scholarship. They also reported feeling more valued by PSU and the School of Education. Although they said that they would have continued their service as scholarship whether or not the reward system valued it, the fact that the reward system now valued their service as scholarship made them feel more confident about, invested in, and satisfied with their work. This was true of junior faculty and mid-career faculty alike.

Junior faculty were not the only ones to get more involved in service as scholarship. Mid-career faculty also reported that they made changes in their work after the policy changes. The fact that service became an "authentic, rewarded, valid part of the mission," made a big difference to many mid-career faculty. These faculty said they had gotten "stale" in their scholarship prior to 1996 and had become frustrated with their academic career. Both their interest in scholarship and the quality of their scholarship improved after they began applying their knowledge in community settings. The 1996 changes became a source of renewal.

In addition, faculty involved in service as scholarship were more satisfied with their work and with PSU because they supported the "messages" the new guidelines sent to faculty and to the external world about what PSU "was all about." One of these messages was that PSU honored and rewarded different faculty strengths and talents. While PSU had always been a place that claimed that they accepted alternative career trajectories, there was always a formal and informal reward structure that prioritized research as the primary and preferred form of scholarship. The new message that "we accept different scholarly strengths" pleased these faculty. Another message was that PSU was committed to its urban mission and "letting knowledge serve the city." Faculty became more satisfied because they felt that PSU was finally aligning their rhetoric and reward system. The dean was proud of this consistency and described its positive spillover effects on new faculty. He felt confident in asserting that junior faculty could be assured that the School of Education not only said that they valued service and teaching scholarship, but in fact "came through" in actual promotion and tenure decisions.

Faculty who engaged in service as scholarship felt this consistency made their workplace more just. Since most of PSU's faculty spent more time on teaching and service than on research, faculty felt the new guidelines legitimized their actual workload as a potential contribution to scholarship and a real contribution to the university. In addition, the new guidelines sent the message that faculty would be rewarded for doing what they wanted to do.

Increased Communication

Prior to 1996, most faculty in the School of Education conducted their work in isolation from one another. However, the 1996 policy changes encouraged more faculty to get involved in service as scholarship and increased the visibility of that involvement. Consequently, communication across department lines increased among faculty involved in service as scholarship. According to the dean and department chairs as well as public relations materials for the School, more faculty were recruited to work on team grant projects with schools and local education agencies and more faculty were publicizing their work throughout the school. A weekly brown bag lunch, annual professional development school conference, and events sponsored by the Center for Academic Excellence were established after the policy changes to allow faculty involved in service as scholarship to share their work and collaborate with each other. Communicating with each other, and more broadly across the college, was both a practical and political strategy on the part of faculty most committed to service as scholarship. They sought to remind and/or prove to the college of education that faculty were regularly engaging in service that it was scholarly in nature.

Enhanced Learning Experience for Students

The 1996 promotion and tenure changes also enhanced PSU's curriculum and student learning experiences. University faculty were more motivated to develop innovative general education courses for undergraduates because their curriculum development, action research projects, and partnerships with community agencies could be presented as the scholarship of teaching or service for promotion and tenure.

In the School of Education faculty invested in deeper partnerships and longer-term relationships with supervising teachers through service as scholarship projects. Master's degree students reported that they had better learning experiences because of the increased communication between faculty and supervising teachers and because of action research opportunities that resulted from these collaborations. The increased time some faculty spent on developing partnerships with schools improved almost all aspects of the School of Education, curriculum, research, and service.

Increase in External Relations and Grant Funding

The development and implementation of a policy to assess and reward service as scholarship brought improved university-community relations, research, and leadership opportunities to PSU and School of Education administrators and faculty. Teachers, principals, leaders of educational organizations, and the State Department of Education expressed greater satisfaction with faculty involvement in the educational problems of city schools and at-risk student populations. The dean attributed the School of Education's success in achieving accreditation and state of education support for new graduate programs in part to the school's expanded involvement in professional development schools.

As a result of the promotion and tenure changes the School of Education was able to create deeper, more long-lasting partnerships with schools. The quality of the interactions between faculty and community partners improved as each had more time to learn what each other was trying to accomplish. A greater trust relationship developed as faculty began to understand that community partners brought important knowledge to the table. Faculty began to learn more in these settings and were more effective after they realized that, as the Dean said, they weren't going out to "try to save the natives from their ignorance."

As a result of improved university-community relationships, and increased faculty involvement in service as scholarship, external grant funding for both service and service as scholarship increased as well (according to the Associate Provost who had studied grant-funding pre and post guideline changes). In the School of Education, there was an increase in grant funding from the State Department of Education and from private and federal funding sources. One of several examples was an education faculty member who received a $5 million grant for math education improvement. This faculty member and the dean reported that had the new promotion and tenure guidelines not been in place, this faculty member would not have devoted her time toward service as scholarship activities and, thus, would most likely not have written the grant.

Continued Opposition to Service as Scholarship

Concerned that the move toward rewarding service as scholarship would hurt the research mission of PSU, and the School of Education, a few senior education faculty were not pleased with the new tenure and promotion guidelines. They feared that fewer and fewer faculty would choose to "carve out" time for research publications, which would lessen the national prestige of the School of Education. They believed that research was the "real hard work" of scholarship and the policy would allow that hard work to be neglected. Also, they feared that unlike teaching and research, which occurred within university walls with human subjects reviews, "community entanglements" could put faculty in awkward positions politically or legally. Some faculty complained that the new promotion and tenure process was more elaborate and complex, requiring more work by candidates and committee members.

This same small group of faculty agreed that the new reward system in the School of Education was "culture building," and they did not like the culture that was being built. For example, they imagined a future where faculty would be able to be tenured and promoted without ever having published an article. Though this was unlikely given the requirement for 20 percent of faculty work to be research, they made this fear public. They said they did not believe a university should consist of "field people." Some faculty felt that, to be fair, new faculty should have to go through the same "harder" standards they had to endure. For example, one such faculty member said, "There is some concern that we're not even sure what scholarship is anymore. Are we really changing our culture here? I mean, are we really an academic, intellectual community or are we becoming like the people we serve, you know, more field based, more practitioner?" They felt that PSU should not become too innovative, otherwise it would raise questions within the state and national system of higher education, and School of Education programs, students, and faculty would not be transferable to other institutions. There was a concern that service as scholarship stripped the faculty member of his/her traditional role as expert. In other words, if the traditional role of faculty in universities was knowledge creation rather than knowledge application, were they still academics if they engaged in knowledge application?

Often these faculty expressed their opposition to the changes in the reward system subtly. They acted as if they were in a "state of disbelief," expressing concern over whether the criteria could be applied effectively or maintaining the position that they really didn't understand the new criteria. This seemed highly unlikely considering the extensive effort university-wide and college-wide to educate faculty about the changes. More likely, by maintaining this position, these faculty could subtly suggest that they were not sure if service really could be scholarship and resist implementing change without putting themselves on the line.

This opposition to rewarding service as scholarship resulted in mixed messages for younger faculty. On the one hand, the provost, dean of the School of Education, education department chairs, and a few senior education faculty personally coached candidates to trust the guidelines and to apply for tenure and promotion based primarily on service as scholarship, if that was their strength. They advised these faculty to carefully document their service as scholarship and assisted candidates as they prepared their portfolios. The provost, dean of the School of Education, and education department chairs simultaneously made conscious efforts to convey the importance of the new guidelines in their addresses to faculty.

On the other hand, there were hallway, coffee room, and closed-door discussions between senior and junior faculty wherein candidates were told not to engage in service as their primary form of scholarship. They were told that if they wanted to move to another institution, they would not be able to compete with faculty who engaged in research. One junior faculty member said she was told, "Even though they tell you that you don't need a lot of published research for promotion and tenure, you really do." The fact that these two sets of messages co-existed made faculty faith in the compliance of the new policies difficult.

Ongoing opposition to the implementation of the new policies meant that while the ground in the School of Education was fertile for successful implementation, it was also uncertain.

Conclusion

The vast majority of academic administrators and faculty at PSU thought that the climate had definitely changed in both form (language) and substance (academic culture) because of the development and implementation of new guidelines to assess and reward service as scholarship. Within the School of Education more faculty considered service as a potential form of scholarship, reflected upon what makes service a form of scholarship, and developed a more sophisticated understanding of how to document and assess their own service as scholarship than five years ago. About 30 percent of education faculty seemed untouched by the policy changes and still referred to their work as teaching, service, and scholarship. Of these, 10 percent were still using these three words to discuss their work, but when asked, said that service could be scholarship "under certain circumstances." The other 20 percent were indifferent or resistant to the idea of service as a potential form of scholarship.

Why did this innovation happen at Patrick State University and what were the elements that worked against and/or for this organizational change? A new president, a reaffirmation of the urban mission, internal restructuring, budget cuts that forced a curriculum transformation, increased emphasis on service-learning, and faculty involvement in the national redefining scholarship movement created the impetus for, vision behind, and success of subsequent changes to the reward system.

How did the tenure and promotion committee assess service as scholarship? PSU's 1998 School of Education promotion and tenure committee used the following criteria to assess service as scholarship: dissemination, professional expertise, the candidate's own conceptualization of their work, a service ethic, originality, impact, and influence and prestige. The committee's criteria in practice and the new policy criteria were very similar, but used slightly different language. The education promotion and tenure committee stressed the link with teaching and research, influence and prestige, and peer review more than the new policy criteria. The criteria used by the committee were simultaneously influenced by a research paradigm and by the new definition of scholarship PSU had developed.

How were education faculty impacted by these changes? Faculty already involved in service as scholarship experienced greater satisfaction with work and their institution, increased communication between faculty, unanticipated grant and research opportunities, better relationships with partner schools and educational organizations, mixed messages, and invaluable tools to "make the case" that their service was scholarship. Subtle structural and culture changes within the School of Education occurred as a result of the development and implementation of the 1996 policies. There was an increase in the amount of service as scholarship, an improved learning experiences for graduate students, a greater emphasis on recruitment for service as scholarship roles, a rise in external grant funding, better relationships between the School of Education and community partners, and a shift towards thinking of service as a potential form of scholarship.

Mid-West State University

In 1988 Mid-West State University (MWSU) was awarded a $10.2 million grant as a national demonstration site for integrating life-long education into the basic fabric of a major, research-oriented, land grant university. As MWSU's life-long learning programs fell under the university's "service" activities, the provost's office saw the grant as an opportunity to reexamine and strengthen MWSU's service mission.

The provost convened two college-wide committees. The first committee concluded that the most effective way for MWSU to strengthen its service mission was to encourage and reward service as a form of scholarship; the second committee developed a guidebook with criteria for MWSU promotion and tenure committees to assess and reward service as scholarship. The provost asked deans and department chairs to give the new guidelines to college-wide promotion and tenure committees to use in the assessment of service as scholarship. The provost did not mandate that every college use the new guidelines but made recommendations and requests for compliance. During the same time at which the two university committees were developing guidelines to assess service as scholarship, two different deans in the College of Education took two different approaches to assessing and rewarding service as scholarship. This case describes both the development of the new university-wide guidelines and their informal implementation in the College of Education.

The Culture of Mid-West State University

Located in a big city, MWSU is a large, research-oriented land grant university in the Mid-West. MWSU enrolls over 43,000 traditional and non-traditional students in every imaginable major and graduate school program. Organized into 14 colleges, about 4,200 faculty (half of whom are full-time) teach only three courses per year, but they are expected to advise large numbers of students and engage in significant scholarly research. All of the colleges have at least one program ranked in the top ten graduate programs in the United States. Because faculty conduct most of their research in isolation and the colleges are large, there is little interaction among faculty either across or within the colleges. In fact, some faculty in the bigger colleges (200 or more) do not know other faculty within their own college.

MWSU faculty and administrators often compare and contrast their own campus with the larger flagship campus, which receives greater state attention and funding. MWSU's sensitivity to being "number two" is a big part of the university culture. In part to combat its second-class status and distinguish itself from the "other" university, MWSU takes its land grant status very seriously. Faculty and administrators articulate the land grant mission as a commitment to applying their expertise to benefit the larger community and society. At the time of this study, both the rhetoric coming from the president's office and the consensus in the departments was that "we ought to be doing external service, it's part of our mission." Academic leadership, faculty, and staff shared a commitment to external service.

The widely held view that Mid-West State University should be a leader in improving society has historically attracted faculty who want their scholarship to be significant and have an impact in communities. One professor said, "It's a practice-oriented group of faculty here." Therefore, getting faculty involved in service as scholarship has not been as difficult at Mid-West State University as at other research universities. Many faculty come to MWSU because of their interest in this kind of work. On the other hand, in the last fifteen years, service as scholarship has taken a back seat to the major reason faculty are recruited and hired at MWSU- to engage in high quality nationally recognized research.

MWSU has a long tradition of engaging in service as scholarship through research-grounded technical assistance and through disseminating the latest research in new ways to new audiences. For example, years before the Smith Lever Act of 1914 established the land-grant service model, MWSU instituted service and research programs to benefit local farming communities. For 75 years, the MWSU Cooperative Extension Service has developed programs to link teaching, research, and service through a community-based clinical approach in nursing, medicine, business, and education. In addition, the university's 14 colleges and numerous centers and institutes provide service in local urban areas and around the globe.

MWSU's reward system centers on the assessment of teaching, research, and service for promotion and tenure. MWSU's promotion and tenure process is completed within each of the 14 colleges, with each dean deciding whether or not to have department and/or college-wide promotion and tenure committees. College-wide committees are elected from faculty across a college. This committee debates the candidate's work based on his/her load, which is negotiated between a candidate and his/her department chair. Then the committee makes a recommendation to the dean who ultimately makes a decision and submits it to the provost. MWSU has a high success rate for promotion and tenure applications. About 80 percent or more of faculty who apply are awarded tenure or promotion, in part because candidates are reviewed on an annual basis. Junior faulty resign or are asked to leave if they are not expected to achieve promotion and tenure.

MWSU has historically accepted nontraditional scholarship more than most major research universities. Despite this history, tension exists between the service and research missions of the campus. This tension is beginning to appear in the promotion and tenure process.

Since the 1970s, MWSU has made a consistent effort to increase the national standing of its colleges through research. This effort has involved recruiting more faculty with traditional research skills and interests and requiring more traditional research for tenure and promotion. By the early 1980s, MWSU had serious identity problems that were playing out in the promotion and tenure process (according to MWSU academic administrators). Promotion and tenure committees struggled to reward teaching and service, while pushing candidates to excel in research.

By the 1990s, the pendulum had shifted toward a more "homogeneous version of what a professor should be," according to one education department chair, reflecting the more traditional research career end of the continuum. Therefore, throughout the 1980s and 1990s, MWSU has struggled with the following question: Would MWSU continue to reward the careers of faculty members who were committed to applying knowledge to social problems in service settings, or would that mission be completely overrun by the institution's desire to become a premier research university?

Because of the size of MWSU, each college has its own history, culture, and reward structure. Therefore, during the 1980s and 1990s, as the university struggled with its identity, the reward system for research and service varied from college to college. Perhaps no MWSU college better embodied the tension between the university's service and research missions than the College of Education.

Founded as a teacher's college in 1952, the College of Education has always had large enrollments. At one time, almost one quarter of the university's student body was enrolled to become future teachers. In the earliest period, the College of Education saw its mission as teaching and providing service to schools; thus, faculty were recruited to carry out this mission, not to conduct research. Faculty were promoted on the basis of this mission as well: teaching and service were given greater importance than research. There was no assessment of "service as scholarship;" all forms of service received credit for promotion and tenure.

By the early 1980s, education faculty were expected to engage in a more balanced mix of teaching, research, and service activities. The College of Education had become one of the most highly recognized colleges on campus and was striving to become the "best" education school in the country. Seven of the ten College of Education graduate programs were ranked in the country's top ten in *U.S. News and World Report*. The College of Education had higher student grade point averages than most other colleges on campus. Superintendents reported that the best teachers came from MWSU. Along with recognition, however, came increasing pressure for faculty to engage in research. Senior faculty in the 1990s were well aware that junior faculty were under considerably more pressure than they had been to publish in the most reputable journals.

Although the College of Education over the last 15 years had pressured faculty to increase their research activities, service remained important. The College of Education led Mid-West State University in the number of off-campus credit programs. It had a strong presence in other parts of the state, creating blurred lines between what happened on and off-campus. In addition, the College had a great deal of research funding that supported outreach activities. This gave the dean of the College of Education considerable influence on campus. Different deans used that influence to push for more attention to the university's service mission at different times.

Rewarding Service as Scholarship: Two Stories

From the early 1980s through 1997 both MWSU and its College of Education engaged in separate and distinct processes to influence the reward system to be more inclusive of service as scholarship. Both processes are described in the next section. Since the two processes occurred simultaneously, the narrative alternates between the university-wide process and that of the College of Education. Appendix D provides a chronological description of events in the university-wide process, and a chronological description of events in the College of Education process.

A New Dean for the College of Education

In the early 1980s, a new dean, Dr. Barbara Schreier, was appointed to the College of Education. Dean Schreier was part of a national educational reform effort called the Holmes Group. Her involvement in the Holmes Group inspired her interest in using professional development schools to get more College of Education faculty involved in nearby urban schools. Professional development schools (PDS) were partnerships between colleges of education and K–12 schools wherein faculty, teachers, administrators and students worked on educational reform efforts together. Professional development schools were also a way for faculty in the College of Education to blend their teaching, research, and service in new ways. The dean considered this work to be "service as scholarship." An associate dean in the College of Education recalled Dean Schreier's involvement in the Holmes Group as a real catalyst for change.

The Dean was involved with the Holmes Group which was creating a new view of what it meant to become prepared as a professional, as a teacher, what different roles teachers might evolve over the course of their career, and what kind of relationships there could be between colleges of education and schools. So to do the work in professional development schools that Dean Schreier was asking of our faculty called for a new faculty role and, I think, that is why you saw a lot of these things coming together.

Under Dean Schreier's leadership, considerable time, effort, and funding were invested in professional development schools (according to the assistant dean, department chairs and senior faculty who worked with her). During 1986–1987 the emphasis on professional development schools and the crystallization of the Holmes partnership affected the college's hiring and a large cohort of faculty (8–10) in Teacher Education and more in educational administration and educational psychology were hired. Several of these faculty were hired on a "potentially tenurable track" and them moved to tenure track positions later. Dean Schreier intentionally hired faculty who could contribute to an agenda of school improvement, and she explicitly told many of these faculty that they would be expected to prioritize their work with the professional development schools. Her goal was to have two thirds of her faculty involved in some way in professional development schools, and there was even talk about having "clinical faculty" or changing the roles of some of the faculty to reflect the new service orientation.

Throughout this time, the dean and the chair of the Department of Teacher Education (the largest department) were encouraging all faculty to become involved in the professional development schools. They believed that MWSU could become a national model for excellence in service. In 1988, Dean Schreier's vision for service for the College of Education became attractive to MWSU's provost who was trying to make decisions about next steps for the College of Lifelong Education. Dr. Schreier was offered, and accepted, a post for one year as both dean of the College of Education and acting dean for the College of Lifelong Education Programs (LEP). As an advocate for service throughout the institution, as well as the College of Education, her involvement in the issue of service became intense. The associate dean recalled:

> When Dean Schreier also became Dean of Lifelong Education at MWSU, she became much more influential in terms of trying to again formulate, prescribe, focus what was meant by service and how that might be evaluated. She pushed very heavily for there to be one-third teaching, one-third research, and one-third service in education and throughout the university.

In fact, Dean Schreier's post as acting dean for the College of LEP sparked a university-wide reexamination of MWSU's service mission.

Restructuring Lifelong Education: A Grant from the Kellogg Foundation

For at least 25 years, MWSU had a College of Lifelong Education Programs. LEP at MWSU consisted of off-campus instruction and some agricultural extension programs. In 1988, Dr. Schreier, now acting dean of the College of Lifelong Education Programs, assumed leadership for crafting and circulating a proposal for reorganizing the lifelong education program. Dr. Schreier and the provost wanted to remove instructional service from the periphery and make it every college's responsibility to expand the concept of life-long education to include service. They came up with a two-part plan to restructure lifelong learning. First, the position of Assistant Provost for Lifelong Education was created to insure continued support for instructional service. Second, the university began phasing out LEP as a separate administrative unit and the responsibility for credit and noncredit off-campus programming and a few service programs was distributed to the remaining colleges.

At this same time, lifelong education became one of the five major university planning platforms identified by the Office of the Provost as part of the university's strategic planning efforts. Planning for the Lifelong University System (PLUS) was intended to strengthen the university's commitment to lifelong education. That same year, Dr. Schreier developed and submitted a grant to the Kellogg Foundation, entitled "MWSU as a Lifelong University: Pioneering the Land Grant Model for the Learning Society of the 21st Century." The proposal asked for funding for MWSU to "become a national model demonstrating how educational services to people of all ages can be woven into the basic fabric of a major land grant AAU university." One academic administrator recalled that developing the grant centered on "Barbara trying to take her vision of university-K–12 involvement and move it across campus."

At the end of Dr. Schreier's acting post in 1988, the provost hired a new assistant provost to take over the work she had started. At the same time, the Kellogg Foundation awarded Mid-West State University the $10.2 million grant for the PLUS platform. As the new grant for lifelong education was being negotiated, the newly hired assistant provost said, "Don't spend any of the money until I get there." Meanwhile, in 1989, Dean Schreier returned to the College of Education to explore ways to assess and reward faculty service in professional development schools through promotion and tenure.

Assessing Service as Scholarship in the College of Education

Dean Schreier believed that certain kinds of service to professional development schools could be scholarship and was very supportive of rewarding service through promotion and tenure. Before and during Dean Schreier's tenure there was no college-wide or department-wide promotion and tenure committee. The department chair made a recommendation to the dean, who gathered her associate and assistant deans together to make promotion and tenure decisions. This gave the dean considerable latitude to reward faculty engaged in service and acknowledge their work as scholarship. At this time, no formal university guidelines mandated the evaluation of service as scholarship, but Dean Schreier worked with her associate and assistant deans to establish informal standards.

Between 1988 and 1992, a large number of faculty hired by Dean Schreier all came up for promotion and tenure, having done significant amounts of work in professional development schools. Although Dean Schreier was supportive of these candidates, she felt that service that was scholarship needed to be documented in very specific ways. MWSU administrators and faculty said that Dean Schreier and her colleagues were "ahead of their time" in terms of conceptualizing methods for documenting service as scholarship. Dean Schreier and her promotion and tenure committee required faculty involved in professional development schools to submit reflective writing, workshop curriculum, articles and grant applications as evidence of scholarship. Two associate deans recalled the process of assessing and rewarding service as scholarship at this time.

> I think this college was somewhat on the cutting edge in trying to define service. We made a real attempt to say there is scholarship in teaching, there is scholarship in research, and there is scholarship in service and that evidence of the quality of the service had to be available to be put forward to be evaluated by others. The scholarly output might be the documents that were used in the workshops, evaluation of the workshop, not just people saying, "blah, blah, it looks good," but rather here is evidence. Or, more importantly, that there be some follow-up authorship of an article about what was learned, that there be some learning from it that others could gain from. So there was always a push for documentation of what was done and evidence of quality that could, in some cases, be sent out for review outside of the university.

> There was support from the administrators for people to do service and for excellence in that area to be something that could be the leading factor whether people were going to get promoted or be given tenure. There was an expectation that if you were doing service as scholarship you should be writing about it. Just doing it, just good works, was not enough, you had to be writing about it and publishing in a practitioner journal or doing something that was describing what you were doing so that it was not just a benefit to MWSU but a benefit to the field more broadly. But it could be things that were sort of reflections on your own experience rather than things that people think of as research studies. The outlets could be in Educational Leadership to reach out to people who are interested in service and practical things rather than what is seen as a research journal.

Despite the dean's predisposition to service as a form of scholarship, there were unexpected problems associated with assessing service as scholarship in promotion and tenure. There was a lot of "gear up time" in setting up the professional development schools. Faculty were spending much of their time developing relationships with K–12 teachers, teaching, and developing new curriculum. While a few faculty found research opportunities at their sites, many did not. Several faculty involved in professional development schools applied for promotion and tenure based on the relationship and infrastructure building aspects of their work, since that had occupied most of their time. These faculty had very little written work reflecting on the experience and very little evidence of their impact on the schools. The associate dean recalled:

> I think people continually struggled with producing evidence of scholarship because faculty, particularly in the development of professional development schools, spent a whole lot of time out there hand-holding, building positive relationships, getting to know the players, working to try to build the kind of relationships that would allow for those to be places where research could be done, where teachers were teaching in ways that we thought were more masterful and that would be good models. And I think that effort to document was difficult.

The associate dean recalled that many of the problems of faculty engaging in relationship building rather than "scholarly" tasks were not anticipated.

> I think the intent was that when one worked out in professional development schools, part of their effort was evolution of that school. Part of that was supposed to result in research, data collection that would yield scholarly publications, and part of it was that we would be teaching our interns or our students in those contexts, and that often one's job might circumference all of those things, and that they would be woven together. However, I think we have some real keen examples of where people got swallowed up by the service and no research emerged and, while teaching might have occurred, there was also not evidence of scholarship or measurable outcomes of the services.

Because of problems in documenting the scholarly aspects of service and the lack of time these faculty had for significant reflection on their work, half of the cohort of faculty working in the professional development schools had well-documented portfolios and the other half had "sketchy" evidence that their service was scholarship for promotion and tenure. The associate dean recalled that some candidates' "stuff included ten pages of 'led this workshop for four hours in this community,' and then six more listings of the same workshop in three other communities." During Dean Schreier's tenure an informal policy allowed faculty to apply with only two areas of strength; many faculty presented service and teaching as their strengths.

Between 1988 and 1992, virtually every one of the junior faculty hired to work primarily in service contexts who applied for promotion and tenure was approved by the dean's committee. Assistant deans who were on the promotion and tenure committee reported that both documented service as scholarship and community service was approved as scholarship for promotion and tenure because the process of assessing service as scholarship was new and the dean wanted to reward the hard work of faculty who had launched the PDSs. In other words, even some faculty without high quality documentation were given the benefit of the doubt. By late 1991, the committee had started looking more critically at portfolios for evidence of service as scholarship, but without any formal criteria to differentiate between community service and service as scholarship, it was not a rigorous assessment. Therefore, toward the end of Dean Schreier's tenure, most faculty involved in service with professional development schools had been promoted or tenured even though evidence of scholarship may not have been strong in several cases.

Although Dean Schreier advocated during her tenure for clinical faculty roles, one-third service workloads, and other ways to integrate service more permanently into faculty roles, the College of Education did not institutionalize any permanent structures. This lack of institutionalization would have ramifications when a new dean, with a different vision of service as scholarship, arrived in 1993.

While Dean Schreier was struggling with how to informally assess service as scholarship in the College of Education, the new Assistant Provost for Lifelong Learning was initiating a grant-funded, university-wide conversation on the same issue.

A New Assistant Provost Initiates University-wide Reform Effort

When Dr. John Curran, the new assistant provost, arrived in 1989, he said that lifelong education wasn't very interesting to him. He wanted to get more involved in how MWSU could fulfill its land grant service mission. He argued that MWSU offered instruction off-campus, but so did many other universities. He believed that, as a research university, MWSU had resources that most of the other universities did not have and, therefore, MWSU could be more useful to the state by doing applied research and taking its scholarship into the community.

Dr. Curran advocated a more comprehensive approach to MWSU's knowledge-extension activities. He was concerned that the existing grant priorities did not provide enough funding for faculty involvement so he met with grant officials and slightly redirected some of the priorities. He shifted the focus from lifelong education with its emphasis on instructional programs and some service to lifelong education as the process of extending research, teaching, and professional expertise to the problems faced by individuals, groups, and the larger society. MWSU adopted the rubric of "university service" and the provost changed Dr. Curran's title from the Assistant Provost for Lifelong Education to the Vice Provost for University Service.

One of the first things the vice provost did was work with the deans, administrators, and faculty on how to spend the $10.2 million Kellogg grant. Vice Provost Curran decided to invest in service projects that would establish long-term partnerships for the university and provide opportunities for faculty to apply their knowledge to social problems. MWSU began a process, which continued throughout the 1990s, of investing the grant in a variety of service efforts, with the largest part of the grant ($2.5 million) going to the Institute for Children, Youth, and Families and the remainder divided among the following service activities: a program to engage faculty in public service to nontraditional areas in labor relations; international business centers to engage small businesses in international markets; a nursing program to provide off-campus degree programs; a master's program in public policy and administration to provide consultation and technical support to state and local government; university service grants of $15,000 to individual faculty for service projects; and interdisciplinary state-issue team grants.

In addition to investing funding in service as scholarship activities, Vice Provost Curran and assistant provosts made alliances with cooperative extension programs and convinced campus stakeholders that directing the new grant toward a reexamination of the service mission was a good idea. Believing that the only way to encourage faculty involvement in external service was to acknowledge certain forms of service as scholarship, the vice provost asked the provost to appoint a committee with a good cross section of respected faculty members in different disciplines to explore the service mission of the university.

In January 1992 the provost's Committee on University Service was convened with the charge of articulating an intellectual foundation for service and making recommendations for further strengthening external service. This committee represented every discipline from electrical engineering to African American studies to education and included well-respected scholars. Only two people on the committee had traditional extension or service responsibilities. The vice provost recalled that the committee was created to "establish the fact on campus that service could be scholarship, based somewhat on Ernest Boyer's Carnegie Foundation report, which had just come out. In some sense, the committee's job was to show the alliance between service and scholarship." The vice provost was very influential in guiding the work of the committee. One of the first things the committee did was deliberate on the meaning of service at the university; they decided to focus their work not on disciplinary or institutional service but external service to the community. Next they created a definition, mission, and vision for MWSU service. As part of this discussion, the committee decided to identify which kinds of service were scholarship and then concentrate purely on service as scholarship.

Over an 18-month period, committee members read and discussed pertinent literature, interviewed more than 100 MWSU colleagues, sought input from 100 service constituents in roundtable discussions conducted across the state, and studied service as it was being undertaken at nearly 20 national peer institutions. In 1993, they produced a report entitled *University Service at Mid-West State University: Extending Knowledge to Serve Society: A Report by the Provost's Committee on Service as Scholarship.* This set of recommendations essentially said that rewards for service as scholarship had to change. "We need to know how to distinguish quality service" was one of the major conclusions. The committee wanted to change the reward system to better acknowledge service as scholarship.

The report was 65 pages long and was divided into two sections, "Defining Dimensions of Service" and "Strategic Directions for Strengthening Service at MWSU." The first section defined service as a form of scholarship, described different kinds of service, the benefits of service as scholarship, and methods of evaluation. This first section also made recommendations for a MWSU agenda to stimulate, support, and reward service as scholarship. The second section of the report included recommendations for spreading the new concept of service as scholarship across the university, including adding to the official MWSU mission statement, placing primary responsibility for service as scholarship at the unit level, creating a measurement and evaluation system to track service as scholarship, rewarding faculty appropriately for engaging in service as scholarship, and strengthening service scholarship through university-wide leadership.

One interesting component of the report was the suggestion that the university not create additional administrative positions to support service as scholarship projects but instead use release-time to engage faulty and staff. The report listed over 20 existing service as scholarship programs in colleges and centers across campus, five to seven of which were connected with the College of Education. Written and intended for faculty, staff, and students, the report acknowledged current service as scholarship projects and described the work that needed to be done to integrate the service as scholarship mission at college and unit levels.

Disseminated throughout the campus, the report emphasized four principles that became the defining characteristics of MWSU's approach to service as scholarship. First, certain forms of external service were scholarship. Second, service scholarship could evolve from and enhance teaching and research. Third, service as scholarship was conducted for the direct benefit of external audiences. Fourth, service as scholarship was consistent with both university and unit-level missions. Just as this committee was finishing their report, a new dean arrived in the College of Education.

A New Dean of Education and a New Vision for Service

Dean Schreier left the College of Education in 1991. After several short-term deans, who had little permanent impact on tenure and promotion at the college, in 1993, Dean Erin Hennessey was appointed to lead the college. The new dean came to the College of Education with her own vision of service as scholarship. She agreed with Dean Schreier that service was a potential form of scholarship but was more conservative about the kinds of service she considered scholarship. She believed that only service that resulted in peer-reviewed publication was scholarship.

Dean Hennessey had two major goals. Primarily, she wanted the College of Education to maintain its high ranking among graduate schools of education and continue to rise in the ranks of major research universities. However, she also wanted the College of Education to be seen by the educational community and the university as fulfilling its land grant commitment to service. In her first year, Dean Hennessey did not take any action in relation to reward structures for service as scholarship or promotion and tenure.

Beginning in her second year, 1994, Dean Hennessey took several steps to implement her vision of service as scholarship and maintain high standards for research. First, Dean Hennessey instituted new procedures for promotion and tenure in the College of Education. She created a college-wide committee and a new promotion and tenure process. Faculty members up for review would meet with department chairs individually to discuss their portfolios. Then, the department members would meet to discuss the candidates and make recommendations to a college-wide committee. The entire faculty would elect the eight-member committee, which would be representative of all education departments. This college-wide committee would review each candidate's portfolio and make recommendations to the dean. Dean Hennessey felt this multithread system would ensure decisions that were more equitable across departments and increase the standards for scholarship because faculty would be holding each other accountable.

Next, Dean Hennessey required that all service result in some form of publication in order to be considered as a form of scholarship for promotion and tenure. While the first step was a formal policy change, the second was more of an informal policy she made clear to department chairs and junior faculty.

As Dean Hennesey was creating a college-wide promotion and tenure committee, she faced a significant challenge. There were still a small group of faculty from the original cohort of faculty hired by Dean Schreier for "clinical service roles," who had not yet been reviewed for tenure. In 1994 and 1995, these faculty applied for promotion and expected that their service to professional development schools would be sufficient "scholarship" for promotion and tenure. A few of these faculty had not published anything from their professional development school service but had concentrated on relationship and infrastructure building.

The dean responded to this challenge by speaking publicly in the college about the need for faculty research productivity. She pressed these faculty members to show more products and influence from their professional development school work. In some cases, she encouraged faculty candidates to work on their writing and reapply in a year. She repeatedly told all faculty who were involved with the professional development schools that they needed to produce research products from their service for it to be considered scholarship.

Dean Hennessey also dramatically reduced the number of professional development schools, an unpopular decision with some faculty. Some faculty heavily involved in service disapproved of the new dean's direction and chose to leave the institution rather than apply for tenure or promotion. The dean recalled this difficult time between her and these faculty:

> There were people who were hired to work in these schools who were not on any kind of trajectory of doing publications, which was a problem. These people had been hired by the prior dean, basically with a promise of, "You do what I want you to do here and you will get promoted." I'd say some of these people had very poor publication records and we gave extensions to faculty who had been involved in these schools, saying you can have a year extension or two-year extension, but your record and what you have been doing is not going to get you promoted. So, that was basically the word. There was quite a bit of talk in the college of holding people to standards of publication and writing. Faculty who were involved in the schools who had, in many people's views, gone sort of native in terms of service—you get involved with the troops out there and you become one of them, forgetting that you are part of the university community and that role has responsibilities in a different way. I think we still have that problem but I think it is clearer now. There is no one who is out there involved in schools who thinks that they can go native with the troops out there and get promoted or get high end-of-the-year reviews.

Dean Hennessey explained to her department chairs and faculty that the role of a faculty member in a research university is to discover new knowledge and disseminate that new knowledge nationwide. Her main critique of faculty involved in professional development schools was that in "going native" with their service, these faculty were having a local, rather than a statewide, national, or international impact. However, faculty who could translate their service into publications could have both a local and a national impact. Dean Hennessey further diagnosed the problem:

> To me, that is where things can fall down, because service as scholarship does not mean that you are just out there providing services. Consulting firms can do that. Private organizations can do that. The university role requires that service benefit the client but also benefit the college and the university and part of that benefit is to bring back what you have learned to influence your own programs, to influence how you teach. The products must address a broader community than a local entity. So we ended up with a lot of faculty who were doing no writing other than local writing. And that is not going to get them tenure. There was a huge tension between faculty involved in the schools doing very local writing, what I viewed as service and not scholarship, and other folks in the

college saying, excuse me, they are not doing any research, there are no publications, there is no national visibility for this, and we are ending up with a shop here that is becoming very isolated and not really generating any knowledge that involves anybody else or making any difference other than in that local school. That is where it fell apart.

In the end, a few of the faculty who emphasized service as scholarship left, a few were ultimately granted tenure after they had published from their service, and one was rejected. In each of these cases, negative feelings remained about the shift in defining service as scholarship. A few faculty reported feeling disillusioned and shaken by the changes and differences between Dean Schreier and Dean Hennessey's approaches toward service as scholarship. Under the previous dean, they claimed, "There weren't people breathing down your back for results, results" as there were now. One faculty member recalled:

> We had a change in the administrative regime of this college, so that before, the long-time dean, Barbara Schreier, and the Teacher Ed department chair, very much valued the kind of work that I was doing. Then Dean Hennessey came on and, I think, Dean Hennessey has more traditional views of what researchers in a research institution, albeit a land grant institution, should be doing. For me and for a few other folks, it felt like the rules of the game shifted just a bit. Her review letters to us were "publish, publish, publish" between now and when you go up for tenure.

While some faculty saw Dean Hennessey's vision for service and scholarship as a disguise for a very simple "publish or perish" position, others saw it as an effort to improve the standards for service as scholarship in the college.

As Dean Hennessey was informally changing expectations for service as scholarship for promotion and tenure, the provost's office formed another committee to make formal recommendations for how to assess service as scholarship across the university.

The Evaluating Service as Scholarship Committee

In March 1995, the Vice Provost for University Service formed a second committee, a service evaluation working group, to work on the recommendations set by the first university service committee. He charged the group to address the following questions: How should Mid-West State University and its various academic units approach the qualitative evaluation of their service programs? What criteria should be used to evaluate service as scholarship? How should these criteria be operationally defined? What are the sources of data and information related to each? How do we know when the criteria are being met?

The first committee included some faculty the provost's office did not know well. However, according to the vice provost, the second committee was "people we had worked with, who had grants from us, who had expressed real interest and so we worked together for a long time chewing on these issues of how you would assess service as scholarship." This second committee spent a year and a half writing a new report on indicators of service as scholarship. They wrote a number of drafts and tried it out in various faculty development meetings. Vice Provost Curran again advocated that "faculty will not take service seriously as a mission of the university—particularly the research university—until they are confident that service efforts can be evaluated as carefully and reliably as is other peer-reviewed scholarship." In fall 1996, the committee published two reports, which are described in the next section.

The Indicators

The committee evaluating service as scholarship and the Office of the Vice Provost for University Service first published a document entitled *Matrix: Four Dimensions of Quality Service* (1996). They next published a larger guidebook entitled *Points of Distinction: Planning and Evaluating Service as Scholarship* (1997). The guidebook included the matrix, appendices with definitions, planning tools, recommendations for developing faculty portfolios, and resource materials. Divided into three sections: Unit Planning and Evaluation, Individual Planning and Evaluation, and Project Evaluation, the guidebook gave advice to faculty, promotion and tenure committees and units preparing to document or assess service as scholarship. Many people on campus referred to these documents—the matrix and the guidebook— together as the "*Indicators,*" which is how they will be described for the rest of this case.

The introduction to the *Indicators* guidebook stated that it was "offered as a tool for the evaluation of a service as scholarship project, be it short-term or long-term, instructional or non-instructional. It may also serve as a planning guide for those initiating service as scholarship projects, assessing a unit or individual's service as scholarship record." The first part of the *Indicators*, the matrix, was a nine-page document, with the text broken down into four categories that were "dimensions" of service as scholarship: significance, context, scholarship, and impact. Each of these dimensions was further broken down into evaluation components. There were sample questions to evaluate each dimension, with examples of qualitative and quantitative indicators that could confirm that each dimension was present in service as scholarship. A brief description of each of the dimensions is provided below.

The significance category was concerned with service project goals, target audience, the issue/opportunity to be addressed, consistency with university and unit missions, and resources. Promotion and tenure committee members were encouraged to ask questions such as: Were the objectives clear? Who benefited from the service? What was the issue or concern addressed and how was that problem studied and framed by the faculty member? What was the importance or size of the problem? Was the project consistent with the missions of the university and the unit? Did the project leverage or create resources for the community or university? Examples of quantitative indicators of significance included the number of participants, projects, events, contacts, and participant hours; indications of demand/need; and the amount of funding received for the service project. Qualitative indicators included evidence of clarity of goals and the fit of the project to needs of target audiences.

The context category related to the appropriateness of the expertise, degree of collaboration present, sensitivity to diversity, and methodological approach. If a faculty member's service was scholarship, then the faculty member was expected to demonstrate sensitivity in relation to diverse audiences and stakeholders and to collaborate with partners in ways that would build capacity for future projects. Service as scholarship that was contextualized fit with the individual and unit's expertise and research priorities, utilized appropriate methodologies, and included a comprehensive evaluation plan. Quantitative indicators included the number of faculty and percentage of faculty time involved, number of new partnerships, inter-institutional linkages, and instances of innovations in delivery. Qualitative indicators included evidence of partnerships formed, successful collaboration, ability to work sensitively with diverse groups, and a good fit between the project needs and expertise employed.

According to the guidebook, service made scholarly contributions if knowledge was generated, applied, disseminated, and preserved. Scholarship was defined as work that used up-to-date knowledge, made a unique and innovative contribution, and was available for possible replication and dissemination. Scholarship generated new research questions and had an impact on both community and academic knowledge. Quantitative indicators of scholarly contributions included the number of publications, papers delivered, new programs developed, professional forums convened for dissemination of service findings by the researcher as well as awards, honors, and citations received for service projects. Qualitative indicators of a scholarly contribution included the use of literature and theory that built on previous works, newly generated theory, replicable innovations, and peer review.

The external and internal impacts category identified service as scholarship projects as those that had a significant impact on the issue and the university, created sustainable change, and encouraged mutual connections/benefits between the university and community. Questions to be asked of service projects in this category included: Were the goals and objectives met? Could the impact be documented? Did the project develop mechanisms for sustainability and, ultimately, university detachment? Did mutual communication and satisfaction derive from the project? Has the project offered new student-learning opportunities, graduate student support, led to innovations in curriculum settings, increased multidisciplinary collaborations, or improved the university's service visibility? Quantitative indicators of impact included number of products generated and distributed, people reached, resources developed, and evidence of increased demand or value placed on faculty involvement. Qualitative indicators included attitudes changed; assessments by students, participants, clients; new skills available in the community; institutionalization of service activities; community satisfaction; and increased student and faculty involvement.

Disseminating the Indicators

Rather than taking the *Indicators'* concept and language of service as scholarship to a governance committee, MWSU took an indirect approach by publishing the report from the provost's office and slowly moving it through all the colleges. The provost sent the *Indicators* out to departments, colleges, and offices, and let the faculty, department chairs, and deans discuss them, provide feedback, and institutionalize them at their own level and at their own initiative. This method of introducing change was consistent with MWSU's culture of decentralization and the way that the provost's office had disseminated other recommended reforms. The strategy taken by the provost's office was not to use the Indicators to change promotion and tenure policy language but to create leadership at the college and unit levels to influence interpretation of promotion and tenure guidelines. The strategy followed the federal model of providing resources to support involvement and assessment of service as scholarship rather than trying to mandate such involvement and assessment.

In fall 1997, the provost sent the *Indicators* to all deans and department chairs with a letter saying that service as scholarship needed to become a more important piece of the faculty evaluation puzzle.

> In a few weeks you will be receiving a set of materials supporting the promotion, reappointment, and tenure process. These documents emphasize the importance of evaluating quality, quantity, impact, and effectiveness of faculty and departmental service efforts. This document, developed by a group of MWSU faculty, under the leadership of the Office of the Vice Provost for University Service, has been circulated widely across the nation and has been the subject at many national symposia and workshops focused on broadening conceptions of scholarship and its assessment in higher education. Although the Guidebook was created to deal with service as scholarship, it contains a matrix of criteria (significance, context, scholarship, and impact) and set of innovative tools for identifying and rating quality and impact of faculty work that apply equally well to research and teaching activities.

The provost also suggested that the *Indicators* could be useful to faculty preparing portfolios and departments planning service as scholarship. The provost was interested in using the *Indicators* to evaluate the entire teaching, research, and service efforts of the university. For example, one of the *Indicators'* evaluation questions, "Is the work useful to the state?" was a question the provost thought should be asked of all of the work at MWSU. The provost gave a speech at the Kellogg grant's capstone conference the previous fall and said that she saw the day when service would disappear because it would be a seamless part of all teaching and research activities in universities.

A letter from the Vice Provost for University Service accompanied the provost's letter and the *Indicators*. The letter underscored the *Indicators* most important parts and offered additional copies. The vice provost indicated that he or one of his staff would be willing to attend department meetings and promotion and tenure committee meetings as the *Indicators* were being interpreted.

The *Indicators* were disseminated in a number of other ways as well. The committee evaluating service as scholarship provided a workshop for department chairs to help them understand the *Indicators* and issues related to documenting service as scholarship. Interestingly, no faculty from the College of Education came to this workshop. The *Indicators* were integrated into the annual planning and review process. The provost's office added a segment to the reporting requirements of the colleges and departments, asking for information on how they were fulfilling "guiding principles," two of which, "access" and "community problem solving," related closely to service as scholarship. Finally, with a second accompanying cover letter, the provost changed the language from "service" to "service as scholarship" in the preface and cover documentation to the promotion and tenure and annual review documentation. In a more formal way this let deans and department chairs know that the provost wanted to reward certain forms of service as scholarship in faculty evaluation. However, the specifics of that evaluation were left to the guidebook that was recommended, as opposed to mandated for use in promotion and tenure.

The *Indicators* were also disseminated through national conference presentations. Because the *Indicators* became a national model for assessing service as scholarship the Vice Provost for University Service and four faculty from MWSU (from geography, large animal sciences, psychology, and teacher education) were invited to take part in a national pilot project on the peer review of service as scholarship- the Faculty Portfolio Development project. They documented their work, developed portfolios, and submitted them to external and internal peer review within their departments, using the *Indicators* to frame their service. This project's peer review component gave the *Indicators* greater visibility within and outside of the university through collaboration with other participating campuses. Several articles were published from this work at MWSU, and the same faculty presented annually at national conferences. In many ways, the Indicators became a national model before they were ever fully implemented in each of the colleges.

In November, 1997 the Provost and Vice Provost for University Service also strengthened the language in the university-wide guidelines to emphasize service as scholarship or outreach. While the emphasis on service as scholarship was placed in several places in the introduction, the following statement is representative of these changes.

> Assessment of faculty performance should recognize the importance of both teaching and research and their extension beyond the borders of the campus as part of the outreach (service as scholarship) mission. Faculty must demonstrate substantive and sustainable achievement in both teaching and research and the infusion of this scholarship in outreach.

During the same two years (1995–97) that MWSU drafted and published the Indicators guidebook on assessing service as scholarship, and was strengthening the language around service as scholarship in the university-wide promotion and tenure guidelines, Dean Hennessey was more firmly establishing her own informal policy in the College of Education.

Institutionalizing Reforms at the College of Education: A "No Excuses Model"

After getting through a two- to three-year period of difficult promotion and tenure cases, Dean Hennessey took additional steps from 1995–97 to ensure her vision for service as scholarship. She began to put structures in place to create what she called a "no excuses" model for service. Instead of having faculty do service in addition to a full teaching load, her office began to pay departments for release time so faculty could engage in service with professional development schools without the department viewing it as a drain on their resources. In return for this release time, faculty members had to document their work through publications, blending scholarship and service. Since all faculty at the college received 25 percent release time for research, and she now paid 25 percent release time for service, the new dean felt that all faculty involved in service should spend at least 50 percent of their time writing publishable articles from their service. She built this writing time into faculty schedules because she felt it was crucial to promotion and tenure as well as faculty roles as scholars in a research university.

After implementing the "no excuses" model, Dean Hennessey began to change the kinds of service the college engaged in. The primary focus of the professional development school model under Dean Schreier was the development of new curriculum, teaching methods, and strategies for teaching to new populations. Dean Hennessey described her own model for professional development schools as more research based, with faculty conducting research in partnership with schools. Despite Dean Hennessey's efforts to decrease the number of professional development schools, she continued to support faculty involvement in a limited number of professional development schools, as long as their work became more oriented toward research. She felt professional development schools provided opportunities to try out innovative research and teaching methods for school improvement, better educational experiences for students, and made the College of Education visible in urban schools.

Dean Hennessey created new service initiatives. Combining her goals of research productivity and service visibility, she increased research dissemination to the state. Her office began publishing a series of one-page research reports that described studies done by College of Education faculty and the implications of the research for educational practice. She sent these reports on a regular basis to superintendents, school boards, principals, and other policy makers and practitioners. Dean Hennessey described this new form of service as a way to have statewide, rather than local impact, on practice. She also established monthly legislative forums for superintendents, legislators, and state board members in which faculty reported on their research and its policy implications.

One of the most interesting moves made by Dean Hennessey was that she created a new administrative position, "service coordinator," responsible for establishing relationships between the College of Education and the educational community. Hiring a service coordinator was Dean Hennessey's solution to the problem of having tenure-track faculty do the "leg work" of relationship and infrastructure building with schools. She hired someone who did not have to worry about promotion and tenure, had considerable service skills, and could act as the link between faculty and various service projects. Within her first few years, the service coordinator developed a technology consulting service, completed needs assessments with superintendents, coordinated a National Conference on Educational Standards, and coordinated the legislative forums described above. In fall 1997, just as Dean Hennessey was beginning to establish her own informal "rules" for faculty engaging in service as scholarship, the *Indicators* were sent to the College of Education.

The Indicators and the College of Education

As previously mentioned, the provost sent the *Indicators* to all of the deans, including Dean Hennessey and her department chairs in fall 1997. Dean Hennessey said that she was not aware of how the materials evolved. Rather, the *Indicators* "just appeared" on her desk one day. She gave the *Indicators* to department chairs and said they should be used as a guide for evaluating service as scholarship, but she did not give them to the newly created college-wide promotion and tenure committee. Interestingly, the dean felt that the College of Education, and it's promotion and tenure committee did not really need the *Indicators* because service was already evaluated fairly.

Despite the fact that she did not explicitly require the 1997–98 promotion and tenure committee to apply the *Indicators* to their decisions, the *Indicators* did manage to indirectly influence promotion and tenure committee members. For example, in the 1997–98 academic year, faculty candidates for promotion and tenure quoted from the *Indicators* in their portfolios and used the ideas presented in them to frame their service as scholarship. Committee members became aware that candidates were quoting from an official university document that stated how and when service was scholarship. Thus, while some promotion and tenure committee members read the Indicators as it was circulating around the university, others learned the language and concepts of service as scholarship through candidate portfolios. There were faculty in the College of Education who were heavily engaged in service, had been a part of the university discussions and committees on service as scholarship, and sat on the promotion and tenure committee. Likewise several committee members were recruited and retained by the institution because of its service mission. Everyone on the committee acknowledged that Mid-West State University had been pushing service as "an important piece of what people do" for the last ten years. Committee members reported that "service was taken very seriously." Therefore, despite the dean's lack of emphasis on the *Indicators*, the College of Education promotion and tenure committee was influenced by the university-wide discussion on rewarding service and these discussions increased pressure to reward certain kinds of service as a form of scholarship.

Promotion and Tenure

Promotion and Tenure Criteria: More Than Good Intentions

This section refers to the fall 1997/spring 1998 College of Education promotion and tenure committee and the actual criteria they applied to assess service as scholarship. The 1997–98 College of Education promotion and tenure committee took its role very seriously. The committee members all agreed that it wasn't good enough at their institution to just be "out there doing good stuff, that wasn't scholarship." Instead of simply blessing all service as scholarship or assuming no service was scholarship, most committee members looked critically at service as scholarship while also trying to give the candidate the benefit of the doubt. The burden of proof was on the candidate to make the case that there were more than good intentions in their service. Once the candidate submitted his/her portfolio, the committee separated good intentions from service as scholarship by looking for the following characteristics: innovative ideas and rigorous questions, critical analysis, academic expertise, local and national impact, peer critique, and connections to teaching and research.

Promotion and tenure committee members reported that they looked first at the ideas presented in the service to see if they were theoretically sound, innovative, and added new knowledge to the field. Scholars involved in service had to pursue important, intellectually rigorous questions for the work to be considered scholarship. The committee felt service that was scholarship was guided by scholarly, as opposed to technical, questions. For example, a service project that focused on how dyslexic elementary students learned the alphabet for the first time was more likely to be viewed as scholarship than a service project that focused on how to train a group of ESL teachers on how to work with dyslexic students. The first project was guided by questions of epistemology, while the other was guided by training and technical assistance kinds of questions.

Along with innovative ideas and rigorous questions, the committee members examined service projects to see if the candidate was "bringing a thoughtful, critical kind of analysis that we associate with academics to the problem." While some committee members expected the candidates to demonstrate that they had followed the scientific method in developing their projects, others simply wanted to see evidence of reflective practice to consider service as scholarship.

Committee members also examined the candidate's use of academic expertise as opposed to administrative or technical expertise. As they looked through products of service projects such as curriculum, evaluative reports, and grant applications, they tried to ascertain if the faculty member had applied his/her knowledge of education literature and theory. The committee was convinced that the candidate's service was scholarship if they could see, as one committee member put it, "the disciplinary lens or the lens of the norms of scientific discourse."

The promotion and tenure committee agreed that service as scholarship must have a significant impact on some audience or group. Committee members wanted to see quantitative and qualitative evidence that the service had a positive impact on a particular community, school, or educational organization. Beyond specific impact, some committee members also felt that, because they were a nationally ranked college of education, they should only reward service as scholarship if it had national visibility and impact within the discipline. One committee member stated:

> If you make a difference in a school that's fine, but nobody cares other than this particular school, and that's not our role as a university, to go out to one school and make a difference. How is your work making a difference beyond that school? How is your work being used by others to have a national impact?

National prestige and recognition tied into national impact. Especially when considering promotion from associate to full professor, the committee expected the person to have become a national figure in his/her field because of their service as scholarship. Letters of recommendation from national experts affirming service accomplishments convinced the committee that the candidate's work had made a national impact. One of the biggest criticisms committee members could level at candidates was that they had carved out a local rather than national service role for themselves, which was insufficient for a faculty member at a major research university.

Peer critique also distinguished community service from service as scholarship. The committee looked to see if the candidate had received peer feedback and used it to improve his/her project. Peer evaluations of the strengths and weaknesses of the projects also counted toward the positive assessment of service as scholarship.

Finally, committee members were more inclined to see service as scholarship if it was only one part of a collection of work that pursued a set of scholarly questions over a long period of time. In other words, the more that the service related to the faculty member's research and teaching the better the case that the service was scholarship. Committee members explained that "it's one thing next to the other thing" in the file that shows a long-term commitment to scholarly questions. Committee members all agreed that the best candidates were ones who seamlessly connected their teaching, research, and service through a set of scholarly questions, over a significant period of time.

Comparison of Actual Criteria with Indicators

The *Indicators* described four dimensions of service as scholarship: significance, context, external and internal impacts, and scholarly contributions. Although the College of Education promotion and tenure committee made no special effort to apply the *Indicators* to its decision-making, there were striking similarities between the *Indicators* and the actual criteria used by the committee during the 1997–98 academic year. For example, the committee's criteria of innovative ideas, rigorous questions, critical analysis, academic expertise, peer critique, and connections to teaching and research, were all characteristics of the "scholarly contributions" dimension in the *Indicators*. Similarly, local and national impact was comparable to the "external and internal impacts" dimension. The College of Education promotion and tenure committee, however, did not assess the degree of collaboration present, community satisfaction with project outcomes, fit with institutional mission, or the size or importance of the problem addressed, criteria discussed in the *Indicators*. The lack of emphasis on the relationship between the faculty member and community agency was consistent with Dean Schreier's emphasis on scholarship as product, as opposed to process.

Required Forms of Documentation

Committee members considered written products necessary to demonstrate scholarship. One committee member said, "What else can we judge, intentions?" The same committee member who described himself as "very conservative" about promotion and tenure described scholarship as "anything that appears in print." Committee members agreed that writing was the best way to understand whether or not the above criteria were present in service projects. If the faculty member wrote about his/her own scholarly process, the committee could see how the faculty member had evaluated, analyzed, and disseminated his/her work.

A variety of written products were acceptable. Self-reflections framing the portfolio and laying out the intellectual process were among the most important forms of documentation of service as scholarship. However, one committee member stressed that it must be a conceptual guide to an entire scholarly career. The committee felt "the candidate almost needs to rewrite that essay every year to reflect on what they are doing." Presentations and published articles describing and analyzing the service as scholarship were very significant. Committee members said that they did not have any problem with documentation of service being in non-refereed or practitioner journals as long as the candidate could prove the materials were somehow getting to a broader audience than just those practitioners. However, the dean preferred that service as scholarship result in more traditional writing.

> It needs to show benefit here and it needs to have benefit in the broader community through writing, not through local writing and not through sort of an oral tradition, sort of talking about it. You have to have professional writing.

While the dean pushed candidates to do more formal writing about their service as scholarship projects, departmental tradition accepted curriculum writing, textbook writing, and other kinds of applied writing as evidence of teaching as scholarship. This tradition created openness on the part of committee members to view nontraditional writing as potential evidence of service as scholarship. However, as the college pushed to increase its national ranking, in part through faculty research reputations, this tradition was being challenged.

In addition to having written about their work, candidates were expected to have, in their portfolios, letters from administrators, teachers, or experts in the field that affirmed the impact of the candidate's service as scholarship on the field. Also critical were statistics, interviews, or reports showing how students were learning more or curriculum had changed as a result of the service as scholarship.

Funding was mentioned several times as one way candidates could legitimize their work as scholarship. Both the dean and committee members reported that ongoing funding indicated some educational funding agency thought the ideas were compelling and important to the field. Grant funding demonstrated that the project fit within the context of important issues and often gave the work a national influence through professional networks with other grantees and foundation reports. Funding was a way that these candidates could say they were contributing to the college. The dean reported one case where she awarded promotion to a candidate with a service as scholarship portfolio even though the college committee turned the candidate down, in part because the candidate brought in significant grant funding.

Problems with Presenting and Assessing Service as Scholarship

As was previously discussed, during Dean Schreier's tenure in the College of Education service was unofficially assessed as scholarship and there were significant problems with documentation. During Dean Hennessey's tenure the College of Education faced four similar types of problems in trying to assess service as scholarship for promotion and tenure. Generally, service as scholarship portfolios included less scholarly writing than traditional research portfolios, making them harder to assess. Second, committee members disagreed about whether to emphasize the products or process of service as scholarship. The third type of problem concerned disagreements among committee members as to the criteria applied to evaluate service as scholarship and the fourth set of problems were inherent in assessing all forms of faculty work.

The first problem concerned documentation. Candidates were not presenting the kinds of evidence the committee wanted to see to confirm candidate's service as scholarship. First and foremost, the candidates did not submit sufficient written products. Instead of writing, many candidates emphasized in their portfolios the relationship-building aspects of their work or qualitative indicators of impact. Since this committee strongly emphasized written products as a qualifying criterion of service as scholarship, often these portfolios were not well received. Some candidates had taken a scholarly approach to their service but had not had the time to write about it yet, while others were really doing community service and presenting it as scholarship. Committee members could not easily distinguish between these two groups. The "writing problem" was not only a committee issue. Despite Dean Hennessey's attempts to build time for writing into their load, faculty reported that there was not enough time for them to write about their service. The Vice Provost for University Service estimated that faculty heavily involved in service cut their writing productivity in half. Some faculty could spend 40 hours a week in a school with no real way to show the impact of the work or that it made a difference. Committee members and candidates often felt there was "less of a paper trail" with service as scholarship than other forms of faculty work, which made it harder to send out portfolios for an external review. Often this resulted in candidates trying to document, and the committee trying to assess, "lost time," when the faculty member was engaging in service not directly tied to written products. Also, when there was a sufficient paper trail, there was the fear that those faculty who were better writers would receive higher reviews than others who were doing better work but did not present it as eloquently.

The second problem was that committee members disagreed about how they should assess service as scholarship. One faction of committee members thought they should evaluate the "scholarly process," while another faction wanted to evaluate the "scholarly products." A committee member described this dilemma:

> This is where it gets tricky because you can not say that writing a textbook or developing an assessment is, in itself, scholarship. It is a matter of looking at the process that the person went through in the development and, in this case, there was a lot of research that went into the development of these assessments. So the scholarly process this person engaged in was very much like someone would do if they were going out to just study kids learning and publish it in the AERJ Journal, but in this case the scholarly product was assessment materials.

A committee member who was herself engaged in service as scholarship was frustrated by the emphasis on "products" of service as scholarship.

> I am skillful at turning a sort of static situation into a dynamic one that is moving forward and doing something. Is not that evidence of effectiveness? Do I have to write about it? Do I have to get everybody else to say I am great before you will think that? I mean, how do I show you that, if what I am doing is part of a process? It is not products always, and, I think, the research mentality is that you are always going to end up with product. I think, in a lot of our service, we do not end up with as many products because a lot of service is a process. And, I can only write about the process so many times.

The committee was also divided about whether or not they felt the "scholarly products" of service had to speak to the research community or whether they could speak primarily to practitioners, a disagreement that partially hinged on the identity of MWSU as a research institution. Some faculty felt that "one of the defining features of a person at a research-oriented university" is that he or she contribute to the "scholarly conversation" and some believed that scholarly conversation only occurred among academics. Therefore, committee members not only disagreed about whether to assess process or product but also the appropriate audience for the product.

A third problem involved a lack of consistency in criteria and indicators used to assess service as scholarship. Committee members felt the process of assessing service as scholarship was much more amorphous than assessing other forms of faculty work. They reported greater consistency in the committee's view of what constituted an exceptional research effort but a more nebulous view of what constituted effective service and teaching. Committee members reported that they seemed to create their own standards for evaluating service as scholarship each year. "It's a definition that gets changed by every committee that meets. It's like walking in quicksand. You're never quite sure if you're going to hit or miss a hard spot as you're striding through this service area and what you are submitting or reviewing." They compared evaluating a research article with, for example, a training module from a service as scholarship project. Faculty felt sure they could read a research article and recognize if it was scholarship, but to evaluate the training module, they would need to know how it was evaluated along with other information. They felt the scholarship was often not self-evident in service as scholarship products, because service as scholarship products were often context dependent. One promotion and tenure committee member said:

> It's harder to make the case because we don't have the typical indicators that we have for research where we can search Citation Index and see how many times people cited your work and said you must really be hot stuff because all of these people are using your name in their work. We don't have those kinds of indicators in service.

Sometimes the committee lacked knowledge of the different kinds of academic writing and newer research methodologies employed in service as scholarship. Also, some committee members had a hard time distinguishing between the criteria to evaluate service as scholarship and the form the most convincing documentation took. For example, committee members would list the reflective essay or letters of support as criteria as opposed to documentation to which they applied criteria.

Fourth, there were problems inherent in assessing all faculty work. Committee members reported that at times they and other committee members were overly critical and at other times not critical enough of a candidate's service as scholarship. One committee member put it this way: "The difficulties come in the assumptions of individuals about these things." In other words, subtle unspoken assumptions that service could not be scholarship invaded committee discussions. Other committee members, however, expressed the view that whether assessing teaching, research, or service, "anonymity, good taste, and colleagueship" prevented the committee from really critically evaluating and turning down some faculty who were not doing service as scholarship, demeaning the entire process.

In addition to these problems there was little constructive communication between faculty candidates and the promotion and tenure committee about improving service as scholarship. Whereas faculty received some feedback on teaching and more feedback on research, the committee was negligent in providing feedback to faculty on the service parts of their portfolios for promotion and annual reviews, which made it difficult for candidates to know how they should improve their service as scholarship.

Despite these problems the committee seemed to have a fairly sophisticated view of service as scholarship, agreed on the general criteria, and believed that overall, it was important that faculty be rewarded for service as scholarship. The next section describes the outcomes of the Indicators on the College of Education promotion and tenure process.

Outcomes

MWSU's university-wide effort to assess and reward service as scholarship, which resulted in the *Indicators*, has had only limited impact on the College of Education. In 1997–98, the *Indicators* did not significantly influence promotion and tenure decisions, faculty behavior, or support structures for service in the College of Education. This was ironic, considering that the *Indicators* had been used as a model for dozens of other campuses to assess service as scholarship for promotion and tenure.

There were several reasons why the *Indicators* had a limited effect on the College of Education. First, the dean did not require the promotion and tenure committee to use them; second, department chairs did not require education faculty to read them; and third, the *Indicators* were not formerly disseminated throughout the College of Education.

Although the *Indicators* were not widely disseminated, a few education faculty involved in service as scholarship were involved in the development of the *Indicators*. These faculty not only read the *Indicators* but used them to frame their portfolios for promotion and tenure. This in turn caused promotion and tenure committee members to read the *Indicators*. In addition, by virtue of their having been the subject of university press and circulated by the Provost's office, many education faculty read the Indicators on their own. Consequently, the *Indicators* did contribute to change at the College of Education, albeit as one factor among many.

Outcomes from the development and implementation of the *Indicators* at the College of Education fall into two categories: outcomes for individual faculty and a cultural shift for the College of Education. These outcomes included tools to make the case; successful test cases; increased faculty satisfaction; a cultural shift, long-term impact on the tenure process, and continued opposition/mixed messages.

Tools to Make the Case

Before the *Indicators*, education faculty had no guidelines for how to make the case that their service was scholarship. Dean Schreier tried to help candidates develop ways to document their service, but at that time, there were no formal or established methods for documentation. In addition to formally establishing the university's position that service could be a form of scholarship, the *Indicators* provided a sound conceptual framework for when and how service was scholarship. Candidates now had a guide to document their service as scholarship and organize their portfolios for promotion and tenure. Once faculty member who was later successful in "making the case" said she organized every piece of evidence by the criteria listed in the new policy. The examples of different kinds of qualitative and quantitative evidence of service as scholarship gave education faculty examples of what evidence to prepare, collect, and write. The four dimensions in the *Indicators* provided a language for the candidates to discuss how and why their service was scholarship. The new policy helped candidates to understand what service as scholarship meant and how it differed from the scholarship of teaching and discovery. Candidates developed a more sophisticated understanding of the concept that resulted in stronger faculty documentation of service as scholarship.

In addition to acting as a guide for documentation for candidates, the new policies also served as a guide and an education for promotion and tenure committee members less familiar with the idea of service as scholarship. Also, since the *Indicators* were now official university policy, if candidates presented appropriate evidence, the policies served as a reminder that the service should be rewarded as scholarship. In this way, the policy provided cultural support to each candidate's documentation.

Promotion and Tenure: Successful Test Cases

After the *Indicators* were given to the Dean of the College of Education and department chairs for use in their promotion and tenure process, four education candidates for promotion and tenure made their cases with portfolios heavily weighted toward service as scholarship in the 1997–1998 academic year. These candidates considered themselves "test cases" for the new university policies. In each of the four cases, the candidates had fewer research publications than other candidates and made the case in their portfolios that their service was scholarship using the language and concepts presented in the *Indicators*. The candidates felt that their cases would indicate whether Dean Hennessey and the college-wide committee would follow the new university guidelines and assess and reward service as scholarship. An important question was: would the *Indicators* provide any "cultural backup" and procedural help for the candidates to successfully make their cases that their service was scholarship?

The "test cases" had two outcomes. Faculty candidates were either granted tenure or promotion or they were given a year's extension with marching orders from the dean to publish from their service as scholarship. After making some effort in this direction, all were promoted within one or two years. As mentioned earlier, in one case, the dean promoted a candidate who brought in significant funding even though the college committee turned the candidate down. Committee members reported that in two of the cases the work first presented was scholarship and in the other two cases it was community service.

Their own successful cases did not convince these four candidates that this meant that service was being assessed and rewarded as scholarship. Rather, the secrecy of the tenure process made them question the process. One such candidate stated:

> In some ways my case was a signal that in fact this kind of service is valued but . . . because we do not know what went on at the college level, my advice to folks coming up behind me is not to use me as a model of anything. I mean, we do not know. It is not clear. We can only speculate about what got valued.

Another candidate hypothesized the "real reasons" her service portfolio was successful.

Well, you see, you never know what goes on in a committee because it is all so secret. It is so ridiculous. I think that I put together a persuasive argument in the essay that I wrote to accompany my materials. I have a hunch that the outside reviewers, important people in the math education research community, recognize this as very important work and so my hunch is that in some ways I was probably a test case. I am one of the first people to come up for tenure (after the Indicators) who has been deeply enmeshed in work in schools and work with teachers both in our professional development school initiative and then all of this work that we have been doing on assessment. I do not have a more traditional research program. The research grows out of work with teachers. I do not have a publication in tier-one refereed journals. So for people on the college committee who do not know a lot about what we do in teacher education, my hunch is that the presentation of my materials and the outside review, and the fact that I have brought in over $4 million in outside grants, meant that the fact that I do not have a piece in the Journal for Research in Mathematics Education could not ultimately be held against me. My hunch is that there were just too many things that people could not discount because I did not have this one additional piece. Now, this is all speculation. Nobody will tell you, but that is my hunch.

The secrecy of the promotion and tenure review process made it difficult to assess the impact of the *Indicators* on these four promotion and tenure decisions. Although it appeared that the *Indicators* had created a more supportive climate for service as scholarship portfolios, candidates still wondered about their success and attributed it to a variety of factors, including funding, personal politics, and the difficulty of turning people down.

Increase in Faculty Satisfaction

The *Indicators* also positively influenced the level of education faculty satisfaction at MWSU. Faculty who were heavily engaged in service as scholarship reported that they felt more confident about their work, and, as a result, spent more time on their projects and improved the quality of their service. For some mid-career faculty who had become stale in their work and disillusioned with research and academic culture, the *Indicators* renewed their inspiration and commitment. These faculty became "really turned on" to the idea that their work could make a difference in the community and simultaneously be valued by Mid-West State University.

The *Indicators* played an important role in validating what many faculty felt was their whole purpose for being at a land grant college—providing expertise to local schools— and thereby increased faculty satisfaction at both the junior and senior faculty levels. Junior faculty interviewed described feeling as if they now had a chance to be tenured doing what they loved. Senior faculty felt that the university was finally validating what much of their career had been about.

Long Term Effects on Promotion and Tenure

In addition to the positive effects the *Indicators* may have had on these four cases, the *Indicators* also had a more subtle, potentially longer term effect on promotion and tenure decisions. One of the main outcomes of the dissemination of the *Indicators* was that the institutional support of service as scholarship muted the "publish or perish reality" toward which MWSU and the College of Education was moving. The Vice Provost for University Service agreed: "I think what we have been able to do is soften that pendulum swing toward research and maybe make it less radical."

Despite the dissemination of the *Indicators*, however, MWSU's College of Education was still a place where considerable pressure was placed on faculty to do traditional research. One education professor summarized this well when he said, "I've never been at an institution where service was more important, but it's still infinitesimal to publishing and researching." Therefore, although the *Indicators* did seem to positively influence promotion and tenure decisions for candidates with service as scholarship portfolios and act as a buffer against the growing tendency to prioritize research over all other forms of scholarship in the College of Education, traditional research continued to be more highly valued.

At least five education faculty involved in service as scholarship reacted proactively to the development of the *Indicators* and the dean's emphasis on producing scholarly publications related to service projects. Rather than being intimidated by this requirement, these faculty used what they learned from the campus-wide and college-wide history of discussions on service to strengthen the quality of their own service as scholarship, effectively demonstrate for promotion and tenure how their service was scholarship, act in politically savvy ways about disseminating their work, and serve as leaders and mentors for other more junior faculty involved in service.

The above-mentioned faculty developed strategies to survive and thrive doing service as scholarship in their College of Education. One of the strategies employed was to win grants that bought out their time for service and brought prestige to the College of Education. Another strategy was to connect their teaching, research, and service scholarship. These faculty described their teaching, research, and service as seamlessly connected in ways that made distinguishing the work for promotion and tenure almost impossible. One recently tenured associate professor explained: "One of the arguments I made in my tenure materials is that I have been about blurring the lines between teaching, research, and service, that each shapes and is shaped by the other two."

This small group of faculty understood that there were other education faculty who had done work with professional development schools that was important but was not scholarship. They argued that each faculty member needed to "make the case that the work was scholarship." Making the case involved trying to better understand the work and communicating that understanding to others. These faculty coped with the lack of understanding of "what they were doing with their time" by producing multiple products for multiple audiences; e.g., academic publications, workshops, and newsletters. They understood that their roles required not only administrative and relationship skills but also a responsibility to share with others what they learned about practice. Presenting their work at conferences was one of their common dissemination mechanisms.

These faculty displayed great confidence, partly because they took an "other options" approach to the work they did toward promotion and tenure. Two such faculty involved in service as scholarship described this attitude below:

> One of the things I said to myself when I knew I was taking a risk on whether I was going to get promoted is, if I can not do this kind of work here and get promoted, I guess I should not be here. And I seriously meant that. I did not want to change into a new person just to get tenure. I had other options in my life besides being here and so I wanted a place where I can do school-based work and if I cannot, then I need to find a different place to be and, I think, we have other faculty who felt the same. Maybe they do not feel like they have as many options as I felt I had. It is not that I have to call all the shots or tell the institution what to do. I know I need to fit into norms, but if I can not push the edge a little bit and engage in the kind of work I want to do, then I do not have to be here.

> Well, I will tell you what. I made a mid-life career change. I am not 30 years old looking at a 30-year career. I am almost 57 years old, and I am pretty clear about what it is I want to do. I am also pretty clear about what I think this place ought to value, and so I simply decided that I could make an argument that this is scholarship. I know it is not the kind of scholarship that some people are going to be looking for, but I know that my work is valued by a lot of people here. I have to convince people that this is worthy of being called scholarship. If the college says to me, "sorry," there are other things I can do in this world. So, I pretty much decided that even if they had said to me, "We will give you an extension," I would not have accepted that. I would have left. So, I worked very hard at putting the materials together, worked very hard at making a persuasive case, and I turned it in and let it go.

Cultural Shift Toward Service as Scholarship

The *Indicators* also subtly influenced the College of Education culture. The *Indicators* served as a positive reminder for some, and a negative reminder for others, of the previous dean's commitment to a reward system that valued community service as well as service as scholarship. For those who believed that service should be valued as scholarship, the *Indicators* provided a new level of institutional support for their argument. These faculty made different choices concerning their workloads accordingly. In as much as they provided a source of credibility for faculty who were arguing for more and better quality service, the *Indicators* were a sort of "cultural weapon." They sent a message that the larger university and other universities were valuing multiple forms of scholarship and, therefore, the College of Education should as well. The *Indicators* were viewed by education faculty, department chairs, and the dean as part of an effort on the part of the provost and president to encourage and hold the College of Education accountable for service to urban schools. When added to the external pressure from the educational community for Mid-West State University to become more involved with urban education, the *Indicators* served as a symbolic push to the College of Education to become more accountable for service.

There were other subtle changes. The campus-wide conversations that surrounded the development of the *Indicators* caught the attention of a few education faculty members. These faculty recalled initiating conversations and debates about the idea of service as scholarship in their departments. Despite the fact that the *Indicators* were not explicitly discussed in the Department of Teacher Education, they did seem to have sparked some additional conversations there about how much time it took faculty to do service in professional development schools, the dangers of assistant professors being in these roles, and how faculty could help each other to engage in scholarship as opposed to just community service to professional development schools. Through these conversations, consensus developed around the idea that service should only be considered scholarship if it is rooted in research expertise: things researched and studied over the years and then applied to appropriate settings. Most of the education faculty agreed that the "service you're doing must reflect the inquiry you're engaged in" for it to be scholarship. While these department-level conversations were somewhat fueled by the reward discussions begun by the previous dean, they were also fueled by the university-wide process that fostered the *Indicators*.

The conversations that surrounded the development of the *Indicators* influenced how faculty and students were recruited into the College of Education. While faculty had always been recruited with the importance of service as part of their "job talk," the idea of service as scholarship surfaced in more interviews for prospective faculty, including in the College of Education. The Vice Provost for University Service pointed out that, "Nobody gets recruited now without talking about the commitment to service and that this is different that the University of ———." In fact, several faculty reported having been told at their interview that "we have a different definition of service at Mid-West State University, based on the land grant ideal of extension and the concept of service as scholarship." The Indicators also influenced College of Education graduate student recruitment. One senior Education faculty member said:

> One of the big attractions for doctoral students coming here is the thought that they are coming to a place where people put a lot of emphasis on working with teachers in schools over a long period of time. That is a valued thing. That is a big drawing card for doctoral students.

One of the goals of the development of the *Indicators* was to change the culture of the institution so that faculty could imagine service as potential form of scholarship (according to academic administrators, committee members, and the grant evaluation reports). A small part of this effort was trying to change the language faculty used to describe service and scholarship so that all faculty would talk about certain kinds of service as "service scholarship." Through the development of the *Indicators*, the term and concept of "service as scholarship" spread to about half of the College of Education. The other half of the College of Education used the word "service" to mean purely community service.

Opposition and Mixed Messages

Despite shifts in the culture of the College of Education, junior faculty continued to receive mixed messages about whether or not service as scholarship would count for promotion and tenure. There were some messages that supported the implementation of the *Indicators*. For example, a few junior faculty were encouraged by senior faculty to do service as long as they engaged in it as scholarship by "making a coherent case for what they are doing and making sure it hangs together as a thoughtful program of scholarship that would say something more." There were strong and clear messages being passed on from senior faculty to junior faculty about what service as scholarship was and was not. One faculty member described arriving at MWSU and asking his department chair whether volunteering at a homeless shelter would count as service as scholarship for promotion and tenure. The department chair explained that this would not be considered service as scholarship because it did not involve application of expertise and knowledge gained through research since homelessness was not his area of expertise, nor was serving soup a form of scholarship.

There were also messages that undermined the *Indicators*. Some faculty distrusted the university rhetoric about valuing multiple forms of scholarship. This distrust recycled itself into messages to junior faculty to "publish or perish." One promotion and tenure member stated this negative message in the following way:

> No matter what an institution says about valuing scholarship in multiple ways, and they may very well mean those things, in academic culture the coin of the realm (at this institution) remains scholarly publications.

Some faculty were counseled to engage purely in research and wait to engage in service until they had tenure and could be more flexible in their career. "As a beginner, you can't risk it," one promotion and tenure committee member said. Therefore, there were conflicting messages about the idea of service as scholarship, and its efficacy for junior faculty applying for tenure. While mixed messages also existed before the development and dissemination of the *Indicators*, the *Indicators* intensified the conflict.

To conclude, the Indicators created minor outcomes in the College of Education. Faculty already involved in service as scholarship were the most influenced by the Indicators, and the *Indicators* slightly strengthened the service culture within the College of Education.

Summary

Why did this happen at Mid-West State University and what were the elements that worked against and/or for these organizational changes? The university-wide process to assess and reward service as scholarship was supported by the following structural and cultural elements: a $10.2 million grant to support and reexamine life-long education and service as scholarship at Mid-West State University; leadership from the provost's office and two faculty committees; a historic land grant mission and tradition of service; and the status of Mid-West State University as the number two research university in the state, which encouraged MWSU to distinguish itself through service. The major factors working against the implementation of the *Indicators* were: the increasing emphasis on research within the campus culture and the decentralized nature of the campus, which made disseminating the *Indicators* difficult and unlikely to reach college-level education promotion and tenure committee members.

In the College of Education, several elements worked toward valuing service as scholarship for promotion and tenure: Dean Schreier's interest in service as scholarship, which was evident in her involvement in the Holmes Group, her expansion of the professional development schools, her work as Acting Dean of LEP, and her attempts to find ways to document, assess, and reward faculty service as scholarship; faculty interest in having their service assessed as scholarship; the historical acceptance of different career trajectories in the College of Education; and a proactive response by faculty engaged in service as scholarship. The forces working against assessing and rewarding service as scholarship in the College of Education included: the College of Education's desire to be ranked as the number one research graduate school, which led to devaluing service that did not result in scholarly publication; the traditional valuing of research over service as scholarship among some faculty, including members of the promotion and tenure committee; the fact that the dean did not require the promotion and tenure committee to use the *Indicators*; and a lack of formal criteria applied to the assessment of service as scholarship in the College of Education.

How did the College of Education promotion and tenure committee assess service as scholarship? The *Indicators* proposed that promotion and tenure committee members use the following four categories to determine whether service was scholarship: significance, context, scholarship, and impact. Even though the *Indicators* only penetrated the consciousness of committee members indirectly, the committee was basically using these four categories to evaluate service as scholarship on their own. For example, when a candidate presented his/her service as scholarship, committee members wanted to know if the candidate's service was guided by innovative and rigorous intellectual questions, which could be loosely folded into the significance category. They evaluated the service for critical analysis, academic expertise, and peer critique, which were parts of the context and scholarship categories. Finally, they looked at the local and national impact of the work, which was included in the impact category. While the *Indicators* did not mention the importance of a connection between teaching, research, and service, this was implied in the context indicator. The committee also did not include the relationship-building aspects of service as scholarship in their assessment of service as scholarship. The fact that the committees' actual criteria were similar to the Indicators, helped in their implementation. However, the lack of a requirement to follow these new guidelines meant that assessment of service as scholarship was inconsistent and often deviated from the intentions set forth in the Indicators.

How have education faculty been affected by the changes in the way service as scholarship is assessed? The *Indicators* have not significantly changed promotion and tenure decisions, faculty behavior, or service decisions in the College of Education, in part because the College of Education had already moved toward assessing service as scholarship prior to the dissemination of the *Indicators*. Nonetheless, the *Indicators* influenced education faculty who were involved in service as scholarship, and, through their portfolios, affected the conversation among committee members. As a result, the *Indicators* did have some minor impact in the College of Education. They seem to have had a positive influence on four promotion and tenure cases and were acting as a buffer against forces that were opposed to the evaluation of service as scholarship. Faculty involved in service as scholarship experienced an increase in satisfaction, with work, and with MWSU, and were given tools to more effectively document their service as scholarship. There were subtle cultural changes in the College of Education because of the development and introduction of the *Indicators*. The *Indicators* influenced the recruitment of faculty and graduate students, acted as a cultural support and additional cover for faculty making the case that their service was scholarship, and encouraged discussion and a slight shift in thinking about the concept of service as scholarship.

Finally, one cannot help but be struck by the strong conceptual framework and intentional planning that went into this effort at MWSU. There were many reports that described in detail all of the planning efforts and strategies used to imbed the service as scholarship mission in the reward system. It is ironic that many more faculty and administrators are aware of the *Indicators* at other campuses than within the College of Education at Mid-West State University. This case demonstrated the importance of dissemination, leadership, and faculty culture when trying to implement university-wide policies in individual departments and colleges. The case also demonstrated how informal policies enforced by deans can be more important than formal university policies in determining a faculty member's fate. While considerable progress was made at Mid-West State University, the final Kellogg report pointed out that "it will take time for service as scholarship to become entrenched on any university campus and the future, though promising, is uncertain."

CHAPTER FIVE

St. Timothy

In 1991–1992, St. Timothy College decided to rewrite its definition of scholarship to be more consistent with its liberal arts mission. This resulted in changes to its faculty handbook and promotion and tenure guidelines, including a written rationale for the new definition and introduction of the idea of aims and stages of scholarship. These changes have had a lasting impact on St. Timothy's reward system for service as scholarship. This case describes the culture and the process by which St. Tims conceptualized, organized, and implemented a new vision of scholarship.

The Culture of St. Tims

St. Timothy College is a small, Catholic, liberal arts college in the Midwest. A small city and several other colleges are close to the campus. Students are traditional age, and the college is mostly residential. There are approximately 2,000 students and 130 faculty. St. Tims, as it is called by many, is 100 years old and is known for excellence in teaching. Teaching loads of three courses a semester, intensive committee work, and research mean that faculty are very busy. Budget cuts have been common yearly events and have had a significant impact on faculty and division chairs. Because the college is heavily tuition-dependent, even the attrition of five students—and the resulting loss of tuition—affects everyone at the college.

St. Tims' faculty of 130 is divided into three divisions: Social Sciences, Humanities, and Physical Sciences. Divisions are broken down into clusters of faculty called "disciplines," which are organized around degree areas. Division chairs supervise budgets, schedule courses, and negotiate faculty workload, but one of their most significant roles is coordinating applications for tenure and promotion. They help faculty candidates prepare their promotion and tenure materials and submit a letter evaluating the candidate's performance.

While St. Tims is best known for its strong liberal arts disciplines, its professional disciplines such as education and business also have good reputations. Although there is ongoing tension between the pure liberal arts focus and the professional disciplines, there is really no second-class status among faculty. For example, each year in a college-wide election faculty are elected in equal numbers from each division and discipline to the Tenure and Promotion Committee, and if any one group of faculty were considered more or less important, this would not happen.

St. Timothy is "somewhat" involved with the local community, according to its dean and division chairs. Service projects tend to be largely teaching related, and faculty in the applied disciplines are more involved. Service projects include professional development and teacher training; summer camps in math, science, computers, and economics; and ongoing mentoring programs for children and teens who are at-risk, have disabilities, or are from Native American, Asian, and Hispanic backgrounds.

Most of the service projects are innovative applications of different disciplines to various community problems and audiences. Some projects have research components, but even those projects are largely inquiries into the teaching and learning process. This method of delivering service is consistent with St. Tims primary teaching mission.

The administration is and has always been very supportive of faculty who initiate service projects, which bring prestige to St. Tims. Faculty learn about outreach opportunities primarily from the administration but also from other faculty. Opportunities are found in requests for proposals, professional associations, local school districts, and state standards committees. One former division chair put it this way: "There is a tendency in the liberal arts college not to have much involvement in the community, but we do more than most private schools."

St. Tims has always had strong deans and strong faculty governing the academic affairs of the college (according to St. Tims' faculty and academic administrators). Faculty traditionally do not want administration having too much power. The faculty feel a sense of ownership of the college and want to be involved in decision making. The Faculty Assembly, a faculty governing body composed of elected representatives from all disciplines, has often disagreed with decisions made by the dean and/or Board of Trustees and has used the forum to discuss their differences. The Faculty Assembly is often a place where underlying tensions between faculty and administration surface.

The college was founded by an order of priests whose governing principle is hospitality; they "created an atmosphere that was congenial, that wasn't educationally edgy," according to one administrator. Although there is not an overwhelming Catholic presence, the Catholic mission shows itself in subtle ways, such as applications for sabbaticals to work on social justice projects. Although over half of the faculty and staff identify as

Catholic, the faculty and Board of Visitors include only a few priests and nuns. St. Tims' governing principle of hospitality nurtured a tradition of community, collegiality, and democratic decision-making. St. Timothy is described by its faculty as being a place with a predisposition toward people working together and trusting each other, a place with few territorial battles, and a place with efficient committees. The low faculty turnover rate is evidence of the faculty's positive feelings. Faculty report working hard to communicate across divisions for the benefit of the college and feeling more allegiance to the college than to their individual disciplines.

The one issue that appears to be creating some tension on campus is the hiring of more faculty with strong traditional research interests. One full professor even said if he had applied to St. Tims today as a new professor, he wouldn't be hired. He and others expressed concern that this trend toward hiring more research-oriented faculty might negatively affect St. Tims teaching and service missions and its ability to reward multiple forms of scholarship through tenure and promotion.

Promotion and Tenure

At St. Tims, promotion and tenure are separate processes but the decisions are made by one committee. The Promotion and Tenure Committee consists of eight members. Seven faculty members are elected from across the college by the faculty, and the dean of the college serves as an ex-officio member without a vote. Only tenured faculty who have been with the college at least two years can serve on the committee. Members are elected to three-year terms, and the committee elects its own chair from within the group each year.

Faculty members who wish to apply for tenure or promotion during the current academic year submit a curriculum vita, an application essay, periodic review letters, self-reviews, course syllabi, letters from colleagues, and supporting documents to the division chair by the end of September. The division chair then writes a letter of support and submits his/her letter and the candidate's materials to the dean. The division chair's letter addresses the candidate's performance in each of the following areas: academic preparation, teaching effectiveness, advisement of students, scholarship and professional activity, and collegial activities. The committee receives all of the applications at the beginning of the academic year and makes recommendations by the end of the year to the president, who recommends them to the Board of Trustees, which ultimately confers tenure or promotion (St. Tims' Faculty Handbook and Personnel Policies).

All tenure applications are reviewed in the fall, all promotions in spring. Every committee member receives a copy of each candidate portfolio and the committee sets aside two full meetings (four or more hours) to discuss each case. Votes are collected by secret ballot and decisions are made by majority vote (St. Tims' Faculty Handbook and Personnel Policies).

Over 90 percent of faculty candidates at St. Timothy receive tenure, and it is not as controversial or difficult as being granted promotion. When faculty members apply for tenure they have to demonstrate *potential for scholarship*; to achieve promotion from assistant to associate, *evidence of scholarship*; and for promotion to full professor, *evidence of sustained scholarly achievement*. Because the guidelines for tenure state that the candidate must demonstrate *potential* for scholarship, only those faculty who have not proven to be effective teachers are denied tenure. St. Tims' faculty understand that effective teaching, as shown by teaching evaluations and peer reviews, is the most important issue for tenure. Since scholarship was historically the deciding factor for promotion, and service did not fit within the scholarship category, there was no serious attempt to evaluate service. Before 1991–92, faculty reported that, in terms of evaluating professional service, "if you wrote something from it, it counted."

Not all faculty at the college experienced the promotion and tenure process in the same way. The education faculty, for example, have experienced both St. Tims culture and promotion and tenure system differently than the rest of the campus.

Education Discipline

At times the education discipline operates like a small island, miles away from the mainland. This small subset of 17 education faculty within the St. Timothy's Social Sciences Division all have offices along the same corridor of a social sciences building. They meet together each week for two hours or more, redesigning the curriculum and discussing grant projects and partnerships with schools. Education assistant professors recall how their narrow research agenda and definition of scholarship changed because of the culture of teaching and service at St. Tims and more specifically, of the education discipline. Part of this culture shift has to do with how much time education faculty spend together. They all genuinely enjoy one another's company and are in close contact with each other, doing perhaps more collaborative than independent work. One relatively new assistant professor said she is impressed with her colleagues because they "let me try new things and they all work real well together."

Between the faculty in the education discipline and the rest of the college, however, there is a strong sense of "us against them." If there is a gap among disciplines, it is and has always been between the education discipline and the rest of the campus. This tension is surprising because St. Tims' faculty are a relatively homogeneous group. Teaching loads, age of faculty, rate of faculty publication, pay scales, gender, and commitment to the teaching mission of the college do not vary much by discipline.

One reason for education's relative isolation is that they spend so much time together working on internal curriculum development and individually out in the field for teaching and professional service that they tend not to be on many campus-wide committees (according to interviews with education faculty and academic administrators). Moreover, the administration of the college is very supportive of the professional service in which education faculty engage, which has caused other faculty to claim that education faculty are too closely aligned with administration. Since there has always been some tension between administration and faculty at the college, the strong relationship between education faculty and administration further distances education faculty from the rest of the faculty.

In addition, education faculty are part of the field of teacher education and, thus, they are affected by the national movement toward greater faculty involvement in developing partnerships with schools. Three education faculty work collaboratively on a $500,000 grant for professional development in science, and one assistant professor recently spent an entire semester in a teacher exchange, where he taught a middle-school class for six months. Such frequent and intense involvement with schools creates a tension between engaging in service and writing for education faculty. One education faculty member said, "There is something to the notion that field education is going in a direction that hurts chances [for education faculty] for promotion and tenure, unless it is converted into articles, and the more faculty do, they may not have time to convert the relationships into articles."

Despite this tension, education faculty at St. Tims are involved in a number of different kinds of professional service projects. In fact, one of the faculty members in education said, "Most of the work education faculty do is service, it is really just what envelope we put it in." This comment underscores the difficulty education faculty have in differentiating between teaching, research, and service for promotion and tenure purposes.

These are the structures, the landscape, and some of the cultural characteristics of St. Tims and its education discipline. What follows is the story of how and why this college decided to engage in a process to reward multiple forms of scholarship.

A New Vision of Scholarship

A History of Discussion on Scholarship

As far back as the 1970s, faculty conferences at St. Tims explored the topic of multiple forms of scholarship. In the early 1980s, the college revised some weak advancement criteria, which required little more than time in rank for promotion. Fueled by St. Timothy's emerging academic ambitions, the 1980s revision made it progressively harder to achieve tenure and promotion. During this time, the requirement for full professor of "sustained scholarly achievement" was being interpreted as having juried publications in one's field—i.e., the kind of traditional research that was mandatory at large universities. In effect, St. Timothy's was becoming a "publish or perish" institution. In the mid-1980s, the Faculty Assembly vigorously debated the issue in response to a proposal to modify promotion and tenure guidelines. In addition, several in-house faculty conferences, the faculty newsletter, and intermittent faculty meetings dealt with the topic.

During this same period, the dean was participating in the national conversation on rewarding multiple forms of scholarship. An important event for him was when Dr. Gene Rice of the American Association for Higher Education (AAHE) gave a speech at the 1988 Council of Independent Colleges Dean's Institute. Dr. Rice spoke about the four kinds of scholarship—discovery, teaching, integration, and application—and the tendency of small colleges to try to increase their prestige by mimicking the discovery or "research university model."

While the dean was contemplating Dr. Rice's speech, a group of St. Tims' faculty were preparing a "release time policy." Faculty wanted to be able to apply for release time from courses to work on discipline-specific research, which they believed would help faculty members advance in rank, enhance the reputation of the college, and relieve them from being overburdened by too much teaching and service. Their rationale read, "If St. Timothy's is to establish itself as an elite institution with a reputation for academic excellence, it must look at the colleges to which it aspires and the opportunities that those colleges provide for their faculties for curricular and scholarly development."

In February 1989, the dean argued against the release time proposal on the floor of the Faculty Assembly. He agreed that many faculty felt overburdened and that the college did not want to discourage active research agendas for they were all proud of recent increases in faculty publications. However, he argued, the cost of the proposal was prohibitive in terms of the reduced course offerings and increased class size. Besides, he said, this college prided itself on being a teaching institution that cared primarily about students. St. Tims would not want to create a two-tiered faculty of teachers and researchers, which more resembled a research university model, when they were supposed to be striving for excellence in teaching and service. Therefore, the dean made a new proposal to the Faculty Assembly: to redefine scholarship in a way that would include teaching and professional service. He argued that more of the high-quality work faculty were already doing in these other areas would count for promotion and tenure.

Despite the dean's new proposal to redefine scholarship, the faculty voted by a margin of four to one in favor of the release time proposal. The Academic Committee of the Board of Trustees agreed with the dean, however, and turned down the proposal, arguing that it would change the character of St. Tims and it would be prohibitively expensive.

In fall 1989, the dean told the faculty that their release time proposal had been turned down by the Board of Trustees, but their proposal had convinced him that the existing reward system needed to change. Several faculty had applied for full professor and had been turned down, despite having engaged in what the dean considered to be spectacular teaching and service scholarship. There were fewer applications to full professor as a result in the three years following these rejections. The dean told the faculty that the current definition of scholarship needed to be reexamined and the criteria for advancement needed to be revised. The dean recalled that he did not initiate anything at the time, because he wanted to locate the faculty discussion within the framework of a report about to be published by Ernest Boyer for the Carnegie Foundation. The report, *Scholarship Reconsidered,* was published the following year in 1991 and the dean began the process of redefining scholarship in fall, 1991.

During the intervening year, several other issues were percolating among faculty, which contributed to the journey to redefine scholarship at St. Tims. A few of these issues had been growing in intensity over the previous decade and simply grew to a climax during this intervening year. For example, St. Tims had been hiring more and more faculty who were primarily interested in conducting traditional research. These faculty were raising the bar for research expectations for promotion and tenure. This created a fear among some faculty, as well as the dean, that in raising the bar, some faculty were being denied promotion for the wrong reasons—especially to full professor. There was consensus among many of the faculty that something needed to be done to make it possible for faculty who were doing scholarship in other areas besides research to succeed in careers at St. Tims. Therefore, just as the bar for scholarship was being raised, there was consensus that the bar needed to be widened. If the bar was going to become higher, faculty wanted there to be more places for faculty to "jump over." This would create a sort of "no excuses model," which required all faculty to be engaged in some kind of scholarly activity.

Another contributing factor was that for some time many humanities faculty had been unsuccessful in achieving promotion with works of art as their scholarship. Faculty felt it was necessary to change the promotion and tenure criteria to make it possible for these faculty to be able to submit works of art, such as plays they wrote, concerts performed, and paintings for review as scholarship. Also, faculty felt the time was right to make changes in the reward system because in some disciplines there were fewer opportunities to publish than in others. The college had been searching for a way to acknowledge the differences in publication opportunities.

All of these issues converged in the late '80s, and increased the faculty's desire to change promotion and tenure guidelines. It was an opportune moment to create a task force on redefining scholarship at St.Tims.

Choosing a Task Force

Once the Carnegie report was published, the dean felt that St. Tims' process could be grounded in the national redefining scholarship movement and therefore St. Tims was ready to embark on a journey to redefine scholarship. In April 1991, the dean asked Dr. Jean Lewis, his good friend and the director of faculty development, to head a task force to redefine scholarship. Dr. Lewis had been a faculty member in the English department for nearly 25 years and the director of faculty development for eight. He knew the school, the faculty, and the issue well. Everyone at the college thought very highly of Dr. Lewis, as was clear in a comment from one assistant professor in education who said Dr. Lewis had the "best vision of what it meant to be a professional." He was also known to be a "task master" and, for this and other reasons, the dean felt Dr. Lewis was an ideal candidate to shepherd this process at St. Tims.

The next step that lay ahead was selecting faculty for the task force. In the late 1970's there had been a committee to redesign the general education or core requirements, a four-year program for undergraduates which still stands today with few revisions. It was believed that the reason the core curriculum was successful was the effort and "duking it out" that was allowed to happen to create the curriculum. Through this experience, the dean had learned important lessons about how to structure St. Timothy's committee processes. The dean understood the need to always include the "potential opposition" in the process to gain their support and make sure people were listening to one another's views.

The dean felt that the success of the redefining scholarship enterprise would depend on the credibility of the task force and the degree to which it was representative and balanced (case study materials on St. Tims' redefining scholarship process, and interview with dean). Therefore, the dean asked each of the three division chairs to nominate two faculty to be representatives of their divisions. He stressed to the division chairs the need to choose faculty who could represent different views of scholarship in their divisions. With the advice of division chairs, the dean appointed the six task force members in April 1991, within one week of the appointment of Dr. Lewis as the task force chair.

Each of the task force members began their service with a letter from the dean defining the task force charge. In the letter, the dean outlined two phases to the project. The first phase was "to develop a working definition of scholarship as we understand it at St. Timothy by the end of the fall 1991 semester." The second phase was to take the new approved definition of scholarship at St. Tims and apply it to current criteria for tenure and promotion. This was to be completed by May 1992. Along the way, the committee was encouraged to read the Boyer materials and collect feedback from colleagues. They were asked to try to arrive at a collegial solution, involving the entire faculty in the deliberative process whenever possible, as had been the tradition at St. Tims in the past. The dean gave the task force a short timeline because, he said, "Task forces always work better under deadlines; it is a gentle way of moving people ahead."

The Task Force Gets to Work: Boyer's Influence

Between May and August 1991, the chair conducted an exhaustive search on the topic of scholarship and asked the task force members to read Ernest Boyer's *Scholarship Reconsidered* (DATE), along with several articles and book chapters discovered through a data-base search. Dr. Lewis circulated multiple copies of *Scholarship Reconsidered* to all college units. He asked task force members to actively seek input from colleagues on defining scholarship, primarily through one-on-one office visits. Finally, that summer, each task force member was asked to write a one-and-a-half page working definition of scholarship and share his or her copies with the rest of the task force in September 1991.

Surveying Faculty on Their Views of Scholarship

In September 1991, the task force began to meet on a weekly basis. During the first few meetings in September, the members shared their impressions of their colleagues' views of scholarship. Faculty were not only eager to discuss the issue, but actually sought out task force members so that they could contribute their views. According to the Director of Faculty Development and many faculty, hallways were buzzing with talk of scholarship. In order to collect more feedback from the entire academic community, the task force asked the director of the Survey Center to help them develop a 22 item "Faculty Survey of Scholarship at St. Timothy."

The 1991 survey had an 80% response rate, with a total of 77 faculty responding. The response rate was comparable across all divisions, ranks, tenure status, and number of years at St. Timothy. The results showed that most faculty agreed or strongly agreed that:

A definition of scholarship at St. Timothy's should include the application of knowledge to consequential problems (i.e., Boyer's "Scholarship of Application").

> Activity relating directly to the intellectual work of the professor and carried out through consultation, technical assistance, policy analysis, program evaluation, and the like should be considered scholarship.

> The definition of scholarship should be congruent with St. Timothy's unique liberal arts teaching mission.

> Publication should not be the yardstick that measures scholarly productivity.

> The definition should include all of Boyer's categories of scholarship.

Many pages of survey results and written comments from the survey were collated and placed in key faculty gathering areas for review. The high degree of faculty comment and engagement with the issue indicated that this was a very important issue to many faculty at St. Timothy's and that faculty members wanted to have their voices heard. The high degree of community decision-making and conversation at St. Timothy indicated that the faculty wanted to take ownership of the future of "their college."

Members of the task force studied the results. They also held an open forum on October 17, 1991, for the purpose of discussing the survey results and any others issues and concerns about the process. The majority of faculty participated in the open forum and/or gave comments to committee members shortly thereafter. The task force took this additional feedback back to their deliberations.

Task Force Deliberations

When the Task Force next met they found a diversity of opinion among the feedback from St. Tims faculty and among themselves. There was some "dialectical tension" that occurred across the table. One faculty member said, "Any broadening of the definition represents a watering down of quality," while another said, "Counting publications is the wrong way to go." Some felt "publications and presentations are the only true tests of scholarship," while others felt all "classroom preparation should count as scholarship." The Director of Faculty Development recalled that good will, good humor, and collegiality characterized the sessions, but at times, it appeared they would never come to consensus. Much of the debate focused on how to do peer review of forms of scholarship other than the scholarship of discovery. However, after thirteen sessions throughout October and November, and four drafts of a new definition and rationale for redefining scholarship, they agreed on a draft, which was sent to the dean on November 12, 1991. The dean approved and submitted the document to the Faculty Advisory Council for discussion at the Faculty Assembly meeting on December 13, 1991.

A New Rationale and Definition of Scholarship

The Rationale for Redefining Scholarship at St. Tims aimed to (a) be consistent with the goals and mission of the college, especially its spirit of community and collegiality, (b) nurture the creative talents of all faculty while fostering rigor and integrity in the scholarship process, (c) recognize scholarship as both process and outcomes, (d) acknowledge those who push back the frontiers of knowledge and those who explain and apply this knowledge, and (e) recognize the need for the community of scholars at St. Timothy to respond to the needs of the world beyond the campus.

The rationale sketched out a history of the meaning of scholarship at St. Timothy and located the discussion within the national movement of hundreds of institutions of higher learning attempting to redefine scholarship.

It then went on to point out the tenets upon which the definition of scholarship at St. Timothy was built. It began with the premise that the key to "maintaining the integrity of the scholarship process was the documentation, sharing, and evaluating of scholarly endeavors" (pg.2).

The definition of scholarship that followed the rationale began with a section entitled the "Concept of Scholarship," which laid out how scholarship manifested itself at St. Tims. It concluded that scholarship at St. Timothy was the bringing to bear of a trained mind on a problem or question and the public sharing of the results of those labors. The next section, entitled the "Process of Scholarship," suggested that scholarship was not only a product, a result, and a contribution to the field, but also the process, which precedes, generates, and shapes the product. The definition suggested that the process of scholarship (whether completed or not) should be periodically shared with colleagues and submitted to the scrutiny of one's peers. The next section, entitled "The Stages of Scholarship," outlined three closely interrelated and sometimes overlapping stages through which scholarship was created: self-development, productivity, and dissemination. Finally, the last section of the definition, entitled "The Aims of Scholarship," outlined the four general aims of scholarship: (a) the creation of discovery of new knowledge, insights, or works; (b) the creation or discovery of innovative pedagogical techniques; (c) the development of a novel integration of pre-existing information or ideas; and (d) the application of theoretical knowledge to consequential problems that results in new knowledge or innovative solutions to problems. One of the examples given for this last aim was applying new theories developed in successful alternative schools to reduce dropout rates in traditional comprehensive schools.

The Campus Approves

On November 21, 1991, the Faculty Advisory Committee placed the motion to approve the new definition and rationale for scholarship on the agenda of the December 13, 1991, Faculty Assembly Meeting. At the meeting, the task force chair delivered the rationale and comments on the genesis and evolution of the project. Energetic discussion about the definition carried over to the next meeting. On February 11, 1992, after discussion, the motion to approve the *Definition of Scholarship at St. Timothy* passed by a vote of 43 to 8. The dean and other faculty recalled that the proposal was so well put together, most faculty agreed easily and couldn't say anything but "yes." However, a minority feared this would mean a decrease in traditional research productivity and they voted "no." There had been so much educating on this process by the director of faculty development that there was really no serious opposition. According to the dean, the committee had "considered every possible possibility." On March 2, 1992, the dean brought the new definition and rationale to the Promotion and Tenure Committee so that they might apply it to the current criteria for tenure and promotion. The Promotion and Tenure Committee discussed this issue during the next five meetings.

Applying Changes to the Promotion and Tenure Guidelines

During the summer of 1992, two members of the Promotion and Tenure Committee drafted a modified set of tenure and promotion guidelines in light of the broadened definition of scholarship. That September, the Promotion and Tenure Committee spent three meetings refining the newly drafted guidelines and then sent copies of the proposed modifications to the task force for the members' input in October. In November 1992, the Promotion and Tenure committee sent the proposal for modifying the tenure and promotion guidelines to the Faculty Assembly for approval. On December 1, 1992, after a ten-minute discussion, there was a move to approve the modified guidelines. There was only one opposing vote.

The new guidelines changed the old policies in several ways. Wording was added to include "the creation or discovery of pedagogical techniques" and "the novel integration of pre-existing information or ideas" as possible forms of scholarship. This wording emphasized that scholarship could be considered as disciplinary, cross-disciplinary, or pedagogical in nature. Therefore, whereas the old document had talked about work "related to one's field" the new one replaced this phrase with "related to one's scholarly interests and expertise." New emphasis was also put on the idea that, regardless of the particular scholarly medium, dissemination and sharing were essential to the integrity of scholarship.

> Scholarly works, whether complete or in process, should be periodically and publicly shared and submitted to the scrutiny of one's peers. This sharing is essential in maintaining the integrity of the scholarly process. In short, scholarship involves the acquisition and advancement of knowledge and the exposure of such efforts to the critical evaluation of others (Faculty Handbook, p. 45).

Although these two changes seem minor, it is important to note that the new rationale and definition of scholarship were included in the revised tenure and promotion guidelines in the *Faculty Handbook*. According to the promotion and tenure committee, faculty, and Dr. Lewis, after the changes it became common for faculty submitting portfolios to frame their portfolio by quoting directly from the new definition and rationale. These changes in 1991–92 reflected a conceptual shift toward recognizing multiple forms of scholarship. That shift changed personal definitions of scholarship and rewards for faculty at St. Tims.

Institutional Support for the Changes

St. Tims provided institutional support to the 1991–92 tenure and promotion changes in several ways. First, the director of faculty development used the resources within his office to support the new policy. Dr. Lewis' office housed a resource center with teaching and learning materials.

Through this office, he coordinated and facilitated a new faculty orientation and mentor program, a series of brown bag discussions on issues of interest to faculty, an annual faculty development conference, book groups, individual counseling, and three faculty development funds. Dr. Lewis added to the office's regular programs workshops on the new terms and definitions. Thus, through its various programs, this office provided a place for faculty to discuss documentation, evaluation, or ethical issues related to service or teaching as scholarship. It was estimated that 60% or more of faculty used the resources in the Office of Faculty Development at one time or another throughout the year.

The faculty workshops specifically educated faculty on how to document multiple forms of scholarship. In addition, the director of faculty development provided individual counseling to nearly all faculty applying for tenure and promotion. He helped them to frame their service as scholarship portfolios and gave them advice for tenure or promotion applications, such as which letters of support to seek. It was clear that the letters Dr. Lewis wrote for faculty had been, and continued to be, a positive force in the education of the Promotion and Tenure Committee on how to evaluate service and teaching as scholarship. However, it was not clear how much sway his letters had with committee members in making the case for a candidate one way or another.

The dean and division chairs supported the new policies by using the language in the new guidelines to discuss scholarship with faculty. This provided symbolic messages that they themselves "bought in" to the new definition of scholarship and changes to the guidelines. St. Tims also supported the changes by providing faculty development funds, awards, and other supports for teaching and professional service activities. For example, the Summer Grants Program provided $1,750 for individual faculty to engage in scholarly, artistic, curricular, and instructional projects undertaken during the summer. The Faculty Development Fund provided awards of $500 to faculty to attend special meetings, workshops, seminars pertinent to one's scholarship. The faculty/student development endowment fund provided awards of $1,000 to faculty/ student partnerships on scholarly, creative, artistic, or teaching-learning enhancement projects. The director of faculty development reported that, while these funds could be used to support faculty professional service projects, fewer than 25% of these funds were used for this purpose. However, so much of the work St. Timothy's faculty engaged in was applied scholarship that there may have been overlap between traditional teaching and research awards and professional service projects in the other 75%.

Within the last few years, the administration had been helping more faculty write grants. This is a likely source of future support for faculty professional service. For example, a large grant related to science teacher professional development, which involved a great deal of professional service, had been partly written and thoroughly supported by the administration. This kind of support had not always been available at St. Tims, as the institution did not have a long history of writing and winning grants. In addition to supporting grant writing for professional service, the administration also provided release time. The three faculty working on the science education grant and a faculty member involved in a Center for Economics Education, which provided service and outreach to local and statewide teachers, were all given release time for their work. The dean and senior administrators felt it was important to support these projects, because they brought positive attention to the institution.

In another attempt to recognize the importance of professional service, St. Timothy's added a Service Award in 1995 to their college-wide faculty awards ceremony. There is also a Leadership, Service, and Involvement Center on campus for student community service and service-learning, from which some faculty have launched projects.

The process of redefining scholarship at St. Tims, from the initial appointment of the task force to institutionalization of the new policies in the *Faculty Handbook*, took less than two years, a remarkably swift process for a college trying to change its reward system using democratic decision making and working through faculty governance. Because of its small size, St. Tims has a history of efficient committees, but this process was expeditious even for them. Although there were many reasons this process was successful, several stand out: Redefining scholarship was a solution to the problem of rising research expectations in a primarily teaching institution, it allowed the college to reward scholarship in the arts, and it addressed discipline differences in the opportunity to publish. All of these issues had arisen in recent years and begged a solution. This process worked because faculty were in charge, they made the redefinition consistent with the mission of the college, and they worked toward compromise. In addition, the task force carefully fostered a spirit of shared ownership among the faculty at large.

The dean also promoted the efficiency of the process by appointing a chair that was respected and known for keeping on task and by setting a short deadline. The two-tiered approach the dean proposed, first rewriting the definition of scholarship and then amending the promotion and tenure materials worked well. The leadership shown by the dean and the director of faculty development were critical to the success of the entire process.

Tenure and Promotion

In the previous sections of this chapter, the history, procedures, and culture of tenure and promotion before the 1991–92 changes, and the changes themselves, were described. In this section, the criteria used by committee members to assess candidates for promotion and tenure during fall 1998 are described, along with the problems associated with assessing service as scholarship.

Criteria to Assess Service as Scholarship

By the time the Promotion and Tenure Committee met in fall 1998, the idea of "service as scholarship" was fully integrated into the procedures for promotion and tenure. While tenure and promotion were separate process-es, one college-wide Promotion and Tenure Committee made all decisions. According to a few of their own members, faculty, and administrators, the 1998 Promotion and Tenure Committee members were more "conserva-tive" in their definitions of scholarship than other recent committees, but they were still open to multiple forms of scholarship if they were well-doc-umented and had strong peer reviews. Committee members said they felt they were "very broad in terms of what we accept," and tended to use a "looser definition of scholarship." For example, they accepted profession-al writing in second-tier and non-refereed journals as evidence of scholar-ship.

In terms of the process, the committee did not break down all of the portfolios by the stages of scholarship, or apply the guidelines literally to each case; however, they referred to the guidelines often. There were no separate criteria to evaluate if or how any specific activity, such as service or teaching, was scholarship. Rather, it was incumbent on the candidate to "make the case" and demonstrate how and why scholarship was demon-strated, and incumbent on the Promotion and Tenure Committee to assess if, and how well, the candidate made the case that their work was scholar-ship.

Because candidates held the burden of proof to demonstrate whether or not their service was scholarship, they were instructed to provide as much evidence as possible. Different committee members were swayed by differ-ent criteria. Overall, the Promotion and Tenure Committee differentiated between community service and service that was scholarship by academic expertise, connections to other teaching and research, self-assessment through systematic reflection, quality of written products, dissemination, and peer reviews.

Academic expertise was critical in assessing service as scholarship. Committee members wanted to see how the candidate's academic training in a specific discipline affected how they constructed and reflected upon their service. Each of the candidates submitted a reflective essay with their portfolio of teaching, service, and research to act as a guide to their work. Committee members examined the reflective essay to see how the faculty member connected their service with scholarly questions and literature in their discipline. They wanted to see that the project demonstrated academ-ic expertise "in action," that the work was connected in some way with what other professors were doing in similar areas around the country and to what was being discussed at national conferences and in national disci-plinary associations.

Committee members looked at how the professional service fit in with the candidate's "trajectory of work." They wanted to see a connectedness between the candidate's teaching, research, and service that made it clear that this service was part of an on-going attempt to address a set of scholarly questions. When candidates involved their students in their service, and their community partners in their research and teaching, these reciprocal movements between teaching, research, and service convinced committee members that the candidate's service was just another expression of their scholarship.

Self-assessment was also a key factor in how the committee assessed service as scholarship. The committee wanted to see the mind of the scholar at work. This meant they looked for evidence that the candidate applied systematic reflection and analysis to the work. They asked questions such as: Did the candidate reflect on the mistakes and lessons learned from the outreach project? Was the candidate intentional and deliberate in the way that he or she conceptualized the problem, designed a solution, and went about evaluating the results?

Dissemination and peer review were other critical pieces of the evaluation process for committee members. Because dissemination was one of the major components of St. Tims' definition and rationale of scholarship, the committee felt comfortable saying that only service projects that had been disseminated qualified as scholarship. Although service projects could potentially be disseminated through video, web sites, or other mediums, the Promotion and Tenure Committee felt strongly that written products in most disciplines were the only way to really effectively disseminate scholarship, so they looked at the quality of the written products.

Along with publication, the committee was concerned that service as scholarship be subject to peer review. Committee members expected candidates to bring some texts related to their service as scholarship (curriculum guides, conference proceedings, grant applications) to peers. Therefore, the Committee looked for credible peer review of the work. They wanted to see whether the service was subject to evaluation by the educational community of scholars or practitioners and to ensure that the service was not simply an event that occurred between the faculty member and a community partner. They felt service as scholarship should involve a discovery process that was shared with others and moved beyond the local site to shed light on practice and scholarship more broadly. One Promotion and Tenure Committee member actually quoted the new guidelines when explaining the importance of the peer critique.

The committee struggled with qualifications of credible peer reviewers, but largely they seemed to believe that only other academics, or in the case of the arts, other performers or professional critics, were "credible" sources of peer review. For example, the committee felt that, in the field of education, when education professors collaborated with high school teachers on professional service projects or acted as experts for task forces on curriculum changes, the high school teachers or task force members were not credible sources of peer review. The committee argued that these community partners were depending on the faculty member for expert knowledge that they themselves did not have. Only external constituents of the projects, with as much, if not more, knowledge of the subject matter than the faculty member, were seen as credible peer reviewers. Therefore, the Promotion and Tenure Committee believed the most credible peer review sources in education were education professors from other universities.

Finally, the committee wanted to see candidates appropriately weigh the items they were presenting as evidence of their service as scholarship. The committee had an informal hierarchy of weighting that gave less importance to participation in voluntary discussion panels, for example, than reviewed conference presentations, invited talks, and published work. The weighting was based on the amount and/or quality of peer review, analysis, audience, and/or prestige associated with each of these ways of disseminating service as scholarship. The committee felt that, as scholars, the candidates should understand this continuum of evidence that supported their scholarship. For example, a presentation on the most recent findings on Attention Deficit Syndrome delivered to a group of high school teachers was not as significant as an ongoing professional development seminar based on the candidate's own research with that same population. The candidate needed to distinguish between these two activities in his or her portfolio and not give them the same weight. In cases where the differences were not self-evident, candidates were expected to describe the degree of peer evaluation and who the different audiences were, in order to give the committee a better understanding of the activities. Committee members pointed out that because evaluating service as scholarship was a new process, it was especially critical that candidates help the committee to understand the differences between dissemination methods and the various audiences the scholarship was intended to benefit.

Problems of Assessing Service as Scholarship

The Promotion and Tenure Committee had several problems in assessing service as scholarship. Reports of collaborative projects did not clearly distinguish between work completed by the candidate and by other parties. For example, often it was not apparent whether the candidate or other parties designed the curriculum, wrote the grant applications, interviewed, collected data, or worked with the children. Even when it was clear which parts of the project were conducted by the candidate and which were conducted collaboratively, committee members disagreed about whether candidates should receive credit for collaborative work.

Another problem the committee faced was inadequate information provided by candidates. Often the candidates did not provide sufficient self-assessment, analysis, or academic context in their professional service portfolios. Instead, candidates simply described their projects. Committee members reported that at times this caused them to speculate on the schol-

arly characteristics of the service projects in ways that hurt the final decision of the committee. In addition, some faculty were not drawing accurate
distinctions between their work as teaching, discovery, application, or integration scholarship. Education portfolios were often seen by the committee
as among the most problematic. Committee members reported that education candidates' portfolios too often had the wrong kinds of information—
they were too dependent on description and lacked reflection and evidence
of professional expertise.

The committee agreed that the composition of the committee influenced
decisions regarding service as scholarship and this was a problem. For
example, education faculty felt that there should always be an education
faculty member on the committee. Otherwise, education faculty felt the
committee would not understand the context of the education field and
education service as scholarship. For the previous five years, the committee
had had one or two education faculty members on it, but from fall 1997 to
fall 1998, no education faculty sat on the committee. During that time, two
education faculty were denied promotion. Education faculty attributed
these negative promotion decisions to the composition of the committee.
Whether there was any truth to this attribution or not, it created negative
feelings between the committee and education faculty. Ironically, there had
been a vote in 1993, when there were no humanities faculty members on
the Promotion and Tenure Committee, as to whether they should move to
a representative committee. The committee, including some education faculty, voted the proposal down. At that time, all faculty felt that the campus
was small enough, with everyone knowing each other, that they could trust
one another to be fair.

The Promotion and Tenure Committee agreed that having someone on
the committee who engaged in service as scholarship, or someone from the
same discipline as the candidate, changed the decisions. Some felt it
changed the conversation, rather than the decisions of committee members,
but all were in agreement that when none of the committee members was
involved in service as scholarship, or were from the same discipline as the
candidate, the candidate's case suffered. There was also a problem of
inconsistency between decisions made from one year to the next. Although
committee members served three-year terms and terms were staggered,
there was significant turnover each year, which meant that the committee
did not have a long memory of past decisions made about service as scholarship. This contributed to a lack of consistency in how faculty on the committee interpreted the meaning of the policy and the criteria they used to
assess service as scholarship.

Committee members admitted the presence of a few "disbelievers" who
made it difficult to come to decisions on service as scholarship portfolios.
It was impossible for a faculty member to make a case that would be sufficient for a disbeliever. Rather these few faculty used the excuse that the

"candidate has not made the case sufficiently" to argue against rewarding multiple forms of scholarship. A few faculty at St. Tims held suspicions that "disbelievers" were not reviewing the service portfolios in good faith. These disbelievers were alleged by their fellow committee members to assume privately that no case could be made for service as scholarship while publicly they seemed open to the idea. A few faculty claimed the disbelievers stance was evident in subtle, nonverbal body language when service as scholarship was discussed. The committee was faced with a problem: What should St. Tims do about this minority group of faculty who did not support the changes and would occasionally serve on the Promotion and Tenure Committee?

Problems also arose when committee members compared service as scholarship to the scholarship of discovery. Some service as scholarship involved traditional research. However, service as scholarship more often consisted of academic consulting, technical assistance, curriculum development, and technological work. In assessing service as scholarship, committee members found themselves trying to fit a round peg into a square hole. For example, there were only a few national awards, journals, or other "national markers for distinction," for service as scholarship. There were many national markers to distinguish research. For the committee to conclude that a professor had not made a significant scholarly contribution through his or her service because he or she had not published in the one new journal for service as scholarship, or received the one national service as scholarship award, was to misunderstand the emerging nature of this form of scholarship and create expectations for markers of service as scholarship that were not really attainable.

Related to this issue were disagreements among committee members regarding consulting activities. Could consulting qualify as scholarship? Some members felt that the role of someone in the academy was to pursue knowledge for its own sake, whereas in consulting the goals were set by the project. They questioned whether faculty's motivations and financial compensation should be taken into account when making determinations about service as scholarship.

Another unresolved problem prompted by the 1991–92 changes centered on faculty confusion about where to locate activities on their resumes; i.e., which parts of their service should be listed under the scholarship category and which parts should be listed under service. Every member of the Promotion and Tenure Committee agreed that there was a problem with faculty mixing in non-scholarly products with scholarship in their portfolios. This hurt some faculty because, as one committee member pointed out, "If you don't negotiate the terrain with some care, it looks like you are trying to pad a weak scholarly record."

In order to minimize inconsistency in evaluating nontraditional forms of scholarship, the committee spent a great deal of time looking at the rationale and definition of scholarship in the *Faculty Handbook* and discussing questions about different modes of scholarship. A beginning-of-the-year retreat and several meetings during the year were set aside for these discussions. The next section addresses outcomes of the effort to assess service as scholarship for tenure and promotion.

Outcomes of the Effort to Redefine Scholarship

Outcomes for St. Tims
One of the key focuses of this study is the impact of college-wide changes in promotion and tenure on education faculty. St. Tims is a small college and there is a great deal of collaboration and collegiality among disciplines. However, because of a history of differences between education faculty and the rest of the college, the fate of education faculty is both intrinsically tied to, and distinct from, the fate of the rest of the college. Therefore, this section describes outcomes for all of St. Tims and, then outcomes specifically associated with education faculty.

The major institutional outcomes at St. Tims were an increase in applications for promotion and tenure; promotion and tenure decisions accepting service and teaching as scholarship; better documentation of service as scholarship; greater faculty satisfaction; more visibility of service as scholarship; and opposition for the changes from a small minority of faculty.

Increase in Applications
After the guideline changes, applications for promotion to full professor significantly increased. Many of the applicants were applying for a second time. For example, five or more faculty who were previously turned down for full professor reapplied after the guideline changes. More faculty whose portfolios included mostly teaching and service applied for promotion to associate and full professor because of the changes. Most faculty felt the guideline changes positively influenced, or will influence, their decision to apply for promotion.

Promotion and Tenure Decisions Accepting Service as Scholarship
The guideline changes significantly increased the number of faculty with portfolios of teaching or service as scholarship who were awarded full professor. In 1993, immediately after the changes, the five faculty who had reapplied were promoted to full professor. One of these five, a faculty member in the economics department, reported that she did not believe that she would have made full professor without the 1991–92 revision. She applied for full professor with only two peer-reviewed journal articles in her discipline. However, she had good teaching evaluations, had won awards for her teaching, and had been involved in a significant amount of faculty professional service. She had designed and conducted economic training workshops for area K–12 teachers, had developed a one-week

summer enrichment program in economics for children, and had taken her discipline abroad, working with teachers in Eastern European countries on economic education principles. Some of her work had been replicated and used in other countries, and she had led the creation of a Center for Economic Education at St. Timothy. Her resume indicated a large number of collaborative and multidisciplinary research projects directed to regional and statewide audiences, publications in practitioner-oriented journals, and a significant number of contributions to college governance. A committee member reported that this candidate's service was seen as scholarship because she applied her academic expertise, disseminated her outcomes, and her model was replicated around the world.

Other faculty also felt that they owed their successful promotion and tenure cases to the 1991–92 guideline changes. A division chair reported that he would not have been promoted without the new guideline changes, which rewarded his scholarship of application and integration with higher education assessment rather than traditional research in his discipline. Another economics faculty member who had previously been denied promotion to full professor prior to the 1991–92 changes was successful in 1993 and attributed his success to the changes in the definition of scholarship. This faculty member's portfolio was based largely on accomplishments in the scholarship of teaching. Other faculty successfully promoted to full professor were engaged in art education, economics education, or other kinds of education with children or community groups and/or K–12 teachers. Although some of these cases were successful based on the scholarship of teaching and integration and not service as scholarship, they demonstrate that the guidelines were being applied in related areas that did not exist prior to the 1991–92 redefinition of scholarship.

Before retiring in 1995, the former dean sat on the Personnel Committee for 17 years. He said that the positive assessment of service as scholarship was a factor in 11 of the 36 college-wide promotions in the 1990s. His predecessor reported that from 1995–1998 there were several successful test cases of faculty who applied for promotion with little traditional scholarship and attributed their success to the expanded definition of scholarship.

Better Documentation

The 1991–92 policy changes significantly altered the documentation process for tenure and promotion. The portfolio became a much more standardized tool in documentation and an expectation of the Promotion and Tenure Committee. The changes made to the *Faculty Handbook* included examples of teaching and service as scholarship, which were very helpful for faculty in preparing their applications. While the documentation submitted five years before the changes may have been six or seven pages, after the changes, the documentation for service and teaching as scholarship started arriving to committee members in big binders and crates. Unfortunately, with the increase in documentation came a tendency on the part of some faculty "to put everything in, and let them decide which parts of it are scholarship," according to one committee member. Because of this phenomenon, the director of faculty development became important in helping faculty decide what to include in their portfolios and how to categorize the items. The director of faculty development played a crucial role in helping faculty craft their portfolios and the policy changes increased the use of his office.

The director of faculty development, dean, and the members of the Promotion and Tenure Committee reported that not only quantity but also quality of evidence of service as scholarship increased. One faculty member who was involved in developing a three-credit course for teachers and a weeklong summer-camp course for elementary students in economic education presented her service as scholarship to the Promotion and Tenure Committee. Documentation included the actual course syllabuses, a summary of the course activities and course materials, a statement on the philosophy of the project, the actual exercises, TV coverage, evaluations, and her mentoring of a graduate student who was involved in the project. In the past, the documentation may have included a couple of lines on a vita under community service, but since the guideline changes, there was an opportunity to shed light on the scholarly nature of the activity through more and different kinds of documentation.

Greater Faculty Satisfaction
There was also a significant increase in faculty satisfaction, according to the dean, division chairs, and faculty. The 1991–92 changes energized faculty who were doing teaching and service as scholarship and could now be rewarded for it. It also encouraged some faculty who were doing community service to deepen their level of involvement with some agencies, become more reflective practitioners, and transform their service into scholarship. Many faculty felt the changes enhanced the level of professionalism at St. Tims, because they were a more dynamic faculty engaged in different forms of scholarship. After the redefinition of scholarship, there was more emphasis on interdisciplinary and collaborative scholarship and a renewed interest in classroom research. The reward system was perceived as more just, equitable, and inclusive by faculty. Faculty morale and enthusiasm improved and there was a stronger spirit of community.

Faculty reported that because of the new policies they could "follow their hearts," and "pursue their passions." Faculty "felt safe" taking risks on new forms of scholarship. A few faculty who had previously not been involved in service as scholarship said the new policies inspired them to get involved. Others said they simply felt more comfortable in their choice to engage in service as scholarship.

Greater Service Visibility

While the policy changes did not significantly increase the numbers of faculty involved in service as scholarship, they did allow more faculty already involved in this work to do more of it, which in turn increased the amount of service that St. Tims was involved in. Although the increase was relatively small, according to the Dean and academic administrators, it was significant. Once faculty felt encouraged to deepen their involvement in professional service activities, some of the professional service that had existed for years behind the scenes became more visible. More faculty knew about one another's scholarly projects in teaching and service after the policy changes.

Opposition

A few faculty remained disgruntled even five years after the changes had taken effect. They feared that the policy changes would "cheapen" the faculty ranks, or "water down faculty work" and quality scholarship would dissipate. These same faculty feared that "people would think everything counts" and thought promotion and tenure "shouldn't become too easy." Since there was no groundswell of easy promotions, this fear was quelled. Nonetheless, a few faculty regretted the redefinition of scholarship and changes to promotion and tenure. The policy changes were in part intended to create a more equitable situation for faculty in disciplines with fewer opportunities to publish in peer-reviewed journals. After the policy changes a few faculty claimed that candidates in disciplines with significant publishing opportunities had begun to publish in more practitioner-oriented and fewer peer-reviewed journals. A few faculty feared this would become a trend and hurt St. Tims' scholarly reputation. In addition, the policy changes were intended to create a more equitable situation for faculty in the arts who previously were unable to present their artwork as scholarship for promotion and tenure. However, after the policy changes, a few faculty claimed arts faculty had an "easier" review because, simply by virtue of a candidate having completed a piece of art, it was now considered scholarship. There was no evidence to support this claim but a few faculty perceived that this was happening.

In summary, the overwhelming majority of academic administrators, faculty and promotion and tenure committee members genuinely embraced the changes to the definition of scholarship, felt the changes were effective in valuing different faculty strengths, and were satisfied that the quality of scholarship had not dissipated.

Outcomes for Education Faculty

While the outcomes mentioned in the previous section apply to education faculty, there were also outcomes specific to their discipline. These outcomes included more favorable promotion and tenure decisions, reactions to promotion and tenure decisions, changes in documentation, greater faculty satisfaction, cultural support for education work, and mixed messages.

Education faculty were not all uniformly trained or adept at traditional forms of scholarship, yet many faculty were trained and skilled in professional service, action research, classroom research, and other kinds of faculty work that would be defined as scholarship in the new policies. Since the field of teacher education was moving in a direction that encouraged these newer forms of scholarship, education faculty were uniformly in favor of the new definition and rationale of scholarship. Education faculty believed the new policies would recognize work that had previously gone unrewarded.

All 17 education faculty were involved in partnerships with schools. Some of these partnerships involved service as scholarship but others did not. Interviews with education faculty made it clear that they did not all understand which aspects of their service with schools would be considered service as scholarship under the new policies and which would not. This confusion remained even five years after the new promotion and tenure guidelines were implemented.

More Favorable Promotion and Tenure Decisions

The policy changes influenced education faculty member chances for promotion and tenure. At first, from fall 1993 to September 1998, a group of assistant professors in education reported that the guidelines caused "possibility to exist where it didn't before." Before the 1991–92 changes, their chances for achieving promotion were "slim and none," whereas now, in their view, their chances had improved. Most education faculty felt that from fall 1993 to fall, 1998 service was assessed and rewarded as scholarship. Education candidates for promotion and tenure, they felt, were more successful because of the policy changes. The dean's files on promotion and tenure confirmed this perception. He indicated that all five education faculty who had received tenure since the 1991–92 changes, as well as three who had received promotions, had in some way benefited from the policy changes. Each of the five education candidates had been involved in service as scholarship, which was assessed as scholarship because of the 1991–92 changes.

Reactions to Promotion and Tenure Decisions

Perceptions changed in fall 1998 when two education faculty learned that they were denied promotion. These negative promotion decisions were a blow to the entire education faculty. Every education faculty member interviewed mentioned the two rejections and that they soured their attitude toward how well the guidelines were being followed. Although the secret nature of the process meant faculty could not know why other faculty were denied promotion, education faculty interviewed assumed that the rejections meant the 1991–92 guidelines were not being followed. The two education faculty had been involved in a good deal of teaching and service, and these faculty members told their colleagues this work was presented as scholarship in their portfolios.

It should be remembered, however, that there was a certain ambiguity around the interpretation of service as scholarship and some education faculty seemed to believe that simply being involved in service meant that it would be considered scholarship. Also, the semester in which these decisions were made was one of the only times in recent history when there was not an education faculty member on the promotion and tenure committee. One assistant professor said the rejection of her colleagues had made her somewhat afraid to apply for promotion, especially with no education faculty on the committee. She said, "Up until this year, the guidelines were working from the faculty perspective in the arts and education." Therefore, most of the negative response on the part of education faculty was a reaction to these recent decisions.

The evidence, in fact, suggests that the 1991–92 changes overall had a positive influence on tenure and promotion decisions for all faculty, including education faculty. A combination of factors appears to have influenced why the two education faculty were denied promotion. These factors included the cultural differences between the education discipline and the rest of the campus; the candidates' over-reliance on the guidelines to explain the scholarly nature of their work, which was not very persuasive; "disbelievers" on the committee; and the absence of an education faculty member on the committee. The absence of an education faculty member on the committee put education faculty at a significant disadvantage. However, it was not clear that the presence of an education faculty member would have made a significant difference in these two cases. The promotion and tenure committee did not seem resistant to the idea that the case might have been made for teaching and service as scholarship in these cases; they simply felt the case was not made. In other words, although there were significant problems with application of the guidelines to actual tenure and promotion decisions, it did appear that post-1992 promotion and tenure decisions for all faculty were based on a broader view of scholarship.

Mixed Messages

Education faculty were especially concerned about the future for promotion and tenure. Despite all of the campus discussion on the new definition of scholarship, junior education faculty reported that division chairs and senior faculty conveyed two conflicting messages to them after the 1991/1992 changes: First, to do scholarship of discovery exclusively in their early careers and, second, to do all forms of scholarship throughout their career but to document everything well. The first message made them feel as if they needed to emphasize traditional research above everything else; the second message made them feel more confidant that they could emphasize teaching and service as long as they documented everything well. The 1991–92 changes had created a safer environment for education faculty to engage in and be rewarded for service as scholarship, but there was still an expectation that they engage in traditional scholarship. For example, one senior faculty member was mentoring a junior faculty who would còme up in three years with no traditional scholarship, but significant amounts of service and teaching as scholarship. He was worried about how she would fare. It was not clear whether education faculty in this situation would be promoted. Division chairs and academic deans agreed that, even though most faculty felt the promotion and tenure process was fair, education faculty were in a more "precarious position."

Changes in Documentation

The change in documentation of service as scholarship was particularly important for education faculty. The examples in the guidelines and support from the director of faculty development helped education faculty write their applications and "explain their world" and the context within which their scholarship occurred. Education faculty admitted that in the last ten years they had not worked as hard as they could have to demonstrate, through their portfolios, how service and applied work in their field was scholarship. In speaking of education candidates who had been trying to demonstrate that their service was scholarship, the dean emeritus said, "It takes practice, and many applicants haven't gotten good at it yet." Many senior faculty at St. Tims and in education mentored other faculty about how to make the case that their service or teaching was scholarship by encouraging them to provide evidence of reflection and analysis. Much of this coaching helped faculty to frame their work in terms that non-education faculty would understand. Therefore, one of the outcomes of this process was that education faculty turned to each other and the director of faculty development for help in improving and framing their service and teaching as scholarship for tenure and promotion.

Greater Faculty Satisfaction

Despite the recent reaction to the two negative promotion decisions, the guidelines positively influenced education faculty satisfaction. Education faculty had more success recruiting faculty from across campus to work on teacher education projects that related to professional service or teaching because their collaboration might now be counted as scholarship for promotion and tenure. Assistant professors in education felt freer to take risks on professional service projects, middle school teacher exchange programs, and grant projects because they knew this kind of activity could be counted for promotion. Education faculty invested more time and energy in service activities that elevated the quality of those service activities to scholarship. One education professor reported that he believed junior faculty now felt that "they would be promoted doing what they believed in."

More Cultural Support for Education Outreach

There was a widespread feeling that the 1991–92 guidelines changed faculty views of scholarship, and education faculty felt it validated much of the work they did. The guidelines provided a cultural support, which allowed education faculty to argue that St. Tims "has agreed to reward this kind of work," and, therefore, so should the Promotion and Tenure Committee.

In a State of Flux

In 1991–92, St. Tims redefined scholarship and attempted to integrate a broader definition of scholarship in their promotion and tenure process. Five years later, St. Tims was in a "state of flux." There were at least five test cases of the new policies that appear to have been successful. Because of the secret nature of the promotion and tenure process, it was difficult to know if someone who was denied tenure was being denied because the new guidelines were not being applied or because their application did not show adequate scholarship. A small number of faculty still maintained that peer-reviewed journal research was the only kind of scholarship. Because the committee engaged in a significant amount of interpretation of the guidelines and because it would have been going against the college policy and culture to admit a more traditional position, it was not clear how many members of the Promotion and Tenure Committee held to the more traditional interpretation of scholarship.

Regardless of the varied positions members of the committee might have held, there was, in their view, clearly room for improvement in the assessment of service as scholarship process. Even the dean admitted, "We haven't been clear enough for this area of scholarship, we need better criteria." The lack of clear criteria to assess service as scholarship contributed to a mild sense of skepticism among some faculty about whether the new policies were being applied.

St. Tims appeared to be moving simultaneously in two directions. On the one hand, they had implemented a policy to assess and reward multiple forms of scholarship. On the other hand, they were hiring more and more young faculty with strong records in traditional scholarship, suggesting that in the future there would be greater pressure for peer-reviewed work and traditional research. While the college was focusing on internal policy changes, the job market was operating in such a way as to bring more traditional scholars to the campus, thus changing the make-up of the kinds of candidates the committee was reviewing for tenure and promotion. These two realities were beginning to collide in the tenure and promotion process. As a result of these two trends, St. Tims was in a state of flux, even after five years of trying to implement this new policy. Yet academic administrators, division chairs, and most faculty reported that the redefinition of scholarship was indeed being applied to promotion and tenure decisions. The dean confirmed this position, saying:

> Because there is a defining document, it cannot be dismissed. Most people
> here are in agreement with the handbook and new people are socialized
> into this view. The discussion as to whether this is a good idea is not an
> issue on campus. This part of our life is on the periphery now.

Therefore, the development and dissemination of a policy to assess service as scholarship was successful at St. Tims. However, the effort to fairly
and effectively implement this policy was still somewhat ambiguous but
appeared to be a work in progress rather than a debate among faculty.
However, St. Tims was still learning how to implement the new policy fairly and effectively.

Conclusion

Why did this happen at St. Tims and what were the elements that
worked for and/or against this organizational change? Elements that
worked in favor of these changes were the small, non-bureaucratic, and
collegial nature of the college; leadership from the dean and director of faculty development; connections to the national movement to redefine scholarship; a need to respond to rising research expectations which did not fit
with the mission or identity of the college; overall faculty readiness to redefine scholarship; and a high level of faculty participation. There were very
few barriers to developing and approving the guidelines, as demonstrated
by the final vote.

However, as St. Tims implemented the guidelines, the college faced the
following barriers: difficulty in identifying criteria and appropriate evaluators to assess service as scholarship; the secret nature of the promotion and
tenure process, which created mystery around whether or not the guidelines were being applied; and a gap between education faculty and the rest
of the college in their experiences with promotion and tenure. Moreover, as
St. Tims continued to hire faculty with strong records in traditional scholarship, it would continue to be a challenge to assess and reward multiple
forms of scholarship.

How did the Promotion and Tenure Committee assess service as scholarship? Candidates held the burden of proof to demonstrate that their service was scholarship. Once candidates put their portfolios forward, the committee looked for a credible peer review of the work, the quality of written
products and other methods of dissemination, the placement of the work
in the literature of the field, and the connection between the candidates'
professional service and scholarly questions. Some of the most difficult
problems facing the committee were assigning individual participation to
collaborative work, descriptive rather than analytic portfolios for professional service, and finding appropriate evaluators for service as scholarship.

Have education faculty been affected by the outcomes associated with
these changes? Most education faculty were positively affected by the

guideline changes. The new rationale and definition of scholarship and assistance from the director of faculty development have helped education faculty to frame their service as scholarship. The Promotion and Tenure Committee operates with a broader definition of scholarship than they did before and this has benefited, and will continue to benefit, education faculty as it has benefited all faculty at St. Tims. In order to take advantage of the new policies, however, education faculty need to ensure that they understand how to transform their service into scholarship and to effectively present their service as scholarship for promotion and tenure.

CHAPTER SIX

Erin College

In spring 1997, changes were made to the Faculty Handbook of Erin College to expand the criteria for rank and promotion to include service as a potential form of scholarship. These changes were a critical step, and part of a series of "clarifications in language" made by the Provost from 1985 to 1997 to expand Erin College's definition of scholarship and align their mission with their faculty reward system. While not officially approved by any faculty governing body, the changes became part of Erin's official rank and promotion process. This case describes the culture of Erin College, the changes made to the Faculty Handbook, criteria used to assess service as scholarship, and outcomes of these policy changes for education faculty.

The Culture of Erin College

Erin College is a medium-sized college in a major city in New England, founded in 1909 to train women teachers in early childhood education. The undergraduate school remains single sex, while the graduate school is now coeducational. Erin College underwent a major reorganization in 1995 developing from two schools (undergraduate and graduate) to four schools, including the Women's College, the School of Education, the School of Management, and the Graduate School of Arts and Sciences. There are 6,700 students, 200 full-time faculty, and 300 part-time faculty within these four schools.

Erin College is a progressive place with a social action agenda. Both historically and today, the administration nurtures and supports faculty members' entrepreneurial and alternative ideas. However, new and innovative projects are hindered by a heavy faculty workload of four courses each semester and extensive advising and committee responsibilities. Erin College is overburdened with meetings, or as one administrator put it, "This place would have a meeting to have a meeting."

Erin College's name is synonymous in the New England region with the highest quality of teaching. The culture of Erin College is student-centered, collaborative, interdisciplinary, service oriented, and committed to faculty and student interactions. Faculty and administrators describe Erin College as a caring place where faculty members mentor students and collaborate with each other on big decisions. Erin College faculty see these qualities as being opposite to the qualities a research university cultivates and have historically prided themselves on not being a research university. Although the fact that the college has a strong full-time faculty, in the last few years Erin has begun to rely more and more on adjunct faculty with strong practitioner backgrounds. Adjunct faculty now outnumber full time faculty 300 to 200; some full-time faculty believe this hurts the quality of education, while others feel it provides students with "linkages to different worlds."

Since its early years as a normal school for kindergarten teachers, Erin College has stressed the philosophical values of serving the community, as well as the educational benefits of service for their students. Erin College's revised mission statement, adopted in 1987, includes "responsiveness to the needs of society and the student" as a major purpose. The Faculty Handbook includes a vision and mission for service-learning at Erin College which was written by the Community Service-Learning (CSL) Council, a committee appointed by the President to integrate service-learning across campus. The vision is that all Erin College students and faculty would "understand community-service-learning as a pedagogy and an organizational strategy for social change."

After having developed partnerships with community agencies for service-learning, many Erin College faculty have begun to see opportunities to link their research and professional experience with the needs of agencies. Therefore, service-learning has been a door through which many Erin College faculty become involved in service as scholarship. In fact, service-learning is integrated into course-work in all of the four schools. Erin College faculty emphasize a strong connection between theory and practice. Most service-learning and other field experiences are accompanied by required seminars for students to reflect on what they learned.

Because Erin College was founded to train teachers, the School of Education is the oldest and largest school and in many ways has shaped the culture of the rest of the College. Immersed in teaching and service, the Dean and faculty have struggled to balance teaching, service, and research responsibilities and make faculty workload and rewards consistent.

Rather than being organized by departments, Erin's School of Education is organized by program areas, defined by the certificates offered by each group of faculty. The organization of faculty into program areas has supported interdisciplinary collaboration in curriculum development, teaching, service, and research.

The School of Education's mission statement identifies programs as "imbedded in schools and other educational settings, and engaged in collaborative study and research." This mission is implemented through relationships between Erin College faculty, students, teachers, principals, and social service agencies. Students are encouraged, and at times required, to seek placements in diverse settings, engage in service-learning, and conduct research to augment their education and enrich community schools. The very intentional approach of having students learn in "real life settings" requires strong partnerships and involvement between Erin College education faculty and community members. Education faculty develop very deep partnerships with both schools and communities and "wear many hats," according to the Dean of the School of Education. Faculty become part of an organizations' inner circle and serve as counsel to teachers, principals, and board members. "Building bridges" is a term commonly used by education faculty to describe their own or other faculty members' work in the larger community. One faculty member reported that, "the intellectual work of education professors is to conceptualize issues of community."

Much of the School of Education's service as scholarship occurs through partnerships between the School and K-12 professional development schools. There are also several centers devoted to service as scholarship projects including some nationally recognized programs in conflict resolution, literacy training, reading, and programs focused on at-risk populations. There are writing institutes for classroom teachers and several faculty reported having written grants in the last year to develop action research programs with schools. Erin College was described by one education professor as a place where "they put a lot of value in understanding the people in the field, with a fair amount of integrity; a lot of faculty say what the practitioner in the field has to say is important."

The School of Education places special emphasis on working with the poorest and most diverse schools. One education professor described a school that is 60 percent Portuguese-speaking where she spends at least one day a week. "It's one of the schools that has the lowest scores in the city, so we are trying to rebuild that school. We have many programs going on there, and I spend much of my time there." When asked why she thought all Erin faculty were so involved in the schools, it became clear that this was an accepted part of the culture. Another education professor characterized her involvement in the following way, "I think it is definitely something about Erin College and this program. Service is considered part of our responsibility, a direct link with the schools is important to us."

One Erin College education faculty member directs a program in which she and others follow 69 at-risk children from second grade through college, with after-school programs, college preparatory programs, and college scholarships. This is an all-inclusive program with parent retreats, teacher conferences, summer jobs, and other activities to guarantee children's success and entry into college. The faculty member designed the project, makes frequent presentations about it, solicits grant funding, conducts longitudinal research on the group of students, and uses the model as a case in her teaching. The program is a huge part of her promotion portfolio and one of Erin College's big service as scholarship success stories.

The Center for Conflict Resolution within the School of Education also stands out as a place that is encouraging service as scholarship. The Center receives grant funding to provide partial release time for faculty to work with schools on conflict resolution programs. The impact of this Center on the community is profound, and it is a good example of how research, teaching, and service are being combined to create educational reform. The Director of the Center said, "We've shaped the whole way of thinking about multicultural education and conflict resolution based upon the expertise of academic people here, developmental approaches to it...This all comes from theoretical ideas that have been garnered by our faculty and the grassroots efforts of community members." Faculty members act as consultants to teachers and principals in schools and, according to the Director, this work "changes the way teaching and learning are done in those schools."

While Erin College has always valued faculty involvement in all forms of service, they have struggled over the last twenty years to find ways to balance their teaching, service, and research missions through the faculty reward system. While the reward system valued all forms of service, there was no formal way to differentiate service from service as scholarship. Between 1985 and 1997 several factors coalesced to cause the Provost to align Erin's mission and reward system and expand its definition of scholarship through amending faculty evaluation and reward policies. The next section describes these factors and steps taken to align Erin's faculty reward system and mission.

Aligning Policy and Practice

A New President: Tenure Abolished

A new President came to Erin College in 1985 and found that the promotion and tenure process was not working. There were some departments on campus where faculty had not applied and/or been awarded promotion in a number of years, and there were many salary equity questions. By the fall of 1986 task forces were established to examine these issues. Tenure was abolished in 1988, although there are still some faculty with grandfathered tenure. The end of tenure at Erin College has had little effect on the campus. The contract system that replaced tenure operates much like the prior promotion system. The contract system provides only a slightly greater chance for promotion than the tenure system did, and very few faculty contracts are not renewed.

A New Reward System: Promotion and Multiple Year Contracts

In 1988 Erin College created a new system to evaluate and reward faculty through a ladder of extended contracts and a promotion system. This was managed by a college-wide Rank and Promotion Committee that conducted both the multiple-year contract review and the rank and promotion process. In the multiple-year contract review, faculty received five-year contracts for normal performance, seven-year contracts for establishing themselves as a teacher, service provider, and researcher, and ten-year contracts for having an established reputation in the larger community and gaining name recognition in the field. Service was considered important for promotion from both five to seven, and seven to ten year contracts. However, no special consideration was given to service as scholarship.

In the rank and promotion process, assistant professors had to demonstrate one year of successful teaching and potential for service and scholarship; associate professors had to demonstrate five years of successful teaching, meritorious service, and scholarship; and full professors had to demonstrate eight years of outstanding teaching, service, and scholarship. The official criteria for successful performance determining rank were academic preparation, relevant experience, teaching, service, and scholarship/professional activity, in that order. At this time the word "service" referred to institutional service, disciplinary service, community service, and service as scholarship. The word "scholarship" referred to research and professional writing.

The new Rank and Promotion Committee was college-wide and consisted of nine members with staggered terms; three new members were added each year. There was no separate Rank and Promotion Committee for the School of Education. However, the committee had representatives from each college and it always included two representatives from the College of Education.

Committee Established to Rewrite Faculty Handbook

Between 1986 and 1988, during the same time that Erin College's tenure system was abolished, the President appointed Dr. Trower, an education professor who was very committed to Erin College and its teaching and service missions, to chair a Committee on Rank and Promotion Guidelines. By 1988, the committee had placed language in the Faculty Handbook that stated that, "teaching was primary, active engagement in the college community and larger external community was essential, and scholarship was important for promotion in rank." The academic criteria for multiple year contracts were established as, "(a) teaching and (b) excellence/strength in service and/or scholarship."

The new language in the Erin Faculty Handbook was non-controversial. It acknowledged and rewarded Erin College faculty for its strengths in teaching and service, as well as establishing a place for rewards for scholarship, making it clear to faculty that Erin's historic strengths in teaching and service would be valued as equal, if not above, strengths in scholarship. Furthermore, the new language strengthened the importance of all kinds of faculty service.

More Changes to the Faculty Handbook

In 1991 Dr. Trower was asked to become the Special Assistant to the President to revise the Faculty Handbook again. At this time minor changes were made to the Handbook in several areas. The definition of scholarship was expanded from publications to include conference presentations, creative and performance arts activity, engagement in professional development activities, grant activities, professional association activity, and professional awards.

Again, Dr. Trower wanted to strengthen the importance of all of the kinds of service faculty provided. Therefore, under the Rank and Promotion Section of the Faculty Handbook he added:

Active engagement in the College community and the larger professional community are essential qualifications for advancement in rank. It may include consultation to professional groups, service on certification committees or licensor boards, membership on community boards of directors, or trustee committees (Faculty Handbook, p.39).

In your resume and application narrative, address college and professional service. Include letters from colleagues and from the professional community that attest to your accomplishments and assist in documenting service. In particular, please state explicitly if you have taken a leadership role in such activities and during what years (Faculty Handbook, p.40).

In addition, the service category was broken down into three sub-categories: committee service, co-curricular service, and community service. Within the community service category, the following lines were included;

Professional Service to the community outside of the College should be addressed. Service on non-profit boards, pro/bono counseling, or community organizing activities that address the mission of the college should be reported and evaluated (Faculty Handbook, p. 39).

These changes were part of a large number of changes made by the Provost at this time to clarify and expand upon previously vague or narrow definitions of teaching, service, or scholarship. While these changes were minor, they were part of a persistent effort over time to strengthen the importance of and rewards for faculty service. However, at this time the changes did not acknowledge service as a form of scholarship, but simply strengthened the overall importance of faculty service for promotion.

An Identity Crisis

Beginning in the late 1980s but predominantly from 1991 on, Erin College faculty began to face an identity crisis concerning their relative emphasis on teaching, service, and research. While the very identity of Erin College was connected with teaching and service, many faculty and administrators were advocating a movement toward higher standards for, and production of, traditional research.

Several forces were pushing Erin College to place greater emphasis on research in the faculty reward system. First, the composition of the faculty was changing. Until the early 1980s not all of the faculty had Ph.D.'s. In the late 1980's and early 1990's Erin hired more faculty with Ph.D's and traditional research training and interests. Many Erin College faculty viewed the introduction of these faculty into their culture as a threat to the predominant culture of teaching and service. Second, when Erin's School of Education started a new Ph.D program in 1988, this also "upped the ante" in terms of research expectations of faculty. More faculty were engaged in traditional research and supervising students engaged in traditional research. Third, some faculty at Erin were beginning to view faculty searches, research grants, and increased publication standards for faculty evaluation as ways to increase the prestige of Erin College and were beginning to push Erin College to move in this direction. One faculty member commented:

> Now what has happened over the last ten or twelve years especially is that . . . well, teaching is still the bread and butter for Erin, you do not survive here if you do not really perform superbly in teaching. But, there has been more research interest because of people with Ph.D.'s, advanced degrees, emphasis on grants, emphasis on writing. But that is always played against the fact that the workload has not changed.

Although research was being given unprecedented attention, faculty were still being recruited to the campus because they were attracted to the strong teaching and service culture of the college. The Provost said that despite recent faculty fears, in the early 1990s Erin College was not generally in the habit of hiring "newly minted" Ph.D's with traditional research agendas. Rather, most of their faculty tended to be hired halfway into their careers with strong applied and community orientations.

To summarize, in the 1990s Erin College faculty experienced growing pressure to do more research and/or produce more academic writing from their teaching and service experiences. Increasingly, faculty were questioning the fairness of the contract and promotion system, with most faculty favoring a return to the teaching and service emphasis, and a minority emphasizing higher standards for research, which was called "scholarship" for promotion. Meanwhile, other changes were occurring within the four colleges that had an important influence on the balance of teaching, service, and research for faculty.

Informal Changes in Rank and Promotion Priorities

The identity crisis over Erin's emphasis on teaching, service, and research was in part a reaction to, and in part fueled by, changes in the late 1980's and early 1990s in rank and promotion priorities. While there were no formal changes in the rank and promotion policies during this time that prioritized research over teaching and service, there were two realities that began to collide. On the one hand, the Rank and Promotion Committee defined scholarship more broadly. On the other hand, the fact that most Erin faculty had well established track records in teaching and service, and less established records in traditional research, meant that faculty who came before the committee with traditional research qualifications "stood out" more favorably in comparison to the others.

From 1990 to 1997, even before the promotion policy officially listed service as a potential form of scholarship, there was a real openness on the part of most committee members to assessing service and teaching as potential forms of scholarship. For example, a former Chair Elect of the Rank and Promotion Committee said that everyone on the committee in the early to mid-1990's recognized that this openness was in the best interest of the college, because teaching and service as scholarship were more likely than traditional research to be Erin faculty strengths. Therefore, scholarship was very broadly defined at the College with recognition and respect for "emerging" forms of scholarship such as action research, qualitative research, classroom research, and service as scholarship. Committee members felt that the openness to multiple forms of scholarship among their colleagues was one of the things they liked best about being at Erin College. For example, a former Rank and Promotion Committee member stated.

> I define scholarship broadly. I think of scholarship as creating a musical composition. I think of scholarship as art work. I think of scholarship as much more than publishing articles in obscure journals that are read by ten people in the universe and, you know, riddled with footnotes, and that that is the sign of an impressive mind at work. I have never thought about coming up with a definition, but I would think it would be as an expression through various modes of creative thinking and critical analysis. I don't think of traditional scholarship as scholarship when I sit on that committee or in my day-to-day workings in effect. One of the reasons I like working here is it is an environment that allows one to think outside the traditional boxes.

Despite the general appreciation for multiple forms of scholarship, the lack of a long history of traditional research had created somewhat of a reverence for it amongst the faculty. The former Chair of the Rank and Promotion Committee described the tension between theory and practice in defining and assessing scholarship during 1990-1997.

I think there was tension. I think it was somehow ironic that you might think that our faculty would be the first to embrace broader, different ways of thinking about scholarship and teaching and service and so it was hard. People articulate certain things and then fall back into old frameworks when they are evaluating applicants for promotion so that even though people could articulate, yes, scholarship is more than that esoteric piece in that obscure journal, once the journal was in front of them, they were drooling. You know, it was like this is real . . . This is REAL scholarship.

Because of the increased reverence for traditional scholarship in the early 1990s through 1997, rank and promotion operated in such a way that the move from assistant to associate depended mostly on teaching and service, but the move from associate to full professor gave additional attention to scholarship and professional activities. Few candidates came forth with no internal service; it was part of the "modus operandi" of Erin College faculty life. Since there were also so many faculty involved in external service, and since the institution was recognized for high quality teaching, almost everyone who applied for multiple-year contracts or promotion had strong teaching and service portfolios. Therefore, scholarship became the deciding factor for the highest promotions and multiple year contracts. Because for many years the word "scholarship" was associated with academic writing, the Provost said, "although it was held in balance at the lower ranks, I think that informally publication became more important than other categories at the full professor level." Therefore while the official Rank and Promotion policies stated that teaching was primary, external service was essential, and scholarship was important, between 1990 and 1997 informal decisions began to emphasize traditional forms of scholarship as primary for promotion to full professor. The move to full professor became a symbol at Erin College of the tension around what the college valued and wanted to reward. While the discrepancy between formal and informal promotion criteria was forming, the College of Education was welcoming a new Dean who would have a positive influence on the assessment of service as scholarship.

The School of Education Welcomes a New Dean
In 1995 the School of Education welcomed a new Dean. Like other administrators, faculty, and staff, this Dean attributed his coming to Erin College to the strong teaching and service mission. The Dean did not believe every faculty member in his college needed to be involved in service, but he believed that most Erin faculty should. He pointed out that, "it takes a special set of skills to work in the community, and not everyone has them." The Dean came to Erin College with a "belief in collaborations," and he wanted to model the involvement he hoped his faculty would have in the community by being active and visible in the community. The Dean spent 35 percent of his time in city and state education departments,

schools, community boards, and other educational organizations. He believed that by developing his own close relationship with these educational partners he would make better decisions about how the school could make a difference in the lives of children and teachers.

As part of his leadership strategy and philosophy of service as scholarship, the dean asked faculty to begin to clarify and document the following aspects of their service projects by answering: "How does this work bring value to those you are trying to serve? If you were to stop this activity, would anyone care, does it make a difference? What is the vision and philosophy behind the work? What are you trying to learn and how can it inform others?" These questions guided the process by which the Dean began to mentor education faculty as they chose service projects and submitted promotion materials. The questions encouraged faculty to transform their service commitments into something more scholarly.

Education faculty felt that when the new Dean came there was a renewed emphasis on service as scholarship. According to one faculty member:

> His philosophy was one of community building and our involvement with all of the schools really expanded. We have professional development schools where faculty receive release time to be the liaison working right in the school. It is not like other colleges where you visit once a month and say hello to everybody. This is a person that is located in that school and really is part of their professional development model. Because of the Dean's background with the schools and the Provost's involvement with communities and service, they both felt Erin really needed to be a partner. When you have leadership that sort of drives it, then it happens. When you have different leadership, nothing gets done because we do not get the time, the money, or the backing.

Within the School of Education the Dean created what he called a "covenant" with faculty, providing instructional course release time for at least some of the activities faculty most wanted to accomplish that year. According to his records, the Dean believed that 27 of the course credits he had released in 1997-1998 were for service as scholarship projects.

The Subversive Administrator and Redefining Scholarship.

In 1992, shortly after Dr. Trower completed his role as Assistant to the President, he became the Provost of Erin College. The Provost called himself a "subversive" administrator and someone who had tried for many years and in various roles to "sneak in various forms of clarification," "make the language more explicit," and "nudge the official promotion policies toward an expanded definition of scholarship."

During the 1990s when Erin College was experiencing an identity crisis over the reward system's emphasis on teaching, service, and research, Dr. Trower was becoming increasingly involved in national efforts to redefine scholarship. Among other things, he was active in a local think tank that had an ongoing project on service as scholarship. This project recommended that colleges and universities begin to reward faculty for their strengths as scholars in teaching, research, and service as scholarship.

By the middle 1990s the discrepancies between formal and informal rank and promotion priorities had caused a growing sense of dissatisfaction among the faculty. Faculty complained to the Provost that Erin College did not significantly reward all of their teaching and service activities, but instead penalized them in promotion decisions for a lack of research. The combination of the mismatch between faculty workload and rewards at Erin College and the Provost's exposure to national efforts to redefine scholarship urged him to make additional changes to rank and promotion policies. By 1997 the Provost was ready to make yet another change to the Faculty Handbook to expand Erin College's definition of scholarship so that faculty would get credit for their service as scholarship for promotion.

The President supported the Provost's decision to embark on and make these changes. The President and Provost were both known on campus as risk-takers and were protective of Erin College's unique strengths through the reward system. They both understood the importance of encouraging more faculty to write about their projects, and then convert and transform their service into scholarship. Because this was a small college, support from the President and Deans was extremely important. There was a comment by one faculty member that, "when the President, the Provost and the college puts an emphasis on something, we all get involved."

The Changes

In the spring of 1997 the Provost made another set of changes under the Faculty Evaluation section of the Faculty Handbook. Under the category of scholarship, the following potential form of service was listed: "Related Professional Activities (external to the College community), e.g., community presentations, professional workshops, or service on community boards or organizations." While this change appears minor, it was the first formal language in the handbook that stated that external community activities that were related to professional expertise were a form of scholarship. Combined with the statement in the scholarship category which said that scholarship was an activity that was shared with peers, this policy change made it possible for service activities that were documented and shared with peers to be considered scholarship. Since the Provost was in charge of faculty development, was a member of and trained the Rank and Promotion Committee, he had ample opportunity to ensure the implementation of this change.

Future Plans

The Provost recognized that one of the weaknesses of the approach taken thus far was that only faculty who worked with the Provost, had recently applied for promotion, or recently served on the Rank and

Promotion Committee were aware of the changes. While it may have been thought that after making important changes to the promotion guidelines, the Provost would immediately notify the campus of the change in an official way, this was not the way things were done at Erin College. Administrators and faculty reported that decisions were typically made by long drawn-out processes where the entire faculty or college tried furtively to come to a consensus before deciding to maintain the status quo or make minor changes, or quietly by administrators so as not to alert the faculty that change was made without them. Since the Provost perceived the change as non-controversial among his faculty and more a shift in thinking than a major deviation from current practice, he simply made the change and then began spreading the word to those he believed it would most effect. Thus, only 40 percent of the 200 full-time faculty knew that changes had been made to the Faculty Handbook. After the Handbook was printed the Provost asked faculty who were involved in service as scholarship, and with whom he had consulted in making the changes to the Handbook, to spread the word to other faculty and advocate for the new policies across campus. One of the ways he did this was by getting more faculty involved in the regional think-tank meetings where service as scholarship was discussed. He discussed this strategy:

> Well, really, I think the critical part is going to be to have somebody who can communicate well with the faculty about this work because you do not have to convert me. Relative to this, I'm the administration and so we need to figure out a way to make it feel more like it is coming from bottom up, knowing that the issue already has my support.

In addition to further dissemination of the policies, the Provost felt that he needed to provide release time for faculty to get involved in service as scholarship and write about their work. However, this was difficult because the college was highly tuition dependent and quite wedded to its reputation for small class size. Faculty had complained to him that their heavy teaching load, internal committee assignments, and community service work left them little time to transform their service into scholarship through reflective writing. The Provost reflected, "the challenge for us institutionally has been to find ways financially to support release time, so that if faculty are spending time in the field, they can also have time to write about the experience." The Provost established a workload committee to examine different options that would slightly increase class size and create more release time opportunities for faculty to publish. The Provost hoped efforts made in this area would be a major step forward for the institution. The release time would help faculty deepen their involvement with service projects, reflect on their work, and disseminate the outcomes more broadly.

The Provost was encouraged that his current role allowed him to help faculty frame their service as scholarship for rank and promotion. He gave examples of several faculty whom he had helped to prepare service as scholarship portfolios and who had been successful. He planned to do more mentoring in the future. The Provost planned to buy copies of *Scholarship Reconsidered* and *Scholarship Assessed* for the Rank and Promotion Committee the following falls of 1998. He planned to buy extra copies for departments so that the "principles of multiple forms of scholarship would be understood from the bottom up." One of the areas he hoped to tackle next was strengthening the suggested forms of documentation for service as scholarship and working with both candidates and the Rank and Promotion Committee on how to prepare and assess documentation of service as scholarship.

Rank and Promotion

This section describes the Rank and Promotion process, criteria used to assess service as scholarship, problems, and required forms of documentation as of Spring, 1998. At that time, the 1997 policy changes had been in effect three semesters: Spring 1997, Fall 1997, and Spring 1998.

The Process

There was a high success rate for faculty applicants for promotion and multiple year contracts between spring 1997 and spring 1998. A longtime Erin College faculty member commented that there were so many safeguards between the candidate's decision to apply and the actual committee review that if a faculty member's application came before the committee and was not successful it meant someone had "really dropped the ball." The high success rate for rank and promotion may seem to contradict earlier statements concerning expectations for research and applications for full professor. In the 1990's there were faculty turned down for lack of research, but there were more faculty who were counseled not to apply or chose not to apply based on the committee's informal bias toward traditional research. Therefore, most faculty who made it through this pre-application process were likely to succeed.

The process toward promotion included several steps. First, faculty completed annual faculty reports, peer reviews of portfolios, early academic assessment meetings, and professional development plans. Second, the Program Director, Dean, and Provost advised the faculty member and approved his/her application. Third, the candidate was able to review model faculty files and was mentored by the Provost, committee members, and senior faculty. Fourth, the Rank and Promotion Committee held sessions for faculty to review promotion criteria and the process, and review previous candidates' files. Finally, there was a mentor system for candidates from the School of Education, and files of faculty who had been promoted were in the Provost's Office for review.

Criteria to Assess Service as Scholarship.

The Committee did not have a formal, written set of criteria to assess service as scholarship. In conjunction with the changes made to the Faculty Handbook in 1997, there were candidates who presented their service as scholarship in spring 1997, fall 1997, and spring 1998. The committee devised informal criteria to assess service as scholarship and applied these informal criteria to their decisions. This section describes the informal criteria applied by the Rank and Promotion Committee to evaluate education candidate's service as scholarship in spring, 1998.

Most education candidate service-as-scholarship portfolios included action research projects, joint research and service projects, and curriculum and policy development within professional development schools. The Provost explained that even in the few years leading up to the 1997 changes, the committee had begun to see arguments that a few candidates' service was scholarship. The simple criterion immediately was established that if a service project was well documented and showed impact, it was listed as service. If there was a "written reflective piece" or "scholarly presentation" attached to the service it was considered as a potential form of scholarship. The Provost explained that while a few service projects were evaluated as scholarship in this way before the 1997 changes, it wasn't until after he officially listed service as a form of scholarship in the promotion policies that the committee truly began to consider it their responsibility to assess and reward service as scholarship. After the 1997 policy changes, the committee spent more time differentiating between community service and service as scholarship through informal criteria they developed together. The Rank and Promotion Committee used the following criteria to differentiate community service from service as scholarship: the contribution of new knowledge to the field, setting in the literature of the field, academic expertise, impact and length and depth, dissemination, intellectual sweat, systematic reflection, intellectual growth, links with teaching and research, connection to the mission of the college, and prestige.

Adding new knowledge to the field, as a test of service as scholarship, was interpreted broadly. Committee members were quick to point out that the new knowledge did not have to be in the form of experimental research or involve complicated statistical equations. Rather the new knowledge created through service could include how to apply educational theories or professional knowledge to new social problems or populations. One committee member described the Erin College philosophy about creating new knowledge:

> Our role as scholars is to continually try to create new knowledge, to continually push the boundaries of what we're already able to know. I think that one of the things that Erin College tries to do is to really live the rhetoric of balancing theory and practice and there is both new knowl-

edge gained in basic research and knowledge to be gained in domains of practice.

The Committee was open to candidate presentations of new and different ways of creating new knowledge through service.

To be considered scholarship, service needed to be placed in the literature of the field and connected to the academic discipline. Furthermore, the committee required proof that the faculty member used specific academic expertise. The candidate held the burden of proof to demonstrate the context of their project, how her or his "service" was framed in educational literature and traditions of practice, and that it was consistent with model service as scholarship projects. Non-education committee members depended on members from the College of Education to locate the service within the education literature for them. It was also critical for the candidate to demonstrate a link between their service project and the latest developments in their discipline. For example, faculty from education needed to demonstrate a connection between a professional development school project and educational reform efforts being discussed at AERA, or by leading educational policy makers and researchers. In addition, the candidate needed to show exactly how their academic knowledge contributed to their service project. "If what they presented was technical and the intellectual conversation was not there, if there was no discourse on the discipline and how to share with colleagues wisdom learned from the work," then the person would not be successful in making the case that their service was scholarship. For example, one education professor described having been called upon to provide service for an educational organization largely because of his administrative skills. This was not considered scholarship because people without academic backgrounds in his area could have provided the service. On the other hand, when an education faculty member was called upon by a school to redesign the curriculum to include the latest methods for teaching about diversity, he applied his academic expertise in service to this school. As one committee member said:

> Presumably there was some problem or a need in the school district that was identified, a faculty member went in and took his or her knowledge of that and applied it to the real life problem in the schools and then came up with some solution and action. That was part of his package of scholarship.

Another important criterion for service as scholarship was impact. Committee members wanted the candidate to show the impact of their work on the educational community, whether through a change in thinking, the organization of a new program, or changes in policy. They looked for qualitative and/or quantitative evidence of impact whether it was a rise in test scores, increases in teacher satisfaction, or widespread use of a new curriculum. The committee believed that in order for faculty service to have a significant and sustainable impact, it must be of a certain length and depth. Erin College faculty had a tradition of creating deep partnerships that lasted many years and the committee felt the best scholarship resembled that model. The committee felt that in most cases "one-shot deals," such as single presentations or consultations were not service as scholarship. Rather, the committee viewed service as scholarship as ongoing, sustained, in-depth projects and relationships with community partners. Consequently, service as scholarship was evaluated not only for the changes made in the educational community, but for the length and depth of the process that created the change.

Dissemination, at a minimum to community, regional, and state audiences, constituted another major criterion for assessing service as scholarship. Erin College committee members examined service projects to see if they were shared with colleagues in the professional community including local teachers, school boards, the state Department of Education, and educational scholars in universities as well as what they called "new audiences" such as parents, or special interest groups. Applicants for promotion to full professor were expected to demonstrate national dissemination of their service as scholarship. One committee member commented, "this is easy with traditional scholarship for the person who wrote five books... it is not as straightforward with service." National presentations at conferences, awards for service as scholarship, grant competitions and coverage of model programs were all evidence of national dissemination. However, the committee acknowledged that since the very nature of much of their candidate's service work consisted of increased involvement, over a period of time, in one community, it was sometimes difficult for candidates for full professor to demonstrate national impact. National dissemination was most clearly demonstrated when an applicant's project became a model that was replicated in other communities.

"Intellectual sweat," reflection, and intellectual growth, were another criterion for service as scholarship. Rank and Promotion Committee members wanted to see evidence of the mind of the scholar at work, which they called "intellectual sweat," in order to be persuaded that service was scholarship. One committee member characterized intellectual sweat as "some sort of systematic approach that was really intentional and deliberate in terms of educational purposes." Another committee member gave an example of how that intellectual sweat demonstrated itself with education candidates who had service as scholarship portfolios. "It couldn't just be a workshop for a school system, but rather it must have a flavor of reflection." This flavor of reflection generally surfaced through a specific set of scholarly skills employed in the projects. " Especially in the move from associate to full professor the committee also felt there had to be documented reflective practice and intellectual growth in service projects to consider them scholarship. The committee wanted to see how the faculty member had grown intellectually through their work on a service project.

It was important to the committee that intellectual sweat, reflection, and intellectual growth were evident in documentation presented for service as scholarship.

Another deciding factor was the extent to which the candidate's teaching, research, and service were seamlessly connected to one another. For example, one education candidate conducted research on at-risk teens in a high school and from this research developed a series of professional development seminars for teachers, designed a counseling program for a youth center and wrote case studies for a master's cohort seminar. She presented all of these projects together at a national conference as a model for how to integrate service as scholarship with teaching and research. Service had a greater chance of being seen as scholarship if it was integrated with teaching and research.

It was also important to the committee that the service was connected with the mission of Erin College, especially teaching and educating others. Relatedness to mission was especially important for the move from associate to full professor, where the committee was looking for the faculty member's scholarship to be related to their department, college, and overall Erin College strategic plan. Committee members agreed that service as scholarship should promote and improve the "life" of the college and help Erin "make a name for itself in and outside the community. " Consequently, the committee looked favorably on service projects that "brought Erin College glory." When a faculty member's service was recognized in the community, and through state and national newspapers, TV, and radio, the prestige which followed the project helped to make the case that the service was scholarship.

What Convinces Them? Making the Case with Documentation.
The candidate was expected to submit as much evidence and documentation as possible to make the case that their service was scholarship. The most compelling evidence included the reflective essay, letters of support, written products from the service, and "verbal documentation" from committee members.

The reflective essay was the central and perhaps most critical piece of documentation because it acted as a guide to the intellectual work of the service project. The Chair Elect of the Rank and Promotion Committee explained:

> In the narrative we are looking for the self-assessment of that work, what the meaning of it has been, what the applicant thinks has been the outstanding accomplishments, why they are putting their energies in this direction and so on.

In order to demonstrate impact the candidate was expected to go beyond the reflective essay and produce letters of support from clients of the service projects. Whereas the reflective essay was written from the perspective of the faculty member, letters of support from external constituencies were crucial documentation that in fact the community felt the service had made an impact and what kind of difference it had made. Letters from principals, PTA's, education department officials, and others often came with pictures and newsletter articles of events faculty designed. These letters confirmed the amount of time, effort, and skill faculty had spent in service efforts, and discussed both short and long-term impact of the programs. Service was not considered scholarship if this kind of documentation was not present.

In terms of written products of service as scholarship, one committee member shared that, "Everyone on the committee is in agreement that scholarship doesn't have to be refereed journals but once we get past other traditional research outlets we are not in agreement." There had been movement over the years toward acceptance of textbooks, and other curriculum products, as scholarship. This trend helped those faculty who had made the argument that they were engaging in teaching as scholarship when they developed course texts and published articles about their teaching practices. The teaching as scholarship documentation also opened the door for documentation of service as scholarship to include "applied writing." Unlike some colleges and universities, applied writing such as professional development seminar manuals, articles in *Kappan* and in regional educational leadership journals, widely disseminated reports, evaluations, and bibliographies of sessions were counted for promotion at Erin College. Faculty were also encouraged to submit "works in progress" as part of their applications. Depending on rank, if someone made the case effectively, even if they had manuscripts in process or a germinating idea, they could be successful. The Dean of the School of Education explained that many of their faculty could publish their work in more traditional journals but chose less traditional writing venues because they placed greater value in reaching practitioner audiences. Often education faculty felt that applied writing venues were "making a bigger difference."

> There is a more comfortable fit in this community then there was at (former institution) concerning nontraditional scholarship. I think there are a number of people who became a faculty member at Erin College because of that viewpoint-not that they are opposed to writing in the narrow sense of scholarship, but they are more in the application stage, the doing. So, if they write a textbook, that is where some may feel more comfortable. I mean, that is where they would like to put their time and their energy rather than feeling as though they have to write just for refereed journals. I think there is a value part of service and scholarship. In many research universities, that would not get high marks.

After the reflective essay, letters of support, and other written products, a critical, but less tangible form of documentation was the knowledge of committee members in the same field who were familiar with that individual's scholarship. This knowledge became a critical kind of "verbal" documentation laid next to the others for discussion. One committee member explained:

> One would hope that the faculty member who is putting forward the file would make the case sufficiently for those of us who are outside of the field, but it often is not the case. What really becomes persuasive is the knowledge that other people on the Committee have of that field.

Overall, the committee members were flexible about how the candidate went about making the case that their service was scholarship. Most committee members appeared to have gone into the process wanting to be convinced by the documentation.

Problems in Assessing Service as Scholarship.

The committee faced several problems in trying to assess service as scholarship. They struggled with evaluating the "content" versus "context" of the service work; assigning merit to preparation for service as scholarship; "the process versus written product;" attributing merit to paid/unpaid, individual/collaborative and interdisciplinary service work; a lack of clear criteria, and long-term committee memory to assess service as scholarship.

The biggest problem the committee faced was the "content" versus "context" problem. Content referred to the educational theory being created, integrated, or applied to an educational problem. The context referred to the setting, audience, or medium to which the content was being applied. Candidates often became so interested in the "context" they were working in that they emphasized these parts of their service projects over the "content." Sometimes faculty became enamored with "learning how to communicate new things to new audiences," and "practice problems" took precedence over what the committee considered "scholarly problems." For example, a professor using an educational theory for teaching dyslexic students became so interested in all of the technical issues surrounding serving dyslexic students that she de-emphasized the theory she applied to serve this population.

Problems also arose when committee members compared service as scholarship to the scholarship of discovery or research. Committee members noted that in traditional research content was laid out in the review of the literature section of research articles. However, when candidates tried to explain the content or (educational theories) which guided their service as scholarship there was no established form to address the major issues in the field, and what impact the service as scholarship had and would have on these issues so most of the applicants came up short.

The committee was unclear about how to assign merit for the time and energy faculty members spent in community sites in preparation for—but not directly related to—service as scholarship. Should this time count for scholarship, community service, or not at all? One example of this situation was a faculty member who had brokered an entirely new relationship between Erin College and their surrounding neighborhood through the creation of a planning board and university-community partnerships. Various scholarly projects had emerged from these relationships years afterwards. However, the initial years of work were more capacity building than scholarship. Most often, the committee relegated "preparation time" to the service category, but since it was so often intertwined with scholarship, it was not always clear how to separate the two.

Another problem was that not all candidates who were making the case that their service was scholarship had developed written products from it. The committee struggled with whether they were evaluating the process of scholarship or the written products from the scholarship. Faculty claimed that overwork and being spread too thin kept them from writing about their service as scholarship. Although faculty said they lacked the time to write, there was also a cultural inclination toward doing rather than reflecting on service work. One education professor involved in service as scholarship said, "We are definitely on the side of doers but doers that don't have the time or take the time to document the significance or the theoretical implications of our work." The appropriate weight that should be given to the products versus the process of service as scholarship came up repeatedly as the committee reviewed service as scholarship portfolios.

Committee members disagreed as to whether paid and unpaid service should "count" as scholarship for promotion. Questions about the value of paid service versus unpaid, and the relationship between compensation for service and a commitment to social justice dominated this issue.

There was also the problem of distinguishing individual merit in cooperative work. Because of the nature of many of the service as scholarship projects, faculty, graduate assistants, teachers, and administrators often worked collaboratively on service as scholarship. There were times when the committee could not tell whether service as scholarship was authentically completed by the candidates or their colleagues. Faculty from the School of Education were involved in more collaborative work than other candidates, and at times there was concern that there be proof in the portfolio that the candidate had personally engaged in the development of the ideas, writing, research, or consultation and that all of the work was not done by their colleagues. While most of the committee members were comfortable with assigning a candidate the same amount of "credit" for collaborative and individual service as scholarship, a few were not. All felt candidates needed to identify their own contributions more clearly.

Related to this issue was the interdisciplinary nature of service work. Sometimes solving community problems required not only the faculty member's academic experience in their own discipline but it also required drawing on academic expertise in other fields. In some cases, the committee found that the faculty member's use of several areas of academic expert-ise diluted the committee's ability to ascertain the candidate's use of aca-demic expertise in their own discipline.

Another problem was that the Rank and Promotion Committee had not provided candidates with guidelines about what they were looking for in the reflective narratives or the criteria that would be used to assess service as scholarship. Consequently, the committee was not getting all of the information they needed to make a decision. Also, the committee was not always consistent in its decision-making from one candidate to another and from one semester to another. Related to this was the changing composi-tion of the committee and the need to reeducate committee members each year. The Chair of the Rank and Promotions Committee noted that, "People look very carefully at what is in the rank and promotion docu-ments. The problem is that things get added on because everyone at the time agrees it is a good idea, but then a new committee comes on and they haven't been part of the discussion." Therefore, there were concerns about the lack of a long-term memory of service as scholarship decisions.

To conclude, the Rank and Promotion Committee began formally assessing service as scholarship in spring 1997 and continued through spring 1998. They had no formal criteria to assess this type of scholarship but created their own which were very similar to Boyer's criteria for assess-ing multiple forms of scholarship. A service project would be considered under the service category if it was well documented and had made an important impact. Service was considered scholarship if in addition to the above there was a "reflective" written piece attached to the service and evi-dence of a scholarly process. The committee was open to multiple forms of writing as evidence that service was scholarship. Despite the fact that they had significant problems in differentiating between community service and service as scholarship, the assessment of service as scholarship for most committee members was a comfortable process, and one that they sup-ported. The next section describes minor outcomes from the assessment of service as scholarship.

Outcomes

Because the 1997 changes were new at the time of this case study and word of the policy changes was not widely disseminated, as of spring, 1998 there were no major outcomes that could be attributed to the policy changes.

However, the new policies were immediately applied in promotion and rank decisions. The awareness of the policy changes by about a quarter of Erin faculty, combined with their immediate applicability to promotion decisions influenced some minor outcomes. Minor outcomes that were associated with the changes to the Faculty Handbook included a range of reactions by faculty, successful test cases, changes in the way faculty documented service as scholarship, increased faculty satisfaction, and mentoring on faculty workload choices.

Reactions to Policy Changes.

There was overwhelming support among those faculty who did learn of the policy changes. Since Erin College had always been a place with an emphasis on external service, the majority of the faculty saw the policy revision as supporting something they had been doing for some time. A professor in education described why she was pleased with the changes and why she was confident others would be as they learned of them.

> Erin has always attracted people that really feel that they are here because of the belief system. Faculty here really care about the people inside and outside the community. So, my gut feeling, knowing many of my colleagues around here for so many years, is that people are happy with the direction of the new policies and people are happy that the administration and faculty are coming closer together in some of the realities of what faculty are doing and how we have to be involved in the community. We do not have a choice. So I think the direction we are moving in is, "Let us try to be fair to people that are really making such a great commitment." And I really feel as though the administration is recognizing our service outside the college and how it impacts the college.

There were other reactions. In the School of Education the Dean said, "Everyone was looking for a way to see how it would be valued and the jury is still out." Some faculty felt their lives would not change much because they were engaged in more traditional scholarship projects. When asked whether the changes had begun to change faculty's views of service as a potential form of scholarship, the dean replied, "This is a comfortable place for that idea to be introduced, they are an application place here." In other words, the changes may have had some small impact on making faculty think of service as a potential form of scholarship but so many people were open to that idea anyway, the policies were not a deciding factor.

According to the Provost, the only force blocking the future successful implementation of the policies were "a small percentage of skeptics with more traditional scholarship backgrounds," who provide an on-going tension between this movement and a more traditional perspective of scholarship. Likewise, there were a small number of opposing reactions to the guideline changes by those faculty who wanted to keep the definition of scholarship as "pure" traditional research. One faculty member on the Rank and Promotion Committee described the "opposition opinion" this way: "We are watering everything down and accepting everyone for rank and promotion because we're basically trying to say that everybody is good." However, this was a minority opinion and did not seem to have much effect on the implementation or dissemination of the policy changes. Therefore, most reactions to this change were positive.

It is important to stress that including service as a potential form of scholarship in the rank and promotion policy occurred on a campus where all service was considered essential for promotion anyway and multiple forms of scholarship were accepted.

Rank and Promotion Test Cases

There were at least five faculty who considered themselves test cases and presented their service as scholarship in their portfolios after the 1997 guidelines. In one such test case a faculty member with very little traditional scholarship claimed that her service was scholarship, applied for promotion, and was turned down. However, the Committee made that decision not because she had not done traditional scholarship, but because her service was not reflective and did not demonstrate a scholarly approach. In their opinion, the candidate engaged in community service, and not service as scholarship.

Another test case was an education faculty member who had gone up for full professor. She had acted as a court advocate for special needs students, consulted with the state on this issue, and designed a summer camp for various disabled groups. The Provost helped this faculty member frame her service work as scholarship by documenting how she had used her knowledge of special education theory and her professional expertise to conduct her work. She was successful. The Provost recalled:

> Her work had been in the City Public Schools as a court advocate for special needs students so she had written all of these court documents which she was not really regarding as scholarship and I said, you know, this is scholarship as long as you place it within that content and implications for both practice and policy with special needs populations.

The Provost described yet another "test case" where an education professor applied for promotion to full professor based on service as scholarship.

> Another person did not have a large list of publications or what have you that had been active for twenty-five years both in the neighborhood and in the community generally, had done a lot of work, was one of the founding members of our Center for Conflict Resolution and worked in the community for violence prevention strategies in the schools and she was successful in framing that as scholarly activity. Erin College is a place where that can happen.

Two additional cases described by committee members came before the committee in 1997 and 1998 and were successful in making the case that their service was scholarship. In these cases service, teaching, and research were all seamlessly blended. For example, one faculty member worked with the Audubon Expedition Institute to bring together a consortium of teachers, schools, and service agencies that eventually created an environmental theme school with new curriculum for K–12 on the environment, a summer teacher-training program on ecological issues, a community bird refuge, and a new masters degree program in ecological teaching. The committee concluded that her service was scholarship because it involved creation of curriculum, original research, conference presentations, the development of a new non-profit, and prestige.

To conclude, after the 1997 changes to the Faculty Handbook, there were several tests of the policy that service might be a form of scholarship, and these test cases appear to have been successful in distinguishing between community service and service as scholarship and rewarding them appropriately.

Increase in Faculty Satisfaction

Faculty who were very involved in service as scholarship and were aware of the policy changes, reported an increase in satisfaction with their jobs and with the college. The changes made these faculty feel as though the college was finally acknowledging and rewarding the service they were committed to in an official way. The Chair Elect of the Rank and Promotion Committee said the policy changes sent a message to people committed to service as scholarship.

> I think some do know and for some it makes a big difference. Yes. Well, a positive difference in the sense that it probably validates for them something that they have believed in and done and continue to do. You know, there is dead wood everywhere so if you want to look at them, this does not impact them. But for the people who are doing some dedicated work, I think it only make them feel better about it.

The Director of the Center for Conflict Resolution echoed the importance of the changes to the morale of the Erin faculty. He believed the changes had already made a difference by stimulating conversations among faculty about what parts of their service were scholarship, provided a new incentive for faculty to become involved, and laid the groundwork for increased faculty loyalty to the institution.

Making the Case: Documenting Service as Scholarship

Both before and after the 1997 changes the provost assisted candidates in preparing their service as scholarship portfolios. As candidates and committee members began to consider the subtle differences between high quality service and service as scholarship, candidate documentation was slowly beginning to improve in both quality and quantity. The guidelines provided a cultural and procedural support for making the case that service was scholarship, a support that had not been there in a formal way before. As the test cases suggested, the committee followed the policies closely, distinguishing between service and service as scholarship. This made candidates work harder on developing quality service as scholarship portfolios.

Faculty who had successfully used the new policies predicted that as the new policies were more widely disseminated more faculty would be encouraged to "make the case" and this would improve their documentation. Similarly, as members rotated on and off the Rank and Promotion Committee, word would spread about the policy changes sending a message that Erin wanted to encourage service as scholarship in all of the departments and colleges. Committee members felt that as more candidates began to understand what was meant as service as scholarship they would begin to document more clearly how their service was embedded in their discipline. One education professor said, "As soon as the faculty understands that that is considered very important, you will see that people not only will describe it better, but show how it relates to their profession."

A Change in Thinking and Emphasis

The policy changes also initiated a change in thinking among the faculty and staff who came into contact with them. For example, the new policies required that the Rank and Promotion Committee work harder at distinguishing community service from service as scholarship. This required a new view of scholarship, service, and faculty roles in the community. Having spent most of their lives invested in field activities, service projects, action research, and other kinds of college/community partnerships, Erin faculty were being asked to be more critical about this work and think about it in different ways. Faculty preparing their service as scholarship portfolios had to weed out the administrative and technical service from their service as scholarship and think critically about the connections between their own research and teaching and service as scholarship.

Mentoring

There was a significant amount of mentoring that was at least partially related to the policy changes. The Provost reported having worked with individuals on a regular basis to help them develop service sections of their dossiers. One faculty member in education who had been successful in applying for promotion to associate professor told a story about how she was putting her portfolio together and was going to include twenty years worth of planning, training, and directing a camp for people with disabilities under community service and her mentor, the Provost, said "no, put it under scholarship." As she looked through the materials she had collected, including training for teachers, philosophical writing she had done related to the camp and other materials, she realized that the project had always been "academic in nature." In fact, after she was encouraged to put the work under scholarship, she then successfully submitted it for an award. Likewise, one senior faculty member saw her mentoring role as, "helping candidates find and fill gaps in the portfolio." She helped candidates to understand where they needed more evidence of scholarship, and gave them suggestions on how to collect or develop additional documentation of service as scholarship.

Faculty in the School of Education said that mentoring for junior faculty on whether or not they could afford to spend time on service as scholarship depended on who the Dean was at the time. Since the current Dean was supportive of service as scholarship efforts, including granting release time, this kind of activity was encouraged in the School of Education.

However, the changes to the Faculty Handbook had also initiated some mentoring that differed from the above approach. A minority of older faculty seemed to be telling younger faculty that, "Even though this service as scholarship stuff may fly here, it may not in your next job, so protect yourself." One senior education faculty member described this advice to junior faculty.

> We have told junior faculty that since Erin College does not have tenure, you have to think about tenure in the profession. You might live the rest of your academic life here at Erin or you may need to go somewhere else and if you do go somewhere else, you need to attend to things that are valued in the profession and think about your life not only at Erin but in the profession. So, what is the nature of your contribution going to be and so, while Erin may have less emphasis on traditional scholarship than the University of Pennsylvania, when it comes to promotion, you had better attend to your publications.

A minority of faculty discouraged junior faculty from engaging in service as scholarship based on an argument that service as scholarship would not be transferable to other institutions.

Service Scholars

Faculty members who were already heavily engaged in service as scholarship reacted to the policy changes in two ways. First, they were increasingly encouraged to improve their service as scholarship and mentor other faculty in this work. Second, they were determined not to let the minority of faculty who were "talking the policy changes down" influence them or other faculty who wanted to make service as scholarship one of their primary activities.

This small group of faculty had several things in common. First, they had all found ways to connect their service as scholarship with their teaching and research. Second, these faculty were able to connect their personal lives with their service. One example of this was an education faculty member who had been inspired to pursue research and professional service in the area of children with autism because of her own personal experiences with an autistic son. She reflected:

> I have a son with autism so naturally I do a lot of community service around the Autism Society. I am on the board, I started a new non-profit for families and advocates, so those are the benefits. Your own personal life begins to sort of lead you in a certain direction.

This faculty member had found a certain coherence between her professional and personal life through connecting her service and scholarship. Another professor did the same:

> But one thing that I have done through service that has worked for me is to try to have my service, my personal life, and my professional life intersect because I have two young children. I mean, why sit on different committees at other schools when I should be doing it there? Because I can't usually go on field trips or do other things. It makes sense to me to take my personal life and my expertise and apply them. You know, I do not run the bake sales. I do other things so I make different contributions. I raise money for the school by writing successful grant proposals for them.

These faculty were well identified leaders on campus who advocated for the college to provide more faculty release time for service as scholarship. These faculty were often involved in a number of institutional change efforts including attempts at multicultural education curriculum changes, community service-learning pedagogy, and service as scholarship. One of these group of "service scholars" described having seen resistance on all fronts from what she called some "more traditional scholars," but said that in terms of service as scholarship more faculty, "who didn't get it, now are moving toward it and may begin to understand the community as a place to grow."

These service scholars were very public about everything they did, and disseminated their work enough that many people on the campus knew of the "fame" of their projects. For example, at least five faculty mentioned the same education faculty when describing the status of service at Erin College, saying things like "But you know someone like Kristy Roberts who has just really been out there and everybody tremendously respects that."

Finally, the public nature of the service as scholarship extended to these faculty members' candidacy for rank and promotion, where they had been quite successful in making the case that their work was scholarship. They were active as mentors for other faculty applying with service as scholarship portfolios. They pushed junior faculty to "document everything," and to work to be recognized for their service as scholarship. One senior education faculty member advised the following:

> What I tell people is, this is the time to toot your own horn; do not be shy; write everything down that you did that you feel in any way has helped you, helped the college, helped your community. And sometimes, I have met with colleagues that say, Well, I did this for five years, but I did not think it counted, and I look at them and say, 'are you crazy? Of course you include that, what an impact you made.' So sometimes you have to almost talk them through because they really feel as though that might not be per-

tinent or, that is something they did but it doesn't count. I tell them this is the time to say it all.

Each of these faculty members were aware of the Provost's changes to the Handbook and a few had consulted with him and helped him to write the changes. They considered themselves as sort of the leaders of the "service as scholarship cause." These service scholars were described by the director of one of the service centers as "social activists, strong feminists, anarchists, or affiliated with some social action group where they're putting their values on the line, writing, speaking out about things, whether it relates to gender issues or sexual orientation or politics." These faculty were reported to be more collaborative than other faculty at Erin, and genuinely seemed to have made careers around the idea of applying their knowledge in scholarly ways to educational problems. While these faculty members took on "service scholar roles" long before the 1997 policy changes, the changes had a definite impact on strengthening and clarifying those roles, as well as securing the roles for the future.

Conclusion

By 1997 the Provost of Erin College, had amended the guidelines for faculty promotion and multiple year contracts to expand the definition of scholarship to include service. While faculty involved in service as scholarship, Rank and Promotion Committee members, and candidates for promotion were aware of the 1997 changes, news of the changes was not widely disseminated. Although Erin College's reward system historically valued and rewarded all forms of service for promotion, it was not until the spring of 1997 that the Rank and Promotion Committee officially began assessing and rewarding service as scholarship. While the policy changes were still new at the time of this site visit and had not been widely disseminated, it was clear that the idea of assessing and rewarding service as scholarship was not controversial at Erin College.

Why did this happen at Erin College and what were the elements that worked against and/or for this organizational change? The faculty inclination toward, and involvement in service and a subset of faculty involvement in service as scholarship, a culture that nurtured alternative and innovative ideas, the Provost's timing and leadership, Presidential leadership, the national network of colleges redefining scholarship, the Provost's position on the Rank and Promotion Committee, faculty complaints about rewards for teaching and service, release time for service as scholarship, a supportive Dean in the School of Education, and the noncontroversial nature of these changes all worked toward this organizational change. Heavy advising, teaching, and meeting responsibilities, a push for more traditional research from a minority of faculty, a small number of faculty members' desire to gain national prestige through increasing standards for traditional research, and a lack of clear criteria to assess service as scholarship were the main elements that worked against this organizational change.

How did the Rank and Promotion Committee assess service as scholarship? There were no formal criteria used to assess service as scholarship. Overall the Rank and Promotion Committee differentiated between community service and service that was scholarship by whether or not the service contributed new knowledge to the field, was widely disseminated, had systematic reflection and intellectual growth, was connected to other teaching and research, was set in the literature of the field, was on-going, was connected to the mission of the college, had an impact on the field, and brought prestige back to the college. The most compelling evidence included the reflective essay, letters of support, written products from the service, and verbal documentation from committee members. The committee struggled with evaluating the content versus context of the service work; a lack of written products; giving merit to paid/unpaid, individual/collaborative, and interdisciplinary service; and a lack of clear criteria and committee memory to assess service as scholarship.

How were education faculty impacted by these changes? The fact that the changes were not widely disseminated, coupled with the existence of a reward system that was already friendly to all kinds of faculty service, meant that there were no major outcomes associated with the changes. The minor outcomes associated with the changes to the Faculty Handbook included the majority of faculty supporting the changes, successful "test cases," changes in the ways faculty documented service as scholarship, an increase in faculty satisfaction, mentoring on faculty workload choices, and increased leadership from service scholars.

Mapping Change Across Four Cases

This study investigated how four colleges and universities developed policies to assess service as scholarship for their promotion and tenure systems. The study sought to understand the impact of these policies on colleges or units of education by exploring how each institution defined service as scholarship and applied this definition to their evaluation process; the procedures used to assess service as scholarship; the outcomes; and elements of culture that helped or hindered the process.

The case summaries of the preceding four chapters were framed by three guiding questions: Why did this happen at this institution and what were the elements that worked against and/or for this organizational change? How did those evaluating tenure and promotion go about assessing service as scholarship? How have education faculty been impacted by the outcomes associated with these changes?

This chapter presents an analysis across the four cases of: 1) the elements of academic culture that supported or thwarted the development and implementation of these policies; 2) the policies and procedures written into promotion and tenure guidelines and faculty handbooks; 3) the actual criteria used by promotion and tenure committees to assess service as scholarship; 4) and the outcomes of this process for education faculty. The concluding chapter addresses the implications of this research for colleges and universities considering implementation of similar policies.

Overview

A similarity across the four cases was the institutional history and context in which these processes occurred. Since their founding, each of the four campuses had a history of valuing teaching and service as equal to, if not more important than, faculty research in faculty evaluation. While the precise time of departure from this tradition differed, each of the campuses began a shift into what Gamson and Finnegan (1996) have called "research culture" by the early 1980s. As market forces brought more faculty with Ph.D's and research backgrounds to these campuses, and the institutions found themselves competing with each other for prestige and resources, each of these colleges became increasingly more focused on research. The term "scholarship" became synonymous with traditional research by the 1990's. Increasingly, success in tenure and promotion, and increases in salary became closely tied with publication productivity.

To different degrees, each of the four institutions experienced significant difficulty in the late 1980's and early 1990's as a disconnect formed between faculty emphasizing teaching and service and reward systems favoring research. Promotion and tenure standards at each of these institutions began to emphasize national over local accomplishments, and published and peer-reviewed writing over other forms of faculty work. Yet, the institutional rhetoric and mission of each of the institutions remained the same—in each case the rhetoric suggested that the institution prized and rewarded faculty teaching and service to the community. During this period some faculty at PSU and St. Tims, who engaged primarily in teaching and service, were denied promotion and tenure. A minority of faculty at MWSU and a majority of faculty at Erin College expressed dissatisfaction with inconsistencies between rhetoric and reward policies.

In the early 1990's, in three of the four cases, an academic administrator determined that something had to be done, garnered faculty support, and launched a process to align the campuses' institutional mission, faculty workload, and the reward system. At the same time, Boyer's *Scholarship Reconsidered* influenced higher education and encouraged campuses to consider certain forms of service as scholarship. Only at MWSU did the impetus come from a grant opportunity and then fall under the leadership of academic administration. However, in all cases, the development and implementation of policies to assess service as scholarship were strongly influenced by academic culture. Elements of academic culture created the impetus for changes and worked for and against policy implementation. External forces, internal forces, leadership, and unique cultural characteristics of each of the institutions led these four campuses to attempt changes to reward systems. Research culture, dissemination and implementation problems, faculty resistance, and novelty all hindered the successful implementation of policies to assess service as scholarship. Each of these elements played critical roles in why and how these four institutions developed and implemented policies and are discussed in greater detail in the next section.

Elements of Academic Culture that Influenced the Development of Policies to Assess Service as Scholarship

External Forces

External forces frequently force institutions to undertake change. Forces that develop over time may lead to a climatic event. Isolated, "cataclysmic events" may also cause institutions to "acknowledge a state of crisis" (Birnbaum, 1988, p. 205) and redirect institutional goals and priorities. In each of the four cases, external forces influenced central administration's decision to attempt to change the reward system. For example, PSU experienced a significant budget crisis, while MWSU received a $10.2 million grant. In the first case, a perceived crisis sparked action, in the second, a perceived opportunity. Both came from outside the university and were unpredicted events that greatly influenced the decision to change the reward system.

Another external force that played a background role, but nonetheless was in operation, was the national teacher education movement that pushed for greater education faculty involvement in professional development school partnerships with K–12 schools. The 1980's Holmes movement certainly fueled Dean Schreier's efforts in MWSU's School of Education, and the professional development school movement influenced PSU's Dean of the School of Education's decision to create a weighting system to balance faculty involvement in teaching, service, and research. This movement within colleges of education was one of the reasons education faculty began to see a need for more flexibility in faculty roles and rewards.

The most significant external force that pushed each of the four campuses to change or amend their promotion and/or tenure policies were market driven pressures to increase faculty research productivity. Part of this change had to do with the changing nature of the institutions and their faculty. The increase in faculty with Ph.D's and development of graduate and doctoral programs meant that more faculty were likely to engage in, or at least supervise, research. Such was the case at Erin College where one professor commented, "the Ph.D program really upped the ante" in terms of research expectations, even though teaching and service expectations remained the same. Another part of this change had to do with the identity that the institution and college of education began to seek for themselves. For example, during Dean Hennessey's tenure at MWSU the College of Education viewed itself as one of the best in the country and was eager to prove that status through *U.S. News and World Report* rankings. Because those ratings are predominantly based upon faculty publication productivity, number and amount of grants received, and student grade point averages, the College of Education's focus for promotion and tenure evolved to primarily and/or exclusively reward research productivity.

Finally, the concept of academic expertise and authority based on a faculty member's status as a researcher was strengthened on each of these four campuses during this time. For example, at both St. Tims and Erin College, it became important for faculty with little published research to be able to explain their distinct role in the university based upon their expertise. The concept of "professional expertise" as the justification for academic positions was evident when MWSU and PSU faculty expressed their distaste for faculty who became like "field people" or rather "went native." Research culture required faculty members' work to demonstrate those areas of knowledge that set them apart from others, rather than collaborative models to bring different kinds of practice and theoretical knowledge together. The increasing tendency toward institutional homogenization on each of these four campuses, wherein each of the institutions were seeking greater national prestige through their faculty members' research reputations, became a major impetus for subsequent changes to the reward system.

Ironically, it was because these campuses had experienced an increase in demand for research productivity, and this push was out of balance with their institutional priorities in teaching and service, that another external force, Boyer's *Scholarship Reconsidered* became so influential to each of the campuses. Boyer's *Scholarship Reconsidered* offered a way for these institutions to return to or create a greater balance between teaching, research, and service. All four institutions were involved in and influenced by the national movement toward redefining scholarship and faculty rewards that involved hundreds of campuses. A speech by one of the leaders of that movement, Dr. Gene Rice of AAHE, inspired the provost to do something about the problems at St. Tims and involvement in a regional think-tank on redefining scholarship encouraged Erin's provost to initiate changes. Ernest Boyer and Ernest Lynton visited PSU's campus and their advice greatly influenced the committee's framework for scholarship. Aware of the fact that faculty would not "buy-in" to the idea that change needed to happen to the promotion and tenure system purely on the basis of what was happening on their own campus, PSU's provost engaged in a very intentional strategy of sending faculty leaders to national conferences and meetings where redefining scholarship was discussed. At these meetings PSU faculty became proponents of redefining scholarship, convinced not only that PSU's present system should change, but offering input as to how it should change.

All of the committees and academic administrators who developed written policies read and framed much of their work based on Boyer and other related works. Committee members often referred to Boyer as they discussed their actual criteria to assess service as scholarship. Boyer's definitions of scholarship had clearly penetrated many committee members' personal definitions of scholarship. Even MWSU's committee members who had not studied the indicators had read and identified with Boyer's writing on scholarship. The Erin committee was about to embark on more extensive reading of Boyer a few months after the site visit. Somewhere around 50 percent of education faculty on promotion and tenure committees at each of the institutions had read Boyer's work on their own. In addition, at all of the institutions candidates educated committee members on Boyer's definitions of scholarship by quoting from Boyer in the reflective essays and throughout their portfolios. Boyer's work provided a common intellectual foundation for discussions of multiple forms of scholarship as well as legitimacy to the effort to recognize service as scholarship for promotion and tenure. In summary, whether it was pressure to increase research productivity, involvement in the professional development school movement, or Boyer's *Scholarship Reconsidered,* external forces played an important role in igniting change in the reward system of these four institutions.

Internal Forces

The research culture that became integrated in faculty evaluation systems in each of the four institutions was not a comfortable fit for many faculty and administrators who had been drawn to their institutions because of the strong teaching and service missions. In fact, a negative faculty reaction to the rise of research culture on at least three of the campuses, (Erin College, PSU, and St. Tims), acted as a major impetus for the campus to redefine scholarship.

Faculty dissatisfaction occurred when faculty expectations for promotion and tenure decisions differed from actual decisions made during periods when the institution, or the College of Education, was struggling between allegiance to a research culture and allegiance to the teaching and service mission. For example, at MWSU a faculty member complained that the "rules of the game changed" when a new dean emphasized traditional research over teaching and service. A PSU faculty member described this period for promotion and tenure as being like "quicksand;" you never knew what you would get when you stepped inside.

The disconnection between faculty expectations and rewards was not the only internal force at play. Different institutional definitions of scholarship and the way the service was framed also played an important role in driving change. St. Tims' faculty and administrators had discovered that their current definition of scholarship did not include scholarly contributions in teaching and service, and therefore needed to redefine scholarship to be consistent with all forms of faculty work. PSU's faculty and administrators needed to make promotion and tenure materials consistent with faculty work, and only decided to redefine scholarship as a method to achieve this goal. MWSU's vice provost's goal was to promote faculty service but realized that the only way to accomplish this within their research culture was to assess and reward service as scholarship for promotion and tenure. Erin College already rewarded service for promotion, but found that defining service as a potential form of scholarship allowed them to both reward service and meet demands for greater faculty scholarship.

Other internal forces were specific to individual campuses. For example, faculty at St. Tims felt they needed to make changes in the definition of scholarship to account for differences in publication opportunities and to effectively reward scholarship in the arts. PSU's increase in service-learning, restructuring, and the new mission and strategic plan all worked together to stimulate change. However, perhaps no internal force was as strong as the leaders within the institutions who drove the changes.

Leadership

Leadership played an important role in why and how each of these four campuses attempted to change their reward system. Leaders at different levels of institutional governance operated in a range of ways to inspire, design, coordinate, and nurture the development and implementation of policies to assess service as scholarship. In the four cases the principal actors who held leadership positions were the (1) provost, (2) deans or Division Chair of Education, (3) mid-level administrators, and (4) service scholars. Presidents played a secondary role.

Provosts played four roles associated with the development and implementation of policies to assess service as scholarship. First, provosts conceived of and launched the initiative; second, they enlisted key personnel to lead it; third, they coordinated the university-wide approval and dissemination of the new policies; and fourth, they facilitated the interpretation and implementation of the new policies with promotion and tenure committees.

The provosts at all four institutions played key roles in initiating the effort to change the reward system. While the provosts at Erin, St. Tims, and PSU all had strong personal convictions that their institutions needed to change to define teaching and service as scholarship, MWSU's provost was less involved but wholeheartedly supported Dean Schreier's grant-writing and assisted in the appointment of the two committees. St. Tim's provost enlisted the "taskmaster," Dr. Lewis, PSU's provost enlisted the associate provosts and faculty committee chair, and MWSU's provost appointed the new Vice Provost for Institutional Service. Only Erin College's provost worked individually on changing promotion and tenure policies. He consulted with faculty leaders involved in service as scholarship and had the full support of the president and deans. However, he would later come to regret not enlisting more faculty and administrators for this effort.

Once it was time to get the new policies approved, provosts helped clear the way to Faculty Senate approvals and to the dissemination of the new policies to faculty across campus. Finally, since the provosts at Erin, St. Tims, and PSU all played a significant role in approving promotion and tenure decisions, as well as in the promotion and tenure committees' interpretation of the documents, these provosts played considerable roles in policy implementation as well. For example, at St. Tims the provost reviewed definitions and terms for scholarship in a retreat with the promotion and tenure committee, while Erin's provost sat on the committee itself and provided an orientation to the policies each year. MWSU's provost was the least involved in this last stage of the process, but also signaled her support by requesting that deans, department chairs, and committee members use the indicators. Erin, PSU, and St. Tims' provosts also attempted to facilitate successful implementation of the policy by helping candidates prepare their portfolios for service as scholarship. All of the provosts and several of the deans helped to fund service as scholarship projects.

The deans of the Colleges of Education, the Division Chair at St. Tims, and education department chairs were the least involved in developing the policies, but were the most important to their implementation. There were exceptions to this pattern, for at Erin College and St. Tims, the provost, not the dean or Division Chair, was probably the most important in the implementation, although the dean and Division Chair had important secondary roles. However, at each of the campuses the policy developed more as a partnership between the provost's office and regular faculty than through local partnerships within education units. Deans of the College of Education often provided advice to candidates about their portfolios, made release time and workload decisions, and his/her opinions were key to establishing a culture around the acceptance or rejection of service as scholarship for promotion and tenure.

Mid-level administrators at MWSU, PSU, and St. Tims were the principle craftsmen, cheerleaders, and shepherds of the process to develop and implement policies to assess service as scholarship. As craftsmen, they built representative faculty committees' and kept the conversations constructive and on track. They framed the committees' discussions in the most current literature on redefining scholarship and made sure the committees were aware of and in touch with experts and other campus communities doing similar things. Also, the Director of Faculty Development at St. Tims, associate provosts at PSU, and Vice Provost for University Service at MWSU crafted democratic processes for soliciting feedback. For example, at each of the institutions these mid-level leaders intentionally involved as many faculty as possible in the process, including dissenting opinions. Focus group meetings, open forums, and dissemination of multiple drafts to key decision-makers were very deliberate ways to make all faculty and administrators feel as if they were part of the decision. "Listening people to death" was used as a strategy to quell opposition by making everyone feel that they were a part of the process.

Mid-level administrators also acted as cheerleaders of the process by spending countless hours spreading the word across campus about what the committee was doing and what it would mean for the future. For example, at MWSU the Vice Provost for University Outreach personally visited each of the colleges and departments. He described service as scholarship in terms that made sense across disciplines and persuaded faculty and administrators to buy-in to his vision for MWSU and service as scholarship.

Finally, once the policies were in place, mid-level administrators acted as shepherds for implementation. PSU, MWSU and St. Tim's administrators all held workshops and meetings for faculty candidates and promotion and tenure committees on the language and criteria in the new policies. Unfortunately, their efforts were not always successful. In most cases failure occurred because mid-level administrators reached the limits of their own authority and the "ball was in someone else's court," such as the dean or promotion and tenure committee, to decide whether to implement the policies. Mid-level administrators held little supervisory power over the actual implementation of their policies, and could not require or demand compliance. Rather, they had to persuade others that the new policies should be followed. Despite the limits of their power, mid-level administrators did the best that they could to ensure successful policy implementation. They acted as consultants on the new policies for promotion and tenure committees, colleges, and departments. Mid-level administrators also did their best to support the first few faculty who applied under the new policies as test cases with service as scholarship portfolios. Interestingly, mid-level administrators really "drove the train" of these change efforts at PSU, MWSU, and St. Tims, while most regular faculty on committees "came along for the ride."

Without successful faculty who served as test cases of the new policies, other faculty would not have fully understood what service as scholarship was, or believed that it would be rewarded. Without regular faculty in each department championing the policy changes and then attempting to spread the word to other faculty interested in service as scholarship, implementation would have been impossible, or at least much less effective. On each of the four campuses there were faculty leaders who had been engaged in service as scholarship for many years. They supported their campuses' change efforts, served on committees, and were among the first to apply for promotion and tenure with service as scholarship portfolios. These faculty served as role models for other would-be "service-scholars." They were part of the impetus for the changes and then did their best to make sure the policies were implemented successfully.

These service scholars had several things in common. All were very public about their service as scholarship, had published articles, brought in grants, and brought prestige to the college through their long-term service as scholarship projects. On each campus service scholars became the living examples of how the policies could work and convinced other faculty that the policies would not dilute scholarly quality. These faculty acted as mentors, helping other faculty document their work and write analytical, as opposed to descriptive articles based on their service. Therefore, service scholars were important both symbolically and practically in the successful implementation of the new policies.

The presidents at MWSU, PSU, and Erin all contributed differently to the process. At PSU, the president provided the vision for PSU as an urban metropolitan university, supported key people in making the changes, provided symbolic support through speeches, and integrated the service as scholarship idea into the new mission statement and strategic plan. Erin's president appointed a campus-wide service-learning committee, provided seed money for service as scholarship projects, appointed and supported the provost, and encouraged faculty to write and publicize their unique service models. MWSU's president's major contribution was placing the right people in the right place at the right time, providing cultural support through speeches, and integrating the issue into strategic planning efforts.

Unique cultural characteristics

Each of the four institutions had unique cultural characteristics and strengths that influenced their organizational change process. For example, PSU had a history of adapting quickly to change, taking risks, and implementing innovative solutions. Changes made to the reward system were part of a larger landscape of change for this institution. Erin's social justice orientation, history of entrepreneurial administrative decisions, emphasis on connecting theory and practice, and the long tenure and popularity of the provost influenced the change process. The history of efficient committees and collegiality at St. Tims supported the development of their policies. MWSU's status as the "#2" state university caused MWSU's central administration and faculty to uphold the land-grant mission as a distinct feature of the university, and inspired central administration's desire for MWSU to become a leader in the area of service as scholarship assessment.

Finally, each of the four institutions had histories in the 1970's and 1980's of reward systems that acknowledged alternative faculty career trajectories and emphasized teaching or service over research. While the emphasis on research in reward systems had changed in recent years, these institutions valued teaching and service as scholarship more easily than institutions without this history. Also, each institution's promotion and tenure committees had been introduced to teaching as scholarship and this helped pave the way for the introduction of service as scholarship. Finally, each of the institutions was unique for the faculty members' strong inclination toward external service.

Elements of Academic Culture that Hindered Successful Implementation

While there were no major forces that hindered the development of policies to assess service as scholarship, once the policies were in place there were significant barriers to implementation. To different degrees and in different ways, each of the four campuses made mistakes in sizing up the potential barriers and opposition to their new policies.

Research Culture

A major finding of this study is that research culture acted as both a proponent of change to faculty evaluation and a major barrier to implementation of policy change. As was previously mentioned, the increase in research culture caused administrators and faculty to protest unfair faculty evaluation systems and request a move back to teaching and service as institutional priorities. Boyer's views of multiple forms of scholarship shaped the new policies that responded to this request. However, once the new policies were implemented, it was clear that research culture still influenced faculty views of scholarship and the system in which faculty and administrators worked. Consequently, the major barrier to the successful implementation of policies to assess service as scholarship were unspoken assumptions on the part of committee members about scholarship, below-the-surface expectations about the purposes of promotion and tenure, and external market-driven pressures to reward research above other forms of scholarship.

Policymakers at each of the institutions believed that since scholarship, narrowly defined as research, received the greatest rewards for promotion and tenure, then broadly defining scholarship to include teaching and service, would equally weight all forms of faculty work. What they did not, and perhaps could not address in their policymaking were the underlying realities of academic culture that had created the situations they were trying to change.

Despite the policy changes and even the culture shift that at least St. Tims and PSU underwent, (where faculty really began to understand service as a form of scholarship), the research culture still influenced the promotion and tenure system. The basic components of research culture that worked against the effective implementation of the policies included the hiring of traditional scholars in the belief that they would improve the status of their institution. The shortage of academic positions and an oversupply of Ph.D's brought more traditional scholars to all four campuses; thus, promotion tenure committees reviewed more traditional scholarship than in the past.

National rankings and institutional reputations were tied to the national research reputations of faculty, grant dollars brought in, and graduate students attracted. In most cases, it was not in the best interests of promotion and tenure committee members, who were stakeholders in this system, to promote and or tenure faculty with local, rather than national reputations. Promotion and tenure served as a gatekeeper for institutions and colleges of education wherein only those faculty who enhanced other faculty members' reputations were let in.

Consequently, although faculty at each of the institutions identified with the service mission and many believed that service could be a form of scholarship, they had self-interest in voting against this premise for promotion and tenure. Research culture operated against successful implementation of the policies to the greatest degree at MWSU, then next at St. Tims, PSU, and least at Erin College. For example, the lack of traditional scholarship at St. Tims had created a thirst for it among the ranks of the promotion and tenure committee. PSU seemed to have found a way of genuinely recognizing multiple forms of scholarship, despite the presence of research culture, but was still struggling with this issue in promotions to full professor. At Erin College, the research culture only operated among perhaps 40% of the faculty, and therefore was fighting a losing battle. However, the rise in faculty with Ph.D's and research interests had changed informal expectations for promotion. At MWSU the very core and essence of the College of Education operated on the research culture model and it was the major predictor of most promotion and tenure decisions. A few MWSU service scholars were able to make the case that their service had made regional and national impact through models that were replicated, awards, grants, and media coverage. These faculty had successful promotion and tenure cases; however, this was unique rather than a strong predictor of future MWSU cases.

The most practical way that research culture worked against implementation of the new policies were through comparisons between traditional research and service as scholarship in relationship to peer review, national recognition, and dissemination. Because service as scholarship was a newer form of faculty work with less disciplinary and national allegiances, fewer journals, and forums to present service as scholarship, there were not the opportunities that existed in research to garner national prestige, national peer review, or raise national rankings. In most cases, it was very difficult for faculty members to demonstrate national impact in a medium that was structurally more locally based. This made service appear as a lesser form of scholarship because it did not bring the same currency that research brought to the table.

Dissemination, Implementation, and Compliance
There were also internal forces which made implementation of the policies difficult. For example, each of the four campuses made decisions about how to disseminate and enforce their new faculty evaluation policies. Whereas St. Tims and PSU successfully disseminated and implemented their policies throughout their institutions, MWSU and Erin College experienced significant problems with dissemination and implementation. Neither of these institutions had found effective ways to get the policies into the hands and minds of the majority of faculty and/or guarantee implementation and compliance in promotion and tenure decisions.

One of the significant differences across these four cases was the relationship between the College of Education and the university. Institutional size, type, and culture largely determined the degree to which colleges/units of education were well-integrated parts of the university community or as

Birnbaum has described, "academic holding companies" – one of many semi-autonomous units under the shared brand name of one university (Birnbaum, 1988). The process to develop policies to assess service as scholarship at each of the four colleges started with the central administration and the more isolated and or insulated the college/unit of education was from the central administration the less involved the College of Education was in the process. The greater the distance, the less College of Education faculty and administrators felt obliged to implement the changes that were passed on to them from central administration. For example, at MWSU the College of Education's status as one of the top-ranked colleges on campus allowed it to operate in virtual isolation from the rest of the university, and therefore it was not easily swayed to comply with university-wide promotion and tenure changes. MWSU had all of the characteristics of a loosely coupled anarchical system (Birnbaum, 1988). Decisions made by the central administration without a particular dean's involvement were unlikely to be implemented unless the dean agreed with the changes or there was some advantage for compliance. Rather, anarchistic institutions are places where each college is more influenced by personal preferences than institutional goals. MWSU central academic administrator efforts at disseminating the policies and ensuring that they were implemented in the College of Education were not effective because there was no strong incentive for the college to adopt the new policies and use them in promotion and tenure decisions. Despite this fact, the indicators had slowly started to infiltrate MWSU's promotion and tenure process. Yet, the lack of consistency in how the policies were disseminated and enforced was a major barrier to their implementation in MWSU's College of Education.

On the other hand, St. Tim's education unit was so completely integrated with the rest of the college there was no question that education faculty would be involved in development, and implementation, of college-wide policies. At Erin College, the changes were not effectively disseminated because of how they were developed. Since the provost had acted as a subversive educator and acted primarily on his own, he had not yet figured out how to effectively disseminate these changes throughout the college. On the other hand, implementation was more under his control, and for those who applied under the new policies with service as scholarship portfolios, the policies were properly implemented and the Rank and Promotion Committee complied with policy definitions of scholarship. Therefore, the barriers Erin faced in dissemination did not alter the implementation of policies in the first few test cases.

Putting a policy in place does not guarantee its implementation; achieving faculty and promotion and tenure committee agreement or adherence to the new policies was a challenge.

Faculty Resistance

Another internal force, which worked against the effective implementation of the policies, was faculty resistance. At each of the institutions there were senior faculty who discouraged junior faculty from engaging in service as scholarship and warned them that if they became involved in service as scholarship they would not be likely to be promoted and their scholarship would not be transferable to other institutions. These same faculty members spoke out in promotion and tenure discussions and within their departments, complaining that the new policy was watering down the quality and thinning the standards for scholarship. They claimed service scholars were becoming like those they served, going native, and thereby abdicating their role as expert. This minority group of faculty worked against the safer climate that the new policies were establishing for service scholars and made it more difficult for administrators to implement the policies and faculty to apply for promotion and tenure with service as scholarship portfolios.

Novelty

Often the response to operating under a new or amended policy can become a barrier to its implementation. St. Tims had been operating under the new system for five years, but the dean still commented that some candidates just had not become effective yet at making the case for teaching and service as scholarship. Both Erin and St. Tim's faculty needed more institutional support on how to document and assess service as scholarship. PSU's policies had been in place for two years but faculty still wondered at times if the criteria were working. This perception of the new policies as experimental and lack of confidence in them because they were new caused difficulties during their implementation.

In addition, MWSU, PSU, and St. Tim's promotion and tenure committee members all reported that in the first few months or years after the changes there were pressures on them to appear to their colleagues as if they were doing a rigorous assessment when they evaluated service as scholarship portfolios. Committee members said there was a saving face aspect of their work right after the policy implementation that made decisions on service as scholarship cases political statements as opposed to objective assessments of faculty work. All of these aspects of the novelty of the policies initially worked against successful implementation.

To conclude, structural forces and elements of academic culture played a major role in causing the policy changes and in preventing their successful implementation. The next section describes and analyzes actual changes made to promotion and/or tenure policies and procedures.

Actual Changes Made to Promotion and/or Tenure Policies and Procedures

Overall, the procedures for promotion and tenure at each of these institutions were very similar. A faculty member prepared a portfolio of his or her work that was evaluated by an elected faculty committee of their peers. The decision was approved or overturned by the dean and/or provost and ratified by the president and board of trustees. Committees all consisted of six to nine members who were elected by the faculty, represented a department or college, and rotated on and off the committee in two or three year terms.

Several scholars have studied and made recommendations on the most effective criteria to assess service as scholarship (Boyer, 1990; Braskamp & Ory; 1994; Checkoway, 1998). Lynton (1995) suggested that service as scholarship, like teaching and research, should be assessed by the following set of measures: depth of expertise and preparation, appropriateness of chosen goals and methods, effectiveness of communication, quality of reflection, impact, originality, and innovation.

Since each of the institutions intended to specify criteria to assess service as scholarship so as to align their institutional service mission and faculty reward system, the best policies would be those that left "little to the imagination," or rather were very specific in outlining how service should be evaluated. In addition, each policy should be evaluated based on how well it met the institution's need and how effectively it worked in assessing service as scholarship.

PSU's changes were by far the most comprehensive and effective in practice. PSU's changes included Boyer's four expressions of scholarship and specific statements describing when and how service was scholarship. The new policies carefully delineated service as scholarship from governance and discipline related service and provided examples of service as scholarship in different disciplines. The guidelines contained specific suggestions for documentation of this type of service. They gave faculty a format to make the case for how their service fit into their overall careers, through scholarly profiles. The guidelines listed specific criteria — very similar to Lynton's—to assess service as scholarship. Finally, they identified both academic peers and community members as appropriate evaluators of service as scholarship. PSU's goal was to make faculty workload — which included a significant amount of teaching and service —consistent with the reward system. By describing each form of faculty work as a type of scholarship they were able to elevate the status of certain forms of teaching and service and create rewards for the work most faculty were emphasizing. Although there were problems once the promotion and tenure committee began analyzing service as scholarship, the problems were not based on lack of clarity in the guidelines. Rather, PSU's policy changes on service as scholarship ensured one of the most successful implementation processes because they were comprehensive and provided very specific criteria, documentation, and definitions for assessing service as scholarship.

The changes at St. Tims were intended to redefine scholarship to be reflective of the unique college mission and faculty workload. The Definition and Rationale sections outlined scholarship as both a process and product with stages of self-development, productivity, and dissemination. The Aims of Scholarship section outlined Boyer's four expressions of scholarship, including the scholarship of application, and examples were provided in different disciplines for each expression. Changes at St. Tim's were included in an addendum to promotion and tenure materials. These changes at St. Tims, like PSU, were effective in creating a system that would value all forms of faculty work for promotion and tenure. However, because materials at St. Tims lacked some of the specificity of PSU's policies, particularly criteria to assess service as scholarship, more was left to the interpretation of the committee. The director of faculty development, candidates, and promotion and tenure committee members all felt there was a need for more specific criteria to assess service as scholarship than was provided in the policies.

MWSU's changes were intended to act as an aid in assessing service as scholarship for promotion and tenure committees. Unlike the other institutions, MWSU's indicators focused purely on criteria to assess this service and were not part of a larger effort to expand the definition of scholarship in teaching, discovery, and integration. It listed dimensions of service as scholarship: significance, context, scholarship, and impact. The indicators provided very detailed quantitative and qualitative indicators in each dimension, as well as required evidence to make the case for service as scholarship. There were recommendations for developing faculty portfolios and advice for promotion and tenure committees. The document was very detailed and comprehensive. Unfortunately, while the document did indirectly reach the College of Education, it is difficult to determine its effectiveness because it was not used by the promotion and tenure committee as a guiding document. Ironically, many of the actual criteria used in practice by committee members mirrored the indicators, although they were not required to read the document.

Erin College's changes were not much more than the placement of two to three additional lines under the scholarship category noting that external service based on professional expertise, and shared with peers, was another form of scholarship. The provost's goal was to begin to develop a platform in the promotion and tenure room from which to differentiate community service from service as scholarship—and have service scholars find success in rank and promotion decisions. It only took a few lines for Erin's faculty to accept the premise that service could be scholarship since the majority of the faculty were already sympathetic to that line of thought. However, the lack of specific criteria to assess service as scholarship and other details, like those listed in PSU's document, made Erin College's Rank and Promotion Committee's role in distinguishing between service as scholarship and community service ambiguous and difficult, ultimately hindering its implementation.

Promotion and Tenure Decisions

Higher education researchers have long found significant differences between written policy criteria and criteria used in practice. The whole concept of a promotion and tenure committee is based on the idea that the members are believed to have sufficient knowledge and expertise to judge the quality of other faculty members' scholarship, even if that faculty member is in another discipline. Because promotion and tenure committees often take the liberty of interpreting written criteria in ways that make sense to them, there is often a variance between written and applied policy criteria. Only two of the cases in this study, MWSU and PSU had specific written criteria for assessing service as scholarship. PSU's written and applied criteria were actually very similar, as were MWSU's which was ironic, considering the promotion and tenure committee had not been required to use the indicator's criteria. St. Tim's and Erin's applied criteria were very similar to those written by MWSU and PSU.

The previous section described each of the four written guidelines to service as scholarship. This section will describe the actual criteria used by the promotion and tenure committee to make decisions on candidates with service as scholarship portfolios.

Criteria to Assess Service as Scholarship

All of the promotion and tenure committees felt that it was the candidates' responsibility to prove that their service was scholarship. Each of the institutions maintained two levels of criteria to assess service as scholarship; one level for assistant to associate professor, and one level from associate to full professor. The same criteria were applied to all but committees looked for "successful" service as scholarship for promotion from assistant to associate professor and "outstanding" service as scholarship for promotion to full professor. Committees evaluating candidates for full professor wanted national over regional impact and dissemination, more quantitative and qualitative evidence of impact, and every form of peer review.

The following criteria to discern service as scholarship were shared by all four committees: professional/academic expertise, peer review, evidence of impact/effectiveness, dissemination, originality and innovation, and connection to teaching and research.

Professional/Academic Expertise

Committee members at each of the institutions wanted to see evidence of the academic knowledge, educational theories, or recent research applied in the school or community setting. For example, how a faculty member used recent research on autism and play therapy to develop the curriculum for a summer camp for autistic children. If this was not explicit in a bibliography, curriculum guide, or other service products, then the specific academic knowledge used needed to be explained in the reflective essay. While PSU and MWSU stressed the words "academic or professional expertise," St. Tims and Erin College stressed that the work needed to be set within the context of the latest literature in the field. The difference is subtle, but suggests that PSU and MWSU were more interested in how the individual faculty member acted as an expert, while Erin and St. Tims were more interested in how the actual service was placed within a discipline's recent scholarly work and traditions of practice.

Peer Review

The issue of peer review of service as scholarship was an important one for the promotion and tenure committees. Promotion and Tenure committee members believed service as scholarship should be open to the public in some way for critique and evaluation. However, the committees differed on who they thought might be appropriate evaluators. At MWSU peer review was emphasized over practitioner review because MWSU wanted to be among the most prestigious colleges of education in the country contributing to the scholarly conversation among academics, and local critiques of faculty work would not achieve that end. At St. Tims the committees' desire to have education faculty at other universities comment on education candidate's work, and not educational practitioners, was symptomatic of a distrust between non-education and education committee members about what constituted scholarship, as well as being a part of a general trend toward raising the reputation of the institution through more rigorous reviews of faculty work. PSU was in the middle on this issue and had specifically written into their guidelines that practitioners such as teachers, principals, community leaders, and state education department officials could be external reviewers for service as scholarship. These evaluators were taken seriously by the committee. However, there was a hierarchy wherein Promotion and Tenure Committee members were more influenced by evaluations from superintendents who were PSU alums, or from other education faculty, and less influenced by reports from teachers, community members, or other recipients of the service. Erin College was so embedded in the city where it was located and there were so many connections between the School of Education and the practitioner community, many of whom had completed Ph.D's at Erin, that there was a long tradition of local critique of the work. Of all of the institutions, Erin seemed the least concerned with the peer review criteria and felt that educational practitioners were appropriate reviewers.

Impact/Effectiveness

Of all of the institutions, Erin College was the most concerned with the demonstrated impact and effectiveness of the service. They wanted to know the numbers of people the service assisted and the quality of the process that was used to deliver the service. They favored ongoing relationships over what they called "one-shot-deals." Committees looked for the following kinds of evidence to demonstrate impact: improved test scores, teacher satisfaction, retention for at-risk students, decreased levels of violence in schools, increased capacity through the development of effective programming and replication of the model. The committees looked for the service to have had an impact in local, state, and national arenas. The national impact was most important for promotions to full professor and less a requirement at the associate level. The next category, dissemination, captures how the committee expected to see the service having a regional and national impact.

Dissemination

Committee members looked at how widely service outcomes were disseminated to determine if it was scholarship. There was clearly a continuum or hierarchy of dissemination: refereed journal articles, invited national conference presentations, and other published work like curriculum guides, textbooks, reports, videos, manuals, conference proceedings, grant proposals, and newsletter articles. The greater the research emphasis in the institution, (i.e. in descending order MWSU, PSU, Erin and St. Tims) the more committees emphasized the traditional end of preferred methods of dissemination. Despite this hierarchy, committees were quite flexible about the forms the dissemination could take, as long as some form was present. Because of Erin College's history of applied educational innovations, their committee was most interested in how the work brought important new things to new audiences. A commitment to historically disadvantaged groups made Erin more sensitive than some of the other campuses as to how their faculty were contributing toward helping the least advantaged in the city and this came through in their bias toward dissemination. However, all of the committees looked at dissemination as a way that the faculty and institution as a whole increased their prestige.

Originality: The Mind of the Scholar at Work

Service that is scholarship makes an original contribution to a field, according to these four promotion and tenure committees. In the process of making that contribution, the mind of the scholar is at work. All of the committees looked for evidence of original, innovative work in which the reflective, analytical, and systematic mind of a scholar was demonstrated. At PSU, Erin, and St. Tims new knowledge could involve doing something new with old knowledge. Committee members wanted candidates to share the scholarly questions that framed their service to demonstrate how they had conceptualized their service as part of an ongoing attempt to answer certain questions in the field. They examined service for good ideas, intellectual rigor, and a certain critical analysis that they believed was characteristic of scholars. The educational problem had to be academic or scholarly in nature, it could not be a purely technical problem such as how to get more funding for an under-supported school. Otherwise the candidate would not have needed their scholarly skills, only administrative or political ones.

The faculty member's self-assessment of the goals and outcomes of the project and evaluation of his/her own work were key indicators of a scholarly mind. The reflective essay was analyzed for systematic reflection over the course of the project and evidence of intellectual growth throughout the service.

Connection to Teaching and Research

Candidates were most successful in making the case that their service was scholarship when there were clear connections between their teaching, research, and service. In fact, at MWSU a few faculty members felt that the only service that was scholarship was rooted in the faculty member's recent research. Otherwise, they concluded, the faculty member was essentially a consultant, in a role that others outside the university could have played, as opposed to acting as a scholar. St. Tims' committee emphasized the connections between the three kinds of faculty activity over an entire career and trajectory of work. In other words, they were not only interested in how the service fit within the candidate's current teaching and research but also how it fit within the entire landscape of the candidate's academic career. This emphasis was consistent with policies at St. Tims around stages and aims of scholarship. Erin College's committee believed that service that was scholarship was seamlessly connected to teaching and research and this was very reflective of the culture of the faculty in the School of Education whose teaching, action research, and service were often happening simultaneously.

Additional Criteria

There were some criteria that were important to one or a few of the institutions to discern service as scholarship and not others. For example, committee members at PSU and Erin College applied a sort of "service ethic" and social justice orientation to service as scholarship. They felt that service as scholarship involved relationship building and development of ethical, reciprocal partnerships.

Erin College and PSU's committees both mentioned that service as scholarship should bring prestige back to the institution. By prestige, Erin and PSU committees meant positive public relations in TV, local and state newspapers, and practitioner journals. Although all of the institutions were places where faculty identified with the mission, Erin College's committee most stressed that service as scholarship should be related to Erin College's mission and benefit the entire college, bringing prestige and accolades back more broadly.

Documentation of Service as Scholarship

The documentation presented for service as scholarship was very similar at each institution. A tradition of documenting teaching scholarship at St. Tims and Erin College had paved the way for acceptance of applied writing like curriculum guides, textbooks, grant reports, and writing for community audiences as potential evidence of scholarship. At PSU and MWSU the history of documenting professional development schools through reports, student test scores, and teacher satisfaction surveys, paved the way for acceptance of different forms of documentation for service as scholarship. At all of the institutions there were reflective essays, evaluations, bibliographies, syllabuses, and interview protocols. There were letters of support from professors at other institutions doing similar work, from community organizations, teachers, principals, superintendents, and graduate students involved in the projects. There were awards from community organizations and various honors conferred as a result of the service. Yet, there was still a continuum in the overall acceptance of these materials as appropriate evidence for service as scholarship. For example, when asked about evidence of service as scholarship one committee member at MWSU said, "Written pieces. What else can we judge, intentions?" MWSU accepted articles in practitioner journals as scholarship but not as uniformly as at Erin College where this kind of writing was more the norm anyway.

Faculty involved in service as scholarship who brought in ongoing grant funding at MWSU were able to use that funding with the dean and committee to show that the service was having an impact, and bringing prestige and benefits to the institution. At St. Tims, Erin College, and PSU, grant funding also held considerable sway with deans and some committee members and confirmed that a candidate's service was scholarship although to a lesser degree. The importance of grant funding can be explained in three ways. First, grants usually required a higher level of documentation and evaluation so the documentation of service as scholarship was likely to be better than the average service project. Second, grants demonstrated a link between the faculty member and a funding agency in the discipline, which helped to place the work squarely in the field, and create an important connection for the college. Third, grants provided prestige, funding, and a regional, if not national recognition of faculty work. Grants were exchanged for lack of publications as a source of peer review because if major funding agencies felt the work was important and continued to fund it, it often convinced the committee that the work must be making significant contributions to the field. In other words, grants answered the question that often underscored much of the tenure and promotion process, "What has and will the candidate contribute toward this college?"

The placement of each of the colleges of education within the institution very much influenced the "informal evidence" provided for candidates presenting service as scholarship. At St. Tims when there was not an education faculty member on the university-wide committee, there was a clear lack of verbal support and context provided for education portfolios, and education faculty suffered for this lack of informal evidence provided in the committee discussion. At PSU, Erin College, and MWSU having someone on the committee who was familiar with the candidate's work served as an invisible form of documentation in conversations that helped make the candidate's case that their service was scholarship.

Problems in Assessing Service: The Swampy Lowlands

Donald Schön (1983) refers to documenting and assessing reflective practice as entering the "swampy lowlands." Committee members described the process of assessing service as scholarship as "mysterious," "nebulous," "messy" and "subjective." All of the promotion and tenure committees described having significant problems in trying to assess service as scholarship. Faculty development efforts, explicit criteria written into promotion and tenure documents, and experiences with test cases, did not diminish the questions that plagued committee members as they reviewed service.

There was collaborative service at all of the institutions, but the most collaborative was at Erin and St. Tims. While all of the committees reported having problems assigning individual merit to collaborative work, committees at Erin College and St. Tims were more comfortable than MWSU and PSU in finding ways to distinguish between a candidate's own work and contributions made by community members or other faculty. Because of its strong social justice orientation, Erin College faculty were concerned about whether paid or unpaid service should count as scholarship and they preferred that faculty provide unpaid service for disadvantaged groups. At MWSU the questions about paid service were concerned with faculty freedom to choose their line of inquiry, and potential loss of objectivity as the agency determined the goals of the project.

Another category of problems could be described as the "not here or not enough" aspect of assessing service as scholarship. All of the committees described problems with poorly documented service. Often not enough information was provided to make committee decisions. Committees complained that the portfolios had descriptive rather than analytical accounts of service, and highlighted relationship-building activities rather than scholarly approaches to problems, conceptual frameworks for service, or the major issues in the field.

Often, candidates did not identify an intellectual question for their service project and demonstrate how they answered it. There was no established way for the candidate to express what they learned from each service project to the outside observer and many candidates did not include self-assessments in their portfolios. Sometimes solid quantitative evidence of impact was not available, e.g. some statistics on teacher and student outcomes were confidential.

The assessment of service as scholarship was often accompanied by questions that did not arise in reviews of teaching and research. For example, at MWSU one candidate told a story of how she had arrived on site for a project one day and was going to collect her data when one of the children became lost on the playground. She stopped to help find the child and her data collection waited until another day. Should committees take into account the unpredictability of school and community settings and the time needed to build relationships so that the service could be successful? What if considering this meant that service as scholarship might hinder the amount of writing and publishing that is expected? Yet another question committee members disagreed on, especially at MWSU, was whether products of service as scholarship should address an academic audience or a practitioner audience. Also, committee members disagreed on who constituted appropriate evaluators for service projects. Because of the heavy emphasis placed on the reflective essay, MWSU and PSU committee members worried about how to distinguish between candidates with persuasive writing skills and good work. Finally, at Erin College and St. Tims, there was disagreement about whether something could be scholarship by virtue of it having been done in a scholarly way (the scholarly process), or whether it is only scholarship once it is written and published (the scholarly product).

Another category of problems arose when the committee tried to compare service as scholarship with teaching as scholarship or research as scholarship. Some of the criteria to evaluate research, teaching, and service as scholarship were the same, but significant criteria and some of the typical indicators of mastery were different. For example, in traditional academic writing the conceptual framework and placement of the educational problem in the literature was usually documented in the first section of the article. However, since service as scholarship did not always result in traditional academic writing, the committee had a harder time knowing where to look for this information. Also service as scholarship often employed newer research methodologies and its findings utilized a practitioner based language. Often in these forms the project's conceptual framework was not highlighted and looked as if no conceptual framework were guiding it. Without being there to observe the scholarly process, they could not recognize the work as scholarship. Also, when committee members compared service to other forms of scholarship they felt less confidant about objective criteria and consistency as to what constituted high quality. However flawed, teaching evaluations and peer reviews of teaching, and peer reviewed journals for research stood for themselves, but service left more to the reviewer in terms of understanding the context and setting.

At St. Tims and Erin College faculty often focused their portfolios on the context of their service project, and the methods they were using to communicate new things to new audiences. Portfolios written this way lacked acknowledgment of the intellectual conversation and major issues in the field, and therefore made it hard for the committee to see the connections between the practice problems and the scholarly problems inherent in the work.

At St. Tims and Erin College committee members felt that there were not clear enough guidelines for faculty on what to present for service as scholarship. At all of the institutions when faculty employed interdisciplinary knowledge for service projects, their specific academic expertise appeared diluted.

Finally, some committee members used the fact that candidates needed to prove that their service is scholarship as an excuse to argue that no service is scholarship. These committee members used subtle and not so subtle body language to argue against the candidate's work as scholarship, when there would have been no evidence that would have convinced them. However, it is possible that faculty who had positive feelings toward any kind of service and who would vote yes for any type of service as scholarship neutralized the influence of these faculty.

Other problems associated with the process of assessing service as scholarship were the same problems faced by committees assessing all faculty work. Since committee members rotated in and out of the committee each year, the committee did not have a long memory of criteria and cases used to assess service as scholarship. Although provosts or deans who sat on the promotion and tenure committee as ex-officio members did serve as the collective memory, if the dean was new and/or had a radically different perspective on assessing service than the previous dean/provost, as was the case at MWSU, then the dean/provost's memory was not only lost, but irrelevant. Also, at times colleagueship kept committees from being as critical as they should of each other's work, although this was more of an issue at St. Tims and Erin College than at PSU and MWSU. Not everyone on the committee was expert on different research methodologies, styles of writing, and things specific to the candidate's discipline. All of these things made the promotion and tenure decision-making process irrational and inconsistent at times.

To conclude, each of the four campuses established policies to assess service as scholarship. Most of the actual criteria used by committees followed the written criteria but a few criteria did not. Promotion and tenure committees experienced unanticipated problems in assessing service as scholarship. These four cases suggest that even when official policies are put in place, they may not eliminate conflict, because policies are always open to interpretation and can not cover every issue. The more involvement by faculty in the development of policies, the more detailed the policies, and the more regulatory power that exists to ensure compliance, the better chance that policies will be followed as intended.

Outcomes

Shakespeare said, "To climb steep hills, requires slow pace at first." Each of these cases is a good example of change at a slow pace. Those campuses where the policies were widely disseminated across the college of education, where the policies had the approval of key stakeholders, and where the most time had passed since policy implementation, experienced the greatest change and the most positive outcomes from policy implementation.

Despite the abundance or scarcity of resources provided for policy implementation, some outcomes were apparent from each campus process. These outcomes varied in degree by campus, and in some cases were only outcomes for those faculty aware of policy changes. There were promotion and tenure outcomes; improved faculty documentation of service as scholarship; increased faculty satisfaction; more and/or improved service; a change in understanding of service as scholarship; an increase in funding, public relations, and prestige; a strengthened service culture; and faculty resistance.

Higher education scholars have noted that it takes a long time to see real outcomes from policy change. While each of the four cases were written within five years of policy changes, there was a wide range (from almost one year at Erin College to five years at St. Tims) since the new policy had been put in place. The fact that the faculty at St. Tims had had five years to adapt to policy changes, and had integrated the policy changes into everyday faculty life, were major reasons for identifiable outcomes from policy implementation. On the other hand, the short period within which the policies were applied at Erin College made identifying outcomes more difficult.

Promotion and Tenure Outcomes

Each of the four institutions were places with 80 percent or higher promotion and tenure success rates before the policy changes. Therefore, any changes to promotion and tenure outcomes were set in the context of places where faculty reported that, "most faculty get promoted and tenured here anyway."

The outcomes related to promotion and tenure were also set against the backdrop of institutions with strong traditions of valuing all kinds of service. However, at each of these four institutions, although to different degrees, the pendulum had shifted in the last five to ten years away from their traditional recognition or emphasis on multiple forms of scholarship and toward traditional research. One of the major outcomes of the policies to reward service as scholarship for promotion and tenure was a slight muting of the trend to emphasize research.

Overall, the policy changes to assess and reward service as scholarship for promotion and tenure ranged from having a neutral to a positive influence on advancement decisions. The policies were the most helpful to those faculty heavily engaged in service as scholarship and least helpful to faculty engaged in community service who thought that their work was scholarship. The policies had no significant impact on promotion and tenure decisions for faculty heavily invested in traditional research. In no case did the policy hurt faculty involved in service as scholarship or any faculty member applying for promotion and tenure.

In the two years following the changes, there were at least four cases at PSU where education candidates applied with service as scholarship as their strongest area for promotion. It appears that in each case these faculty would not have been successful without the policy changes. The policy changes at Erin College only slightly influenced the success of faculty applying with service as scholarship portfolios. At the time of the policy changes the Rank and Promotion Committee was already operating in ways that prioritized and rewarded all service and had been for some time. One of the most significant influences the policy changes were having and would have in the future on Erin College rank and promotion decisions was to give candidates and committee members a more sophisticated understanding to differentiate between community service and service as scholarship. Because of the new policies, Erin's committee became more discerning about service as scholarship and several candidates who applied after the new policies were successful.

Tenure and promotion decisions at St. Tims were being made with a broader view of scholarship than prior to 1992. Candidates who had strong evidence of service as scholarship, including written documents, were successful, whereas those faculty who depended on the guidelines to make the case for them were not successful. While there were two recent cases where education faculty were denied promotion and claimed to be involved in service as scholarship, there was insufficient evidence suggesting that the new policies were not applied. Rather, evidence suggested that most of the education faculty had benefited from the policy changes in promotion and tenure decisions over the last five years.

MWSU education faculty with strong service as scholarship portfolios were successful after the policy changes, but mostly because they had turned their service as scholarship into publications or brought in grant dollars. However, the Indicators seemed to have a subtle impact on these positive promotion and tenure decisions. They reminded the dean and the promotion and tenure committee that the central administration recognized service as scholarship. They also provided a framework for candidates to make more persuasive cases in their portfolios. MWSU's College of Education Promotion and Tenure Committee applied many of the criteria outlined in the indicators in making their decisions about service as scholarship without having been required by the dean to do so.

At each of the institutions the new policies were most easily applied in decisions concerning the move from assistant to associate professor, but most debated in the move from associate professor to full professor. Because of the fact that at each of these institutions there was some history of faculty promotion from assistant to associate professor with little traditional scholarship, a great deal of emphasis was put on the evaluation for full professor. The evaluation for full professor became the embodiment of a culture war between those faculty who had supported the policy to reward multiple forms of scholarship and honor the service mission, and those faculty who wanted to increase the prestige of the College of Education or institution by hiring and promoting more traditional scholars. This phenomenon was most present at MWSU, PSU, and St. Tims and present only to a small degree at Erin College.

Another common finding across institutions was that the period directly after the policy changes was a difficult time for junior faculty and others interested in applying for tenure or promotion. Faculty candidates did not know whether to trust that the new policies would be implemented fairly by the first few promotion and tenure committees that were required to apply them. Whether the changes were incremental, two, three, or five years old, there was a feeling among faculty at each of these campuses that it was still too soon to tell whether the new policies would be implemented as intended. The confidence in the guidelines was strongest at St. Tims where they had been in place for five years, but even their faculty questioned whether they were being followed. These questions left the institutions in somewhat of a state of flux with faculty watching every test case and interpreting for themselves whether or not they thought the new policies were being followed. Test cases strongly influenced faculty behavior in terms of their decisions about whether to apply for promotion and tenure and at what time. While it appears that the policy changes slightly increased the chances that faculty involved in service as scholarship would be tenured or promoted, the secret nature of the promotion and tenure process made it difficult to know all of the reasons why each particular decision was made. Overall, policies to reward service as scholarship for promotion and tenure had a greater impact in areas other than actual promotion and tenure decisions. The next section describes these more significant outcomes.

Changes in Amount and Quality of Service

While the development and implementation of the new policies slightly increased the amount of service as scholarship on each campus, the policies had a greater impact on the depth and quality of service experiences. Because of the safer atmosphere created for faculty involved in service as scholarship, faculty spent more time in service settings and developed deeper partnerships with schools and community organizations than before the policy changes. The increased amount of time faculty spent at their service sites resulted in their being able to serve more teachers and students, have longer and more meaningful interactions, and develop more strategies to connect their teaching, research, and service activities in these sites. For example, after the policy changes at PSU principals and teachers found that the partnerships with PSU education faculty became more mutually beneficial and involved higher quality interactions because faculty felt like they could devote more time to service as scholarship.

The discussions about service as scholarship that surrounded the development and interpretation of the new policies acted as a lever at all four institutions to push faculty involved in community service and transform their service into scholarship. All four schools had faculty engaged in service who tended to prefer "doing" to systematic reflection and writing. Especially at Erin College where faculty were deeply entrenched in community service, faculty who came into contact with the new policies were forced to consider how to differentiate between their own community service and service as scholarship activities and to evaluate for themselves what they would need to do to transform some of their own service into scholarship. At PSU and MWSU the policies forced faculty working with professional development schools to reevaluate their work in light of the new criteria for service as scholarship and to change the ways in which they approached their work. At St. Tims the policies were forcing the education faculty to consider what kinds of dissemination, peer review, and documentation designate work with schools as scholarship. This reflection would be likely to improve the quality of their service as well.

Making the Case through Documentation

The most consistent and significant outcome across each of the four cases was that the changes to promotion and tenure policies were most useful as faculty development tools to prepare candidates to make the case that their service was scholarship. Once the policies were published, they became the authoritative guide for faculty involved in this type of work. Faculty quoted from the policy and used its conceptual framework concerning service as scholarship throughout their portfolios. They organized their reflective essays using the criteria listed in the policies for service as scholarship, demonstrating how their specific community work met each criteria. Most of the policies provided examples of appropriate documentation and the candidates used this as a guide to document their work. The policy not only served as a guide for these faculty, but also a sort of procedural contract between them and the promotion and tenure committee. If a candidate demonstrated that his/her service was scholarship using each of the university's criteria and provided every possible kind of evidence suggested in the policies, then candidates expected to be tenured and/or promoted. The policies became symbolic and cultural armor for faculty involved in service as scholarship as they made their cases for promotion and tenure. This armor held the most sway at PSU and the least at MWSU, but nonetheless was present in each case.

Another outcome that accompanied policy implementation was the support of individual faculty by key offices. Part of the reason faculty were using the new policies to frame their portfolios was that there was extensive development work, mentoring, and outreach to faculty by provost's offices, faculty development offices, and dean's offices in the form of individual consultations, workshops, letters, and guides.

Related outcomes were increases in the amount and quality of documentation for both teaching and service as scholarship. After these policies went into effect, portfolios became a much more standard tool for documentation. Each of the four committees experienced a shift in the last few years from a listing of community service activities, to binders and collections of curriculum guides, videos, letters from community organizations, and articles in practitioner journals describing service as scholarship. The new policies changed the culture around documentation of service so that there were better explanations in each portfolio of why particular service projects were scholarship. Often the increased documentation of service as scholarship, combined with the tendency for faculty to quote the guidelines in their applications, were the first and most significant way committee members were educated on both the policy changes and the shift in thinking about service as scholarship. Despite the fact that several committee members complained that the "notebooks got bigger," most promotion and tenure committee members reported that the evidence for multiple forms of scholarship had improved because of the new policies.

However, the increase in documentation of service as scholarship was not completely positive. After the policy changes, some faculty became confused about where to list certain activities in their portfolios and there was a tendency for some faculty to include everything and let the committee discern what it was and where it should go.

Faculty Satisfaction

Among those faculty who were already involved in service as scholarship, the policy changes increased faculty satisfaction with work and with their university. Faculty reported that they were more satisfied because the new policies (1) created a greater congruence between the stated rhetoric of their college/university's service mission and its actual reward system;

(2) acknowledged their service as a potential form of scholarship; (3) elevated the importance of service as scholarship in the reward system; (4) in some cases, made it possible for faculty to be evaluated more proportionally to their actual workload; (5) and legitimized the scholarly role these faculty were playing in the educational community. While most of the faculty involved in service as scholarship would have been likely to engage in this work regardless of the new policies, the policies had both a psychological and symbolic effect of lessening the stress and resentment these faculty felt at being overworked by their institutions. After the new polices were put in place, these faculty felt that their work was more appreciated and respected, their roles as community scholars better understood, and their place within the university more secure.

Faculty at each of the four institutions agreed that they did not want there to be only one kind of professorship at their college. They wanted their colleague next door to be able to emphasize teaching as scholarship, while they emphasized service as scholarship and other's research as scholarship. Faculty involved in service as scholarship at all of the campuses felt that the new policies were more just, equitable, and inclusive of different faculty careers.

There were faculty at each of these institutions who felt their careers were reinvigorated when they realized they could engage in service as scholarship and this work would count for promotion.

The very existence of formal policies stating that the university valued service as scholarship and the first few test cases at each institution made faculty involved in service as scholarship feel safer about the chances that their service would count for tenure and promotion. For example, at St. Tims one assistant professor in education felt that the policy changes allowed him to spend more time on service, and go "where my heart is" because of the greater likelihood that the work would contribute toward his portfolio for promotion. Faculty involved in service as scholarship at PSU felt "some breathing room," and were not as "scared as they used to be" because of the policy changes. While this safer environment was in part created by the new policies, it was also contingent and dependent upon the support of the dean and promotion and tenure committee. Nevertheless, in each of the four cases the new promotion and tenure policies positively influenced faculty satisfaction for those involved in service as scholarship.

Change in Understanding of Service as Scholarship

To different degrees, the development, dissemination, and implementation of the new policies caused a shift in thinking toward service as a potential form of scholarship on each of the four campuses. Because of widespread faculty involvement in the development of the Rationale at St. Tims there was a genuine culture change around the meaning of scholarship. After the new policies were implemented, almost the entire faculty at St. Tims considered teaching, service, discovery, and integration as potential forms of scholarship. In the five years after the policy changes, new faculty were socialized into this view of scholarship. This was also true at PSU, although it was not as widespread. PSU faculty were aware of and for the most part agreed with the language and assumptions in the policies around service as scholarship, but at least half of the faculty maintained the traditional rhetoric of "teaching, research, and service" to describe their work.

At MWSU the university-wide process to define service as scholarship altered some education faculty thinking about service as a form of scholarship. However, because the development of the policies was not based in the College of Education and was poorly disseminated within the college, the indicators did not have a widespread effect on changing faculty views of scholarship. Despite this, faculty and administrators at MWSU had a very sophisticated understanding of service and the ways in which it manifested itself as scholarship. The emphasis on the land grant mission, faculty experiences with service as scholarship, and campus-wide conversations had had an impact on the general understanding of service as scholarship.

At Erin College the policy had not yet changed faculty understanding of service or scholarship. Most Erin faculty understood "service" to mean community service. Yet when faculty at Erin were given examples of service projects that would be considered service as scholarship by the new policies, there was a strong faculty consensus that certain kinds of service were scholarship.

Increased Funding, Public Relations, Prestige

As a result of the policy changes, service as scholarship activities became more visible both on and off-campus. This resulted in increases in funding and better public relations. As a result of the policy changes, PSU and MWSU experienced increases in external funding from state, grant, and private giving for service as scholarship. In addition, more existing grants directed part of their general funds toward service as scholarship. Each institution and their faculty received significant positive public relations, and local, state, and national coverage of both individual faculty service efforts and the institutional process to reward multiple forms of scholarship. For example, both MWSU's indicators and PSU's promotion and tenure documents became national models used by dozens of other campuses to reward service as scholarship. Academic administrators and individual faculty presented at national conferences, consulted nationally on these policies, and found research and writing opportunities based on their work. As part of the national conversation on faculty roles and rewards, many of the academic administrators who led these changes published articles in higher education journals.

Strengthened Service Culture

While the new policies grew out of each of the institution's existing service cultures, they also strengthened and enhanced them. For example, before the policies faculty at MWSU, PSU and Erin College were often recruited with service as part of the "job talk." After the policy changes more faculty were recruited to these colleges and universities because of the promise that not only the rhetoric, but also the reward system, would now acknowledge service as scholarship. This recruited more faculty to the institution who wanted to engage in this kind of work.

In at least three cases, PSU, St. Tims, and Erin College, the development and implementation of these policies had unexpected, overall positive effects on the relationships between the college/university and the community. In addition, the new reward system at PSU made the curriculum work better and at St. Tims encouraged more interdisciplinary and collaborative scholarship in teaching and service. The process helped all four institutions to clarify their missions and enhanced communication across disciplines.

Mixed Messages and Faculty Resistance

There were very few negative outcomes associated with these policy changes for two major reasons. One reason had to do with dissemination and the other with the process of developing the policies. At Erin College and MWSU the policies were not disseminated widely enough to create negative reactions or significantly influence faculty behavior one way or another. At St. Tims the process was so collaborative and created so much consensus that few faculty were surprised when the policies were applied to promotion and tenure decisions. Rather, there was an overall readiness for the policies to be implemented. In addition, at PSU and St. Tims, the lack of a groundswell of easy promotions engendered widespread acceptance of the policies. In other words, since the policies were helping faculty involved in service as scholarship, but not hurting traditional researchers, they were not largely controversial. This having been said, some minor negative outcomes surfaced from the margins of faculty life at these four campuses.

As a result of the implementation of the new policies, faculty candidates at PSU, MWSU, and St. Tims received mixed messages about promotion and tenure. For example, at St. Tim's faculty were socialized into a broader view of scholarship and regularly encouraged to apply for tenure and promotion with portfolios that reflected this view. Yet, the institution was simultaneously continuing to hire faculty with backgrounds and interests in research rather than teaching and service. Some promotion and tenure committee members would praise these traditional research portfolios publicly, sending a message to faculty that when the institution had a choice, they preferred traditional scholars. Likewise, in hallway conversations and even some division meetings, faculty at St. Tims were told that "we value all forms of scholarship here, but until you get tenure and promotion to associate professor, only do traditional research."

On each of the campuses, but primarily at PSU and St. Tims a minority of faculty spoke out against the new policies claiming that the new policies were hurting the institution's already fragile research reputations. There was no evidence that suggested that this had happened. For faculty engaging exclusively in traditional research, the policies did not appear to have any influence. In addition, some faculty were finding more opportunities to publish articles about their service as scholarship than they had had available before.

Some members of each of the promotion and tenure committees complained that the process of evaluating faculty work had become more difficult and time consuming because of the new policies. The lack of agreed upon standards for evaluating service as scholarship meant that these committees were swimming in some uncharted seas and this made this part of their work harder.

There was also a feeling by some faculty at each of the campuses that the new policies were not being followed and this caused resentment and lowered morale. Because of the secret nature of the promotion and tenure process, faculty conjectured and made assumptions about unfavorable promotion and tenure decisions absent concrete data. Individual faculty interpreted promotion rejections as proof that the policies were not being applied. The promotion and tenure committee could not counter this assumption because of the secret nature of their deliberations. This was a difficult but perhaps inevitable outcome that accompanied implementation and expectations for the changes.

Summary

To conclude, this study investigated how four colleges and universities developed policies to assess service as scholarship for their promotion and tenure systems. Major findings suggest:

External forces, institutional isomorphism, internal forces, leadership, and unique cultural characteristics caused these four campuses to attempt changes to the reward system. Research culture, dissemination and implementation problems, faculty resistance, and novelty were elements that hindered the successful implementation of polices to assess service as scholarship.

The most effective policies were detailed and comprehensive and guided candidates and committees through the new terrain of documenting and assessing service as scholarship.

The following criteria were shared by all four committees to discern service as scholarship: professional/academic expertise, peer review, evidence of impact/effectiveness, dissemination, originality and innovation, and connection to teaching and research.

Outcomes of policy changes include: a slight increase in faculty members' chances of achieving promotion and tenure, improved documentation of service as scholarship, increased faculty satisfaction with work and institution, more and/or improved service, a change in understanding of service
. as scholarship, an increase in funding, positive public relations and pres-

tige, a strengthened service culture, increased prevalence of mixed messages delivered to promotion and tenure candidates, and some faculty resistance.

The process to develop and implement policies to assess service as scholarship decreased the tendency for each of these campuses to exclusively reward research for promotion and tenure while strengthening overall service culture. Whereas this chapter provided an analysis of findings across four cases, the next and final chapter discusses the implications of these findings.

CHAPTER EIGHT

Designing Cultures that Reward Service as Scholarship

This chapter is divided into five sections. Section I provides a brief summary of the scope and findings of this study. Section II outlines the limitations of this research. Implications of this research for policy and practice are discussed in the third section. The fourth section presents recommendations and the chapter ends with a discussion of areas for future research.

Section I: Study Overview

Understanding how colleges and universities develop policies to assess and reward service as scholarship is important because commentators inside and outside of higher education have criticized colleges and universities for neglecting the service aspects of their missions (Bok, 1990; Harkavy & Puckett, 1991; Levine, 1994) and have called upon faculty to respond in applied, socially useful ways (Hirsch, 1996). Although many educators in higher education have touted the need for and importance of service (Boyer 1990; Elman & Smock, 1985; Gamson, 1995; 1999; Lynton, 1995; Rice, 1991), there are few concrete examples of colleges and universities that have actually integrated service as scholarship into their promotion and tenure systems. If academic leaders want to expand their institution's definition of scholarship to include service and make rhetoric and rewards consistent, they need to understand the factors most likely to cause colleges and universities to make changes to their reward systems.

For service to be truly integrated into the reward system of the university, it must be accepted and integrated into the culture of faculty. However, the dominant academic culture elevates research over all other kinds of professional work (Crosson, 1983; Gamson & Finnegan, 1996). Very few colleges and universities have attempted to fundamentally amend or change their cultures to value teaching and service as highly as research for promotion and tenure. Boyer's (1990) *Scholarship Reconsidered* challenged higher education to assess certain forms of faculty service as scholarship for promotion and tenure. Research has not completely identified the cultural assumptions, central tendencies, faculty training, or other elements of academic culture which impact when, how, and why service as scholarship becomes fully integrated into promotion and tenure reward systems. This study provides a window into the elements of academic culture that support or hinder the assessment of service as scholarship. The study also sheds light on potential levers for change by explaining how and why these four colleges and universities decided to alter the status quo and make changes to their faculty reward systems.

Studying how promotion and tenure committees assess service as scholarship in the education discipline is important for a number of reasons. Faculty are increasingly called upon to link their service with scholarship (Edgerton, 1995). In the future, more faculty members will be asked to offer judgments about the quality of nontraditional forms of scholarship and academe will need assessment strategies that cover an expanded definition of faculty work (Edgerton, 1995). Furthermore, Diamond (1995) argues that no single definition of scholarship will be agreed upon by all disciplines and trying to establish one could be counterproductive. Consequently, Lynton (1995) and Diamond (1995) have both called upon the disciplines to explore their own measures of quality for service as scholarship. Of all the disciplines, education faculty report engaging in the greatest amount of external service (Kirchstein, 1997). There is a long history of education faculty engaging in action research, consulting, and professional development activities with schools and other educational organizations (Campoy, 1996). Because education faculty are among the most likely to engage in service as scholarship, it is useful to study the criteria used to assess service as scholarship in the education discipline. Campuses that want to reward service as scholarship need well-developed criteria to differentiate between community, disciplinary, and governance-related service and service as scholarship.

Little research has been done which tests newly developed criteria for assessing service as scholarship in practice. Likewise, Diamond (1995) has pointed out that formal and informal statements of promotion and tenure criteria are only one factor influencing how faculty on promotion and tenure committees make decisions. Other factors include disciplinary and professional values, personal priorities and interests, and institutional and department priorities. For these reasons and because policies are open to interpretation, it is important to understand the differences between written criteria and criteria used in practice and why those discrepancies exist. This study describes and analyzes written criteria and criteria used in practice for assessing service as scholarship, thus filling a gap in the literature.

Examining the outcomes of policies to assess and reward service as scholarship is timely because so few colleges and universities have attempted to integrate service as scholarship into their promotion and tenure system and it is not yet clear what outcomes result from such an "experiment." If the true test of the soundness of a policy is its usefulness in practice, as some policy-makers have suggested, then it is important to know whether these policies achieved their goals. Information concerning the successes and failures of policies to assess service as scholarship can help other campuses craft similar policies or consider alternative strategies to accomplish the same ends. Also, there is a well-established literature indicating that extrinsic rewards influence faculty behavior (Serow, Brawner & Demery, 1999) and that policies can contribute to culture change. This study provided an excellent opportunity to test whether new policies to assess service as scholarship influence faculty behavior or changes in university or college of education culture. Although a secondary reason, it is important to know the outcomes of policies to assess service as scholarship because women faculty devote more time to service activities than do men (Riley, Baldridge, et al, 1978; Long & Fox, 1995) and it is important that women faculty members' careers are not negatively effected by the decision to pursue service as scholarship.

The purpose of this research was to understand how colleges and universities develop policies to assess and reward service as scholarship, the elements of academic culture that help or hinder that process, how promotion and tenure committees apply new or amended policies to promotion and tenure decisions, and the outcomes of this process for education faculty.

The development, implementation, and outcomes of policies to assess service as scholarship in promotion and tenure were studied by selecting four institutions (one from each major Carnegie classification; baccalaureate, masters, doctoral, and research). These four institutions were identified by the New England Resource Center for Higher Education and American Association for Higher Education as having recently developed exemplary programs for assessing service as scholarship. Yin's (1994) case study methodology guided the research design, data collection, and analysis. Four site visits were conducted in the spring and fall of 1998 and interviews were conducted with administrators and faculty leaders involved in the policy changes and promotion and tenure committees, and with junior and senior education faculty. Documents such as promotion and tenure materials, internal memorandums, newsletters, and committee notes were reviewed as well. Finally, data was analyzed and each of the four case studies was constructed.

Findings

This study investigated how four colleges and universities developed policies to assess service as scholarship for their promotion and tenure systems. Major findings across these four cases were outlined in the previous chapter.

Briefly, this study showed that policies to assess service as scholarship can serve important functions in: (1) making an institution's service mission, faculty workload, and reward system more consistent, (2) decreasing the exclusivity of research in promotion and tenure decisions and expanding faculty members' views of scholarship, (3) increasing faculty satisfaction, chances for promotion and tenure, and the quality of documentation among service scholars and, (4) strengthening the quality of faculty service and a university's service culture. The study also confirmed the previously cited rise of research culture in the 1980s and early 1990s in all four types of universities and explored the barriers research culture presents to assessing and rewarding service as scholarship for promotion and tenure. The process to develop and implement policies to assess service as scholarship decreased the tendency for each of these campuses to exclusively reward research for promotion and tenure while strengthening overall service culture.

Section II: Study Limitations

This research was limited to four institutions. One of the four campuses was operating on a contract system, which was unusual. All four of the institutions had very strong service missions, and other unique cultural characteristics. Institutions were not randomly selected, but identified by NERCHE and AAHE as exemplary for having developed policies to assess service as scholarship. Universities that have become innovators in this area are likely to be unique in some other ways. Therefore, one should not generalize across all colleges interested in implementing policies to assess service as scholarship. While the study included a college or university in each Carnegie classification, and this provided a useful comparison of issues across different kinds of academic cultures, the findings for each type of university cannot be generalized to all similar types of universities. In addition, the study focused on colleges/units of education and while some findings were reported for the institution as a whole, the study cannot be generalized to whole institutions or to other disciplines.

The number of faculty interviewed at each university was small in comparison to the size of the faculty. While the participants were chosen to include a representative group of faculty in each of the three categories, key informants, and others assisted in the identification of participants, so the sample was not randomly selected. Therefore, findings are not generalizable to a broader population. It may be that five to ten more interviews at each institution may have uncovered additional data or shed a fuller light on the institutional or college of education culture.

Because of the confidential nature of tenure decisions, some of the participants may have been reluctant to be too open or revealing about how decisions were made. Because many of the participants may be advocates for their system of rewarding service as scholarship or have recently benefited from it, there may have been a halo effect over my findings, wherein participants may have filtered out the more negative or ambiguous consequences of the policy. Some of the limitations of interviews are that informants may have recalled events inaccurately, or given the researcher answers that they thought she wanted to hear (Yin, 1994). Also, this research captures faculty opinions and recollections in one moment of time and their attitudes and beliefs may vary from year to year. This was most apparent at St. Tims where the interview data from education faculty was greatly influenced by the timing of the visit.

Another limitation of this study was the use of self-perceptions of what occurred. While research has shown a correlation between perceptions of reality and the presence of that reality, this research does depend on self-perceptions. The use of multiple sources of evidence, and the fact that 12–16 faculty and administrators were interviewed on each campus were intended to mitigate this limitation, but nonetheless the consequences of using self-perceptions are not clear.

It was both fortunate and unfortunate that there was a variance of 1–5 years since each college implemented their policies. The differences in time were a disadvantage because it made it more difficult to compare outcomes across institutions. Because the effort to integrate service as scholarship into traditional reward systems is relatively new, and because this study is not longitudinal but rather investigates a rather short slice of time, this study is intended to capture short term consequences of the policy, not long term consequences. The subtleties of the consequences of personnel decisions based on a recent policy change will take time to be felt, and this study was not able to capture all of the long-term consequences.

This study does not answer questions about rewards other than the promotion and tenure system, and only explored outcomes for tenure-track education faculty. Because of the confidential nature of the promotion and tenure process it was not possible to ascertain with certainty the number of faculty who would not have been promoted without the change in policies.

Despite these limitations, this study is significant because it is the first of its kind to study how colleges integrate service as scholarship into their reward system. It is the first study to examine the organizational change process that led to these changes and to explore the criteria used to assess service as scholarship in promotion and tenure.

Section III: Implications

What do these findings mean for practice? The following statements present policy implications based upon the findings and conclusions of this study. The main audience for these implications are those who want to establish policies to assess service as scholarship. The fourth section provides recommendations based on the findings for the education discipline, and leaders of research universities.

For Those Who Want to Establish Policies to Assess Service as Scholarship

The experiences of these four institutions suggest a set of lessons for academic leaders (Presidents, Provosts, Deans, department chairs or faculty) considering developing policies to assess and reward service as scholarship for promotion and tenure as well as higher education leaders attempting other kinds of organizational change. The cases are instructive for their successes as well as their failures. In PSU and St. Tim's cases, campus leaders met their goals of redefining scholarship to include service, disseminating and implementing new promotion and tenure policies, and completing the first test cases. Erin College and MWSU experienced problems in dissemination and implementation that resulted in few major policy outcomes. However, all four campuses experienced outcomes from policy development and attempts at implementation. In addition, all four campuses faced similar barriers in implementing these policies. Lessons drawn from these four examples are provided below in the areas of managing academic culture, assessing service as scholarship, and managing outcomes.

Managing Academic Culture

Match rewards to faculty talents and institutional mission.

While institutions have unique features and cultures depending on their missions, histories and goals, increasingly they are responding to pressures that emphasize their similarities (Birnbaum, 1988). Institutional isomorphism, where institutions model their research standards for faculty after the most prestigious universities in order to increase their national standing (Jencks & Reisman, 1968), occurred in each of the four cases. Institutional isomorphism caused four different types of universities with different missions to begin to exclusively reward research or prioritize research for promotion and tenure. This occurred despite the fact that each campus had a strong and distinct service mission and was a different institutional type. For example, PSU had an urban metropolitan service mission, MWSU had a land-grant service mission, and Erin College had a social justice service mission. While St. Tim's service mission was not as imbedded in their culture as it was in the others, there was a significant history of applied scholarship. Before the 1980s, most faculty understood St. Tims as a place that valued teaching and service over traditional research.

Whether it was a majority of faculty (at MWSU), or a minority of faculty (at Erin College), on each of the four campuses during the late 1980s and early 1990s the faculty experienced a metamorphosis in which allegiance to discipline and national reputation slowly began to take priority over more local issues such as teaching and service. To different degrees, faculty at each of the institutions developed into what Gouldner (1957) has called "cosmopolitans" rather than "locals." Faculty became more influenced by invisible colleges or networks of colleagues at other institutions, and believed that scholarly work was always tied into larger discipline-related national issues, rather than local issues. This became most true at MWSU and less so at Erin College where the principle was operating but there were still more "local faculty." The idea that faculty work should be linked to a discipline's "invisible college" became an important and ingrained mental model in faculty members' minds.

Birnbaum (1983) has pointed out the dangers inherent in this kind of homogenization in higher education. Different kinds of institutions are needed to fulfill the different roles and responsibilities in American society and if all institutions begin to mimic Harvard in reward system and in emphasis, we loose an important and valuable diversity within higher education.

This study suggests that institutions with strong teaching and service missions which develop faculty reward systems that favor research will likely experience a fragmentation of sorts, where faculty become dissatisfied with the disconnection between institutional mission, faculty interests, faculty workload, and rewards. Says Gamson (1997), "We need to get over the traditional research culture that has sapped the vitality of most of our colleges and universities by drawing faculty away from commitment to their institutions and communities. The denigration of applied research and problem solving has further eroded higher education's connection to the world. The domination of research and publications in tenure and promotion decisions has had a chilling effect even on those faculty members who wish to engage as citizens outside of their institutions" (p. 13).

In addition to the havoc this disconnect causes for faculty, campuses that extol the virtues of faculty service while rewarding research miss out on major opportunities to actually become leaders in what they do best. Most colleges and universities can only hope to be in the middle to bottom percentile of research output and prestige. On the other hand, these same colleges can be leaders in the areas of knowledge application and transmission. Since many baccalaureate, masters, and doctoral universities attract faculty who are most skilled in engaging in teaching and service as scholarship, it makes sense to match institutional rewards with the areas in which their faculty most excel and that are most consistent with the institutional mission.

Boyer's Scholarship Reconsidered *may help institutions return to their roots.*
Ironically, just as isomorphism caused these four institutions to move away from their teaching and service missions and toward research, it became a necessary prelude to the development of policies to assess service as scholarship because it forced these institutions to re-examine their missions and faculty strengths. This reexamination led to the adoption of Boyer's multiple forms of scholarship that allowed institutions to regain some balance between institutional mission and faculty rewards.

National efforts to redefine scholarship have had a significant effect on muting the trend toward solely rewarding research as scholarship for promotion and tenure. These efforts were effective because they came at a time when baccalaureate, masters, and some doctoral campuses were questioning how they had gotten so far away from their teaching and service missions and at a time when research institutions needed an alternative way to acknowledge those faculty who wanted to work in research universities but emphasize teaching and service. Boyer's (1990) *Scholarship Reconsidered* provided a framework for colleges and universities to acknowledge the talents of those within their ranks who were responding to the public's call for faculty to respond in socially useful ways. In other words, national and institutional attempts to redefine scholarship helped many colleges and universities to redirect their efforts away from trying to imitate institutions that were trying to become Harvard and toward their own unique strengths.

There are roles for leaders at every level.

Singleton, Hirsch, and Burack (1997) studied successful campus service programs and found that three kinds of leadership were needed to make them work: entrepreneurial, advocacy, and symbolic leadership. In addition, institutional savvy was key. This study found four kinds of leadership present in presidents, provosts, deans, promotion and tenure committee members, and service scholars. Presidents and provosts made the greatest contributions in the areas of symbolic leadership and advocacy; mid-level managers and service scholars in the areas of entrepreneurial leadership and institutional savvy. The lesson for other campuses considering the development of similar promotion and tenure policies is that there are many concrete contributions different campus constituencies can make throughout the process.

Provosts can play a critical role in sparking conversations about rewarding service as scholarship on their campuses, provide a vision, launch the effort, choose the right people for leadership positions and support them, help to guide committee work toward campus ratification, provide faculty development and promotion and tenure committee training and guidance, and articulate over and over again why the campus is pursuing this effort and why it is important. In addition, presidents and provosts can provide structural and financial support to promote service as scholarship on campus. However, it is critical that Provosts do not make changes on their own; rather, the process needs to be campus wide. PSU's Provost showed foresight by sending faculty leaders to national conferences where redefining scholarship was discussed. He created and built faculty allies. This is only one example of the kind of behind-the-scenes supportive strategies that can be used by high level administrators to move the process forward. Many academic leaders in this study spent a great deal of time providing faculty development sessions and workshops on the new policies and helping candidates as they prepared to "make their case." These efforts increased faculty confidence in their work, elevated the quality of documentation of service as scholarship, and thereby supported implementation.

Mid-level administrators have been described as the invisible leaders of higher education (Young, 1990). Mid-level administrators are crucial to the development of policies. They can act as cheerleaders, work to fashion democratic processes, gain faculty consensus, draft documents and keep committee processes on track. However, there are limits to their power and they alone cannot be responsible for implementation.

While at some campuses the cultural capital of leaders who had been there a long time aided the change process, (e.g., Erin's Provost, St. Tim's Dean and Faculty Director, and PSU's Provost), newcomers also played a key role in guiding change (e.g. PSU's president and MWSU's Vice Provost). Consequently, this study suggests it is not necessary for academic leaders to have been at an institution for a certain amount of time before they can make a difference in this regard.

Leaders need to be able to understand, manage, and change cultures.

Schein (1992) has said that the next generation of leaders will need to: understand the culture in which they are embedded, surmount their own taken-for-granted assumptions, orchestrate events and processes that enable groups to evolve toward new cultural assumptions, have the ability to induce cognitive redefinition by articulating and selling new visions and concepts, recognize that cognitive redefinition only occurs in the heads of many members if they are actively involved in the process, and have the willingness and ability to involve others and elicit their participation in change processes. Indeed, these are exactly the kinds of skills academic leaders developing policies to assess service as scholarship will need. These skills will help them to understand the barriers they face in their own academic culture and the resources they need to make the policies succeed. It is crucial that leaders have in mind who will be implementing the policy and who will be making sure the policy is followed at every step of policy development.

Kerr (1982) has noted the tendency for colleges and universities to resist change and stick with the status quo because it is the only option that cannot be vetoed. Each of these four campuses were attempting change against the resistance of a very powerful status quo since some degree of research culture had permeated each of their faculty evaluation systems. Bergquist (1992, p. 228) has claimed that "to understand the resistance experienced in any collegiate organization to a new idea or innovative program, one must first determine the way in which the idea or program will be interpreted by those now there—in light of their past history in the organization and the organization's dominant culture." Campus leaders interested in making changes to the reward system need to spend ample time "sizing up" how the changes will be accepted or rejected by their campuses' dominant academic culture. They need to understand all of the elements and resources that kept the former practice in place and assume that there is more than just a piece of paper between their idea and it's implementation.

Leaders also need to take timing into account and whether the institution is in a place of readiness to launch a particular organizational change. For some institutions, there may be times when the development and implementation of policies to assess service as scholarship may not be best for the institution.

Schein (1985) has stated that a culture can be changed only when "implicit and silent assumptions" are "brought to the surface and confronted" (p.306). In this study the leaders of all four campuses made assumptions that if they expanded the concept of scholarship to include more than research, and then confirmed the new expanded definition of scholarship as official policy, research would no longer maintain a privileged position in faculty evaluation. However, as Thomas Kuhn (1970) pointed out in, *The Structure of Scientific Revolutions*, it is difficult to change the surface of an organization or process without altering the very paradigm that created the organization or process. These campus leaders did not consider the effect of faculty hiring choices, the national stature and prestige associated with research, the well-defined indicators of quality in research and less defined indicators in teaching and service. They did not confront the assumption faculty held about "scholarship" from their graduate school training and socialization. The political nature of promotion and tenure decisions, potential faculty resistance, methods of dissemination, and who would be held responsible for ensuring policy compliance were not addressed, or only partially addressed, in the strategies used to develop and implement the policies. In other words, leaders did not always have a full view of the culture in which they were embedded or surmount their own taken-for-granted assumptions. Academic leaders should take note of this mistake and initiate conversations throughout their policy development that take into account such barriers and entertain potential solutions. In addition, faculty expectations for scholarship, and for reward systems, need to be considered by academic leaders in designing and implementing faculty assessment.

Leaders need to take advantage of crisis, opportunity, and institutional culture to shape change.

Academic leaders in each of the four institutions utilized unexpected events (such as a budget crisis or 10 million dollar grant) and more foreseeable aspects of their institution's culture (such as the tendency toward collegial decision-making or history of applied scholarship) to move their institutions forward in an organizational change process.

Siehl (1985) identified several triggers that induce culture change: environmental crises, environmental opportunities, and internal revolutions. Academic leaders can shape how environmental crises such as budget deficits, or internal revolutions like faculty dissatisfaction with the reward structure, are interpreted by the campus and how they impact future directions.

Bolman and Deal (1991) have suggested that one way to view organizations is through a symbolic frame in which "cultures are propelled more by rituals, ceremonies, stories, heroes and myths, than by rules, policies and managerial authority" (pp.15–16). Unique cultural characteristics of each of these campuses or foreseeable aspects of institutional culture were also used by academic leaders to shape change.

It is important that academic leaders work with what they already know about their institutions, as well as internal or external crises and opportunities that arise unexpectantly, to move their institutions closer toward their institutional mission.

Deans, department chairs, and senior faculty are critical to successful policy implementation.

All universities, but especially large universities with fairly autonomous colleges of education, need to be mindful of getting the local units (the colleges and departments that will later be asked to interpret and implement the policies) involved in decision-making. In cases where there is an autonomous College of Education, the deans, department chairs, and senior education faculty need to be on-board from the very beginning of new policy development. If this is not possible, it is better that each college be asked to develop their own separate policies to assess service as scholarship so that it is thoroughly discussed and decided upon among faculty and administrators within the College of Education.

Deans exercise a great deal of indirect power over faculty through their control of resources (Wolverton, Wolverton, & Gmelch, 1999). The larger, more complex, and more competitive the environment, the greater potential for Deans to experience role conflict and ambiguity (Ryan, 1980). Deans can become caught between the expectations of their departments and those of central administration (Baldridge, 1971). In this study, deans were especially important in the larger universities in establishing a culture around acceptance or rejection of the idea of service as scholarship. Because deans of colleges of education are so influential in overseeing reward systems, new policies to assess service as scholarship are unlikely to be implemented if they do not have dean support.

Department Chairs are reported by both tenure track and non-tenure track faculty to be the most important players in faculty's work roles and workload, chances for promotion, salary/compensation, role in governance, professional development support, academic freedom, and professional status (Chronister & Baldwin, 1999). Because department chairs oversee workload assignments and recommendations for promotion and tenure, their approval of new policies to assess service as scholarship is also key to policies' success.

Senior faculty most often hold key positions within departments, serve as chair of promotion committees, and select and mentor junior faculty. Consequently, they can act as roadblocks for change, thus, maintaining the status quo, or as shepherds of cultural change within a college. For this reason, their involvement in policy development is crucial. In this study senior faculty resistance and opposition at times worked against successful policy implementation. If leaders had made more concerted efforts to gain their support from the beginning, they may have avoided this problem.

The process used to develop and implement policies is important.

Each of the four campuses in this study were chosen for having made exemplary attempts to assess service as scholarship. Yet even among these four campuses there were successes and failures in implementing the policies. While each of the campuses succeeded at some level, their success was relative to the situation on their campus and how well or poorly service was assessed before the changes. Nonetheless, the findings from this study suggest that the process used to bring about the changes, the "means" to the "end" can have a significant impact on campus community, faculty satisfaction, and the development of faculty consensus on institutional mission and purposes. For example, PSU, St. Tim's, and MWSU's leaders, facilitated highly democratic inclusive processes. They developed many ways to solicit feedback, include dissenting opinions, distribute multiple drafts to key decision-makers, and as one administrator put it, "listen people to death." The double strategy of genuinely including a diversity of opinions in each stage of the process and quelling potential opposition by making everyone feel as if they were a part of the process, led to greater campus community and faculty satisfaction among all involved in policy changes. On the campuses where faculty were involved in the development of policies they felt more responsibility and ownership for them and there was a greater chance they would be disseminated and understood.

Academic leaders on all four campuses understood the importance of the "process" in creating change. Erin's provost regretted not having involved more faculty in development of their policies for this reason. Academic leaders who pay careful attention to the process as well as the products of policy change and try to create as democratic and inclusive a process as possible, may not only make the policy implementation more successful but also enrich academic community and individual faculty views of scholarship.

Making formal and informal performance expectations explicit is key to successful policy implementation.

This study suggested that when informal performance expectations are used to make promotion and tenure decisions and these informal expectations are not made clear to candidates, both the institution and their faculty lose as faculty become preoccupied and unproductive as they struggle to understand what is expected of them. Consequently, academic leaders should strive to make informal and formal performance expectations consistent. Changes to promotion and tenure policies need to be formally announced and re-announced so that they are made available to every faculty member in clear unambiguous language. Also, informal promotion and tenure committee preferences for certain kinds of documentation, such as the relative value of journal articles and grant funding, should not be secrets but explained to candidates when they are first hired. The process by which committee members decide whether and how well the candidate has contributed to the college needs to be made explicit.

Assessment of Service as Scholarship

The best policies are specific and comprehensive.

Gamson and Finnegan (1996) have pointed out that faculty are socialized "to be members of their disciplines in graduate school and become steeped in values, beliefs, and methods espoused by invisible colleges (p. 172)." Therefore, "when the institutional mission is not used to define the criteria and standards within faculty personnel policies, faculty are encouraged to apply the professional standards by which they were socialized, that is, the culture of research (p.172)." For this reason and because the area of assessing service as scholarship is, as Russ Edgerton (1995) has described, "messy," and a relatively new effort, the best policies will allow for flexibility but will leave little to interpretation. In this study, PSU's policy provided the best example of a specific and comprehensive policy, but even in this case, committee members struggled with areas that were not clearly defined.

The best policies to assess service as scholarship: separate out service as scholarship from disciplinary related service, governance, and community service; provide examples of service as scholarship in different disciplines, and of external service that is not scholarship; list specific guidelines for documentation of service as scholarship; require a scholarly profile or narrative where faculty can make the case that their service is scholarship; provide specific criteria for assessing service as scholarship; and identify appropriate evaluators of service as scholarship. Effective policies account for differences between indicators of quality for teaching, research, and service.

Especially for the move from associate to full professor, policies should address specific ways service as scholarship can achieve regional or national recognition, adequate dissemination, and peer review.

Scholarship Reconsidered is an important resource.

On all four campuses, Boyer's *Scholarship Reconsidered* played a significant role in guiding the committee discussions, policy implementation, and the assessment of service as scholarship. Boyer's *Scholarship Reconsidered*

provides a strong intellectual foundation for campus discussion about multiple forms of scholarship, for the development of policies, and for the
assessment of service as scholarship. It should be considered a primary and
effective resource for other campuses developing and implementing similar
policies.

*Institutional policy-makers and committees need to consider key ques-
tions before reviewing candidates.*

In each of the four cases in this study, institutional policy-makers failed
to address important aspects of assessing service as scholarship in the written policies. Promotion and tenure committees then found that they had
multiple questions and/or disagreements about how to assess certain
aspects of portfolios in the middle of reviewing candidates for promotion.
Since consensus had not yet been achieved on these issues before the discussion began, this sometimes lead to inconsistency in decisions. Policy-
makers need to work with promotion and tenure committees to come to
some consensus and clarity on the interpretation of the policies and what
they mean for the assessment of service as scholarship. At the very beginning of the academic year, policy-makers should work with promotion and
tenure committees to consider the following questions before they start
reviewing candidates with service as scholarship portfolios: Will relationship-building, and the development of ethical reciprocal partnerships count
toward the evaluation of scholarship? If so, how much? Will we assign
individual merit to collaborative work and how? Will we consider paid and
unpaid service equally? Will we allow for fewer publications in lieu of different kinds of writing products? Will we accept newer research methodologies like qualitative inquiry, phenomenology, or participatory action
research, where the findings are presented in a more practitioner and perhaps less theoretical construction? By answering these and related questions first, promotion and tenure committees can eliminate some of the
inconsistency that occurs when these decisions are made on a case by case
basis.

*Assessing service as scholarship may change the nature of faculty evalua-
tion and faculty roles.*

Making Outreach Visible (Driscoll and Lynton, 1999) describes a
process of documentation where service scholars were, "trying to fit their
service scholarship to the protocols of traditional scholarship," and struggling. One service scholar, Warren Rauhe, is quoted as saying, "My outreach activities are not meant to be a substitute for traditional research
scholarship. They represent a new paradigm." As the participants in
Driscoll and Lynton's (1999) Kellogg-funded project documented their
service as scholarship, they found that some criteria traditionally used to
evaluate research, such as the universal categories of goals, questions, and
methods, were also applicable to the documentation and assessment of

service as scholarship. However, they also found that they needed to use other criteria specifically relevant to service as scholarship, and not used to evaluate teaching and research. Likewise, the documentation and the assessment of service as scholarship in these four cases unearthed some important challenges to the typical indicators of quality scholarship.

The traditional criteria of academic expertise as a criterion for scholarship assumes that the faculty member is an expert and that their unique knowledge in a subject area is the chief characteristic that makes them a scholar in any given situation. Yet in service settings where faculty work with practitioners and community members on collaborative projects they are trying to create as Judith Ramaley (1998) has said, "reciprocal movements between the university's knowledge and community knowledge." The faculty member is acting as a facilitator of the many sets of knowledge he/she and others bring to the table and perhaps is "learning" as much as they are "teaching." Service as scholarship may suggest a new role for faculty who are not as "set apart" from those they serve as teachers are from students or researchers are from their subjects, and whose expertise is not only content knowledge but also skill knowledge in integrating, synthesizing, connecting and accepting knowledge in partnership with other "experts" in community settings. Complementing this trend is the new emphasis on undergraduate teaching, qualitative research methodologies, and the service mission of higher education that are quietly changing how higher education works.

The traditional criteria of peer review suggests that only those colleagues who have the same or greater content knowledge as a faculty member are appropriate evaluators of the scholarly nature of the faculty member's work. Although student evaluations are taken seriously in evaluating teaching as scholarship cases, peer review of teaching and curriculum review by other faculty members are often considered higher forms of evaluation for this reason. Service as scholarship questions the premise that those who receive services or are partners in delivering service are not appropriate judges of scholarly quality. If one were to imagine the service as scholarship enterprise as half in the domain of academe, and half in the domain of practice, then why not give legitimate voice to those who live in the practitioner world and can judge the usefulness of a new model in practice? Braskamp and Ory (1994) have stated that nonacademic colleagues, including recipients of outreach, can provide a "unique and valuable perspective to faculty evaluation," and encourage campuses to "rely more heavily on the perspectives and judgments of a greater variety of sources (Braskamp & Ory, 1994)."

Finally, the tradition of academic writing as the preferred method of dissemination of scholarship is being questioned. Faculty who engage in service as scholarship apply theory in service settings to solve problems. These faculty are asking, "Is scholarship a process or a product or both?"

In other words, are service projects without writing products automatically disqualified as forms of scholarship? Furthermore, to whom should the service as scholarship be disseminated? If one of the main purposes of knowledge application is to make a significant change in the way practitioners act and think, then isn't dissemination to practitioner communities an appropriate measure of scholarship? Rewarding only the product and not the process of scholarship in assessment is limited (Braskamp & Ory, 1994). If assessment of service as scholarship values only written products faculty will be encouraged to engage in short-term projects rather than more complex, controversial projects because they will be rewarded for writing more articles from more products (Braskamp & Ory, 1994). Promotion and tenure committees should find ways to balance the weight they give to the process and the product of scholarship.

The acceptance and assessment of service as scholarship may begin to change faculty roles. As more and more campuses rethink how they evaluate and reward their faculty members' outreach, more and more faculty may begin to see their roles as a scholar and teacher differently.

Assessment needs to include faculty development.

In each of the four cases in this study faculty received inadequate feedback in yearly reviews and after promotion and tenure decisions on how to improve their service as scholarship. The assessment of service as scholarship needs to include an element of faculty development so faculty understand "which behaviors to improve and which to retain (Braskamp & Ory, 1994)."

Candidates need help.

Many of the candidates with service as scholarship portfolios in this study would not have been successful without the assistance of a more senior faculty member or administrator who guided them in documenting and presenting their work. Integrating service as scholarship into reward systems is much like creating a new culture. New members must be oriented into the new system. More experienced and senior faculty should take leadership in mentoring junior faculty in engaging in, and documenting service as scholarship for promotion and tenure. "By not mentoring we are wasting talent. We should be concerned with capitalizing on young professional's talent (Wright and Wright, 1987, p. 207)."

Candidates for promotion and tenure who use service as scholarship portfolios need help from other faculty, department chairs, promotion and tenure committees, deans and others in crafting their case. They need help in clarifying the scholarly questions that guided their study, identifying the literature and conceptual framework employed in descriptive terms. Candidates need help considering how to document their service as an ongoing process, rather than as the outcomes of different activities. They need to be guided to consider the audience and purpose of the information in their portfolio, to document individual contributions and expertise instead of the entire project team's impact, and to locate the activity in the department and institutional mission. In addition, faculty should be encouraged to integrate their teaching, service, and research as much as possible. Universities might consider establishing formal or informal mentoring programs in departments or colleges to facilitate this process.

Managing Outcomes

Finnegan and Gamson (1996) have demonstrated that a new cultural schema cannot be adopted wholesale without the resources to support it. In each of the four cases the new cultural schema introduced was a new definition of scholarship, and a policy to reward service as scholarship for promotion and tenure. In each case, resources were required for the successful implementation of the new policies. Each of the campuses needed three important resources to ensure effective policy implementation: an effective dissemination strategy; the acceptance and backing of senior education faculty, department chairs, and the dean; and time. It is important for academic leaders to try to predict which resources will be required to successfully institutionalize their policies and build as many of them into their implementation plan as possible. In addition, academic leaders need to prepare to manage unexpected and/or unintended outcomes from policy changes.

Successful policy implementation requires academic leaders to minimize the mixed messages that result from new faculty reward systems.

Randy Bass (1999) described the tenure process much like the panopticon in Foucault's *Discipline and Punish.* Faculty behavior is controlled by the threat of an unclear evaluation. While the faculty in this study did not experience their tenure systems quite as starkly, there is something to be said for the intense stress and anxiety that faculty endure when policies are left vague, and rhetoric and actual rewards are inconsistent.

In each of the four cases, faculty experienced significant dissatisfaction before policy changes and mixed messages after policy changes. Recognizing service as scholarship may be one way to reduce the anxiety felt by faculty about their chances for promotion and tenure, but it does not necessarily wipe out informal expectations and mixed messages about promotion and tenure communicated by colleagues. Academic leaders need to put every effort into narrowing the gap between rhetoric and actual reward systems, and between formal policies and what faculty are told informally by senior colleagues and promotion and tenure committee members about what it takes to get promoted.

Faculty are a university's most important investment. A faculty member who is tenured and becomes a permanent faculty member will cost that institution an average of two million dollars in compensation over a lifetime (Brown & Kurland, 1996 in Malone, 1999). Studies have shown the importance of early experiences of new faculty to long-term job satisfaction, commitment, motivation and productivity, (Boice, 1992; Chronister, Baldwin, & Bailey, 1991). Yet many faculty experience an absence of mentors, sense of isolation, and absence of clear feedback in their first few years as faculty (Whit 1991; Sorcinelli, 1992). A recent study of academics revealed faculty dissatisfaction with work environments, disillusionment with career progress, and consequences of stress (Gmelch, Wilke, & Lovrich, 1986). When faculty experience ambiguity about their role as academics, and what faculty activities their institution values, as were experienced by faculty in these four cases, the outcomes for individual faculty include increased tension, anxiety, emotional exhaustion, depression and decreased job satisfaction. The outcomes for organizations include decreased organizational commitment, job involvement, job performance and increased turnover (Fisher & Gitelson, 1983 in Malone, 1999). Therefore, it is in the best interest of colleges and universities to work hard at minimizing the mixed messages that can arise from implementing new faculty reward systems.

In addition, it is important to note that this study has important implications as a critique of traditional promotion and tenure systems. Promotion and tenure have been the main features of the academic reward system for faculty for most of the 20th century (Chait, 1995). Chait (1995) notes that despite the controversy promotion and tenure has not changed significantly in the last decade. This study suggests that there are many problems inherent in how faculty evaluation works as a system. Academic leaders and faculty need to take a good hard look at the assumptions promulgated and reinforced by their evaluation system and if they do not support their mission, consider re-engineering faculty evaluation and promotion and tenure.

Policies to assess service as scholarship may increase faculty satisfaction.

It is not fair for institutions to publicly claim that they reward faculty service and then exclusively reward research for promotion and tenure. Faculty know this. In this study, the development and implementation of policies to assess service as scholarship had a powerful psychological and symbolic effect in reducing the stress and resentment faculty felt at being under-valued, over-worked, and under-paid. The policies made service scholars feel safer, more appreciated and understood, and thereby made them feel more committed and loyal to their institutions. The policies also had a symbolic purpose: they acted as a procedural contract, or symbolic armor, wherein faculty engaged in service as scholarship assumed that if they met all of the criteria for assessing service as scholarship, they would be promoted.

All around the country faculty are engaged in service without any formal rewards. For example, in a 1995 survey of faculty in the New England region conducted by the New England Resource Center for Higher Education (NERCHE) 92% of faculty said they were encouraged to engage in professional service, but only 31% said explicit criteria were used to document and evaluate professional service in promotion and tenure decisions at their university. In the, "Faculty Attitudes and Characteristics: Results of a 1995–1996 survey," 78.2 percent of all faculty in the study reported having performed service in the community in the last two years, and 59.2 percent of faculty noted that their institution was committed to the welfare of the local community (Chronicle, 1996). The lack of a consistent reward system for service as well as teaching activities leaves faculty with mixed messages about how to spend their time. If for no other reason, policies to assess service as scholarship should be created in order to satisfy, value, reward, and retain those faculty who fulfill their institution's service mission.

Policies to assess service as scholarship may help women faculty. Most of the service scholars interviewed in this study were women. On average, women publish less than men on average and earn lower salaries but report spending more time on teaching and service (Long and Fox, 1995). Most reward systems value research productivity above all other types of faculty work. Therefore, the outcomes of policies that revise the reward system to increase rewards for teaching and service are critical to the status of women in the academy. Creamer (1998) has stated:

> The profile of faculty across this country has remained so stubbornly homogeneous because of the reluctance to relinquish traditional measures of faculty productivity. A narrow definition of what constitutes a contribution to knowledge represents only a fragment of academic discourse, and it awards the privilege of an authoritative voice to only a few scholars. Expanding the definition of scholarship will benefit minority, female, and male academics alike.

While faculty satisfaction increased at all four institutions in this study, it is likely that policies to assess service as scholarship will have the greatest influence in institutions where rewards had previously not existed for service as scholarship and in places where a significant amount of faculty time is devoted to service as scholarship.

Test cases influence perceptions of policy success or failure.

In each of the four institutions the very first faculty to apply for promotion under the new guidelines were watched very closely by other faculty. The outcomes of their cases were interpreted as proof of the success or failure of policy implementation. Provosts, Deans, department chairs, and promotion and tenure committee members need to manage the messages that emanate from the first few test cases of new policies. Inevitably, an entire department or college may be looking at these cases and making judgments as to whether or not new policies are being followed. This is both fortunate and unfortunate and the culture around this issue needs to be carefully managed by policy advocates. Because of the secrecy of promotion and tenure decisions, it is not always clear whether a candidate had a suitable portfolio to make the case that their service is scholarship. Yet, if the candidate claims publicly that they were doing service as scholarship, and was rejected, it appears to their colleagues as if the policies were ignored. Likewise, there may be candidates with community service portfolios who are successful, and this sends a message that the policy is working even though it is not discerning between community service and service as scholarship. Academic leaders need to manage these messages by encouraging candidates, promotion and tenure committee members, and faculty not to speculate on the meaning of every case, while encouraging them to look for a pattern over a series of cases to confirm progress toward policy objectives.

Service scholars need to be supported.

C. Wright Mills (1959) said that, "scholarship is a choice of how to live, as well as a choice of a career." Service scholars are faculty with rare gifts for discovering and applying knowledge in community settings. They have chosen a particular kind of scholarship, which they find consistent with their values, to frame their career. Singleton, Hirsch, and Burack (1997) found that service scholars across several campuses consciously attended to links between service and high quality scholarship, garnered and creatively deployed institutional support and resources, had the flexibility to respond to changing situations and opportunities and conducted effective missionary work to other campus members to increase service visibility. Service scholars in these four cases employed the same set of skills and were important leaders in policy development and implementation. Service scholars need to be nurtured, supported, made visible, employed as mentors, and encouraged to serve on promotion and tenure committees. Whenever possible, service scholars should be consulted for their evaluation of other faculty members' service as scholarship-either as promotion and tenure members or as internal reviewers. Faculty who engage in professional service as scholarship, and universities that struggle with how to reward their work, are like pioneers on frontier land. They are part of a movement toward a different way of thinking of knowledge, scholarship, faculty roles, and the relationship of the university to the community. This movement needs to be supported.

Section IV: Recommendations

To those who want to build a service culture.

> A young, untenured professor does not need to be a heartless or craven careerist to find herself cut off from the very social problems and people that initially drew her to her discipline (Ansley & Gaventa, 1997, p.47).

This quote describes the experience of many new faculty who want to engage in service but are drawn away by pressures of research culture. The rise of research culture within colleges and universities is very instructive for those who are interested in constructing or strengthening service culture within colleges and universities. Finnegan and Gamson (1996) have argued that research culture is a cultural schema that grew through the support of resources. Key resources within academe include graduate school training, faculty hiring processes, travel funds, faculty and staff personnel lines, promotion and tenure systems, salaries, awards, and perhaps most of all "reputation and standing in the academic hierarchy" (Gamson & Finnegan, 1996). These resources were and are used to construct and strengthen research culture throughout higher education. These resources exist at the national level through disciplinary associations and at the local level in departments. If, as Gamson & Finnegan (1996) suggest research culture owes its prominent place in academic culture to this blueprint of resources, might not the same blueprint of resources be used to grow service culture within higher education?

For those faculty and policy-makers interested in strengthening the service culture of higher education, one attractive strategy is to try to access and use the same list of resources that increased the prominence of research. In other words, advocates of service culture would influence graduate student training and socialization so that graduate students developed skills and interests in service as scholarship, and create multiple opportunities across disciplines for young scholars to learn how to apply knowledge in community settings. Service advocates would work with disciplinary associations or create alternative associations which over time would develop discipline-specific approaches to apply knowledge, methods to assess service as scholarship, and spawn the creation of journals, web sites, and multi-media outlets where faculty involved in service as scholarship could disseminate their work across their discipline nationally. Endowed chairs and post-doctoral fellowships emphasizing service as scholarship would be created. Furthermore, advocates would find ways through Carnegie classifications and *U.S. News and World Report* to rank universities by their contributions to solving the problems of their communities and to applying knowledge in innovative ways. Once it was in the best interest of deans and department chairs to reward service as scholarship based on external market-driven pressures; merit pay, salaries, and promotion and tenure rewards would follow.

However, there are others who argue that advocating for service as scholarship in colleges and universities is about more than just how faculty get rewarded. They see advocating for service as scholarship as a revolutionary attempt to change the values of higher education. Rather than creating similar national structures to assess and reward service as scholarship, which might strengthen the role of faculty member as expert, increase the differences between disciplines, and maintain the cosmopolitan nature of rewards, these advocates would question why regional and local contributions should not be given primacy. They would argue for graduate training and reward systems to value more collaborative scholarship, the skills of faculty who work on the borders of theory and practice, and for higher education to rethink the primacy of academic expertise among all of its values. In other words, they would not use the same resources to build a service culture, because they do not agree with the values and assumptions beneath those resources, and would rather transform higher education's values while building service culture.

Both views require a reinvention of higher education, an expansion of its view of itself and its role in society, and internal restructuring to better align faculty to collectively meet the needs of students and society. While it may not be likely or desirable that all of higher education will reorganize to meet society's needs for service as scholarship in either of these ways, advocates of service as scholarship can still use these strategies to craft colleges and universities with stronger service cultures. Some institutions will choose to emphasize research or teaching to the exclusion of their other missions. However, for those institutions that take up the call to transform higher education to become more involved in service, this is a good time to press for change. There are major generational changes within the faculty that present opportunities for retraining faculty and graduate student training (Rice, 1999). Collaborations between government and private businesses are breaking down knowledge boundaries between research universities and communities (Walshok, 1999). Finally, the growth of service-learning and participatory action research, and accountability pressures from state governments and the public make this a particularly good time for advocates of service culture to begin transformations that can take hold.

To the Education Discipline

This study set out to explore how colleges or units of education assess service as scholarship for promotion in tenure. Rather than finding a unique set of criteria developed by education faculty to assess service as scholarship, or a unique application of general criteria suited for education, this study found that the education discipline applied the same criteria in the same way as other disciplines. Academic leaders with a birds eye view of policy implementation across campus noted that education faculty were more receptive to the idea of evaluation, technical assistance, curriculum development, and professional development with schools as forms of scholarship than many other colleges where the polices were implemented. Nonetheless, this study showed no apparent education disciplinary lens framing the assessment of education candidate's service as scholarship. There were two likely reasons. First, in each case the criteria were not written by education faculty but an interdisciplinary group of faculty. Second, most of the criteria were modeled after Boyer's *Scholarship Reconsidered,* a source that was considered an authority in the emerging field of service as scholarship and therefore a model that did not need to be revised. It was not clear from this study whether discipline-specific criteria for assessing service would have been beneficial, and in which types of universities. However, the lack of involvement of education faculty in development or critique of policies to assess service as scholarship does have implications for the future of the education discipline.

Tierney (1999) has studied the current state of education faculty. Using NSOPF and NEA data as well as through site visits to twelve Colleges of Education, Tierney determined that education has become the field with the oldest faculty; education faculty ranked last in the time they spent on research activities and the highest in the time they spent on administration, contact hours with students, and "other activities;" and education faculty published fewer refereed articles than any other field. Tierney noted three implications from this data that are pertinent to this study. First, since senior faculty are frequently most vested in the system and least likely to accept changes in workload, roles, and responsibilities, and there are more senior faculty in education than in any other discipline, change within schools of education may be difficult. Second, there are fewer education faculty between 35 and 55 where, traditionally, leaders emerge. Third, because education faculty publish less than their peers, their intellectual importance to a college campus may be thought of as questionable.

Finkelstein (1995) argues that by attempting to make a place for themselves within universities as experts, education faculty have created hierarchies that differentiate them from K–12 teachers and others in the educational community outside the university. One of the mechanisms used to create this gap was the primacy of research in education faculty member roles. Despite attempts to gain legitimacy through research, Tierney's data shows that education faculty are often undervalued because they do not produce as much peer-reviewed writing as their peers in other disciplines, but do engage in a greater amount of teaching and service.

National efforts to redefine scholarship in the last ten years have presented a significant opportunity to the education discipline. They have come at a time when NEA, NASSP, AFT and other major educational associations, are extolling the virtues of college of education-school partnerships in settings like professional development schools. If university reward systems change to acknowledge teaching and service as scholarship, they will create greater capacity for education faculty to spend time on teaching and service, and for many colleges of education, finally be rewarding what education faculty do best. This is a timely, but so far unrecognized opportunity for education faculty to take leadership in defining criteria to evaluate what Donald Schön (1983) has called "reflective practice," and link their own teaching, research, and service to K–12 issues and student learning outcomes in both undergraduate and graduate education and teacher preparation. Education faculty could work with other disciplines on campus and teach them skills in knowledge application and in working with communities. Rather than being the least appreciated for their publication productivity, education faculty could finally be appreciated for their skills across Boyer's expressions of scholarship and for developing ways to assess and improve their own practice.

To all types of colleges and universities, including the research university.
    A major focus of this study has been the attempt by faculty and academic leaders to amend or transform research culture to assess and reward service as scholarship for promotion and tenure. The question arises: should all colleges and universities, including major research universities, dismantle or amend reward systems that prioritize research? The obvious answer is no. Just as we need institutions that prioritize teaching and service for promotion and tenure, we need research universities that lead the world in cutting-edge research in order to sustain diversity within American higher education and meet societies needs for new knowledge.
    This study demonstrated that institutions with strong teaching and service missions, service cultures, faculty strengths in service as scholarship, and a history of innovation, are most inclined to integrate service as scholarship into faculty evaluation and most likely to benefit from its inclusion. Consequently, public masters and doctoral institutions, often referred to as "comprehensive colleges and universities" are probably more likely than top-tier private research universities to adopt and benefit from policies to assess service as scholarship. A provost at a private research university might consider implementing such policies and conclude that they would result in their faculty engaging in less traditional research. If traditional research is the only or primary goal of the institution, faculty evaluation policies that assess service as scholarship might not be the best choice.
    On the other hand, there are reasons for all types of colleges and universities, including research universities, to consider rewarding service as scholarship and integrating Boyer's expanded view of scholarship into faculty evaluation. First, there has been a public call to all of higher education, not just certain kinds of universities, for greater knowledge application and service. Second, just about every U.S. four-year college espouses a service mission and attracts some faculty with skills in applying knowledge in community settings. If institutions intend to have even a few of their faculty fulfill their service mission, it is only fair that they reward those faculty members for their work. Consequently, institutions need appropriate measures to assess the quality of service as scholarship. Third, institutions that assess and reward service as scholarship are able to acknowledge different faculty strengths, match rhetoric, workload, and reward system, and create or sustain a service culture. This in turn can increase faculty satisfaction, which may increase institutional effectiveness. Fourth, for some disciplines,

faculty reward systems that acknowledge multiple forms of scholarship lessen the disadvantage professional schools and certain disciplines experience because of their faculties' tendency to prioritize teaching and service over research. Finally, polices that reward service as scholarship may enhance the quality of faculty service by creating more incentives for faculty to improve in this area. These policies may also create a more equitable playing field in promotion and tenure for women faculty who report spending more time on teaching and service. Therefore, there are reasons for all types of universities, including research universities to consider integrating multiple forms of scholarship into faculty evaluation.

Research universities are most valued for their ability to create new knowledge. In 1983, Ernest Lynton first noted the great disconnection forming between academic knowledge generated by faculty and the growing needs in society for applied knowledge. A gap was forming, and continued to form, between the knowledge generated by research universities and the actual application of that knowledge in practice. At the same time, Crosson (1983) noted a "professional subclass of service specialists" forming at the edges of research universities; faculty with skills in discovering and applying knowledge, but only being rewarded for the former. Since 1983, this field of service specialists has grown. For example, in 1997, when the first Ernest Lynton awards for service as scholarship were awarded, there were 12 nominees, in 1998 there were 15, and in 1999, 159. This study confirmed the presence of service scholars at all types of universities, including the research university. If faculty with strengths in discovering and applying knowledge exist within research universities, shouldn't they be brought in from the edges of their universities and rewarded for all that they do well? If service scholars are fulfilling a part of their institution's mission that very few other faculty are equipped or interested in addressing, don't research universities do themselves a service to make a place for them?

In "Reversing the Telescope" Lynton (1998) argued that institutions need to stop viewing faculty work in isolation and begin seeing the ways that faculty work contributes to common department, college, and institutional needs. It does not make sense for research universities to require all faculty to engage in service as scholarship. However, if service is an important part of the mission, it also does not make sense for research universities to ignore a faculty member's contribution to the collective work of that faculty in meeting all parts of that mission.

Research universities are the gatekeepers of higher education and have a disproportionate influence on the future direction of all colleges and universities (Checkoway, 1999). If higher education is going to take the lead in narrowing the gap between knowledge creation and knowledge application, then research universities must be involved and help to lead the way. Since research universities train the greatest number of future faculty, they could make a major contribution to preparing future scholars with skills in knowledge application and integration, and for roles that extend into their communities of practice. Since other universities look to research universities for leadership, they can begin to reward those faculty fulfilling the service aspects of their mission. Finally, Hollander (1999) has commented that one of the best things about research universities is that they are thinking places with deep discipline specific knowledge about issues and rich research methodologies with which to study phenomenon. Research universities can contribute to their own service mission, and the service mission of higher education by studying the most effective processes for the transmission of new knowledge to local community problems and issues as well as the reward systems, and structures within universities that make this work possible.

Section V: Topics for Future Research

This study demonstrates the need to conduct additional research on the development and implementation of policies to assess and reward service as scholarship. The organizational change process that created these changes is difficult and complex. Part of what makes the process so complex are all of the invisible participants and influences which impact why and how change does and does not occur.

Future research might examine the graduate student socialization and faculty socialization process that encourages faculty research interests and discourages faculty from involvement in service as scholarship. Furthermore, the role of disciplinary associations in encouraging faculty involvement in research over teaching and service should be studied.

Second, the findings suggest that service scholars would have likely engaged in service as scholarship without the benefit of official policies to reward their work. Service scholars reported that their decision to engage in service as scholarship had more to do with how they defined themselves personally and how they defined their role as an academic than it did with extrinsic rewards. Yet the findings also suggested that the policies influenced faculty behavior in terms of satisfaction, documentation of service as scholarship, and increased involvement in service as scholarship. This raises questions about the appropriate balance of intrinsic motivation and extrinsic rewards that deans and department chairs should encourage in order to elevate the status of service in their units. An additional line of inquiry for future researchers might study how and why these service scholars became committed to service as scholarship and what sustains them in the absence of extrinsic rewards. How can academic leaders nurture the interest and capacity for service as scholarship in their faculty?

A third line of inquiry might focus on the relative benefits of defining service as scholarship vis-à-vis simply rewarding all forms of service for promotion and tenure. The Erin College case raises an interesting question for related research. If an institution is not significantly influenced by research culture and is likely to value all forms of service equally to teaching and research for promotion and tenure anyway, is there a strategic advantage for faculty, the institution, or community in assessing and rewarding service as scholarship? An additional line of inquiry might compare similar types of universities and investigate how the concept and process of assessing service as scholarship versus rewarding all forms of service might improve the quality of service or faculty satisfaction. Do universities and faculty view their work and roles differently when service is assessed as scholarship as opposed to purely service?

Finally, it would be interesting to explore the impact of promotion and tenure systems that assess and reward service as scholarship more deeply. For example, one might explore the long term effects of policies to assess service as scholarship on faculty satisfaction, faculty recruitment, faculty definitions of scholarship, university-community relationships, and student learning outcomes. Interviews conducted with faculty and administrators five years after policy changes at St. Tim's suggest that it takes at least five years or more for an institution to fully adopt a new policy and for long-term effects to be seen. Further research could look at the costs and benefits of such policies across institutional types, differences in process, and discipline.

Conclusion

This book began with a story about Dr. Molly Hourihan and her outreach to a women's shelter. As she turned inward and looked for ways to document her work as scholarship, it became clear that faculty professional service is not one faculty member's story, but rather a story situated in a discipline, a college, and a university with its own rewards and culture. One of the major issues influencing the success of Dr. Hourihan's faculty professional service is the degree to which her university is prepared to support her.

Market forces in higher education push institutions toward the adoption of research culture and toward prioritizing research above teaching and service in faculty evaluation systems. Four colleges/universities in this study resisted this pressure (to some degree) and valued service as scholarship for promotion and tenure. However, this response is not the norm, and presents the question: Why would/should colleges and universities institute faculty reward systems that go directly against powerful market-driven forces? Why would colleges and universities make a decision that seems to go against their competitiveness in the academic market, academic socialization, disciplinary association interests, and the likelihood for major research funding?

One answer supported through this study are that external forces like budget crisis or grant opportunities, and internal forces like faculty dissatisfaction and academic leadership, can act as stimulus to move institutions to amend or change their reward systems.

Another answer implied by this study is that academic leaders and faculty took a good hard look at their colleges and universities and saw that their service mission, and their college's capacity to apply knowledge to community problems, was one of their institution's greatest strengths. At that point, academic leaders and faculty led their campuses toward rewarding service as scholarship because they thought it would move their institutions closer toward fulfilling their mission. They believed that if they were true to their service missions, and rewarded their faculty for who they were, and what they did best, that other benefits would follow. They recognized that their institutions would never have the research resources of Harvard, but that Harvard would never have their unique mission and faculty talent in transmission and application of knowledge. They decided to take a risk by loving what their institution already was, and building toward what it could become. Colleges and universities which follow in their lead and recognize, reward, and seek to improve upon what they do best, will likely improve their own institutional effectiveness and make a major contribution to the needs of society and diversification of American higher education.

Interview Questions for Faculty on Promotion and Tenure Committees

Introduction

The purpose of this interview is to better understand the reward system for faculty professional service at_____. I am interviewing faculty who are on the promotion and tenure committee, other faculty within the department, the Department Chair, and the Dean to understand the criteria and procedures for assessing service as scholarship for tenured and tenure track faculty.

I would like to tape record our conversation in order to save me the task of taking notes and to assure the greatest level of accuracy. Is that okay with you? The information you share will be kept strictly confidential, in that no names or departments will be associated with information used in the final report. If, for any reason you would like me to turn off the tape-recorder so that you may go completely "off the record" just indicate your wishes.

As a result of preliminary analysis of interview and survey results, I may need to contact you by phone to either ask additional questions or get clarifications. Do you have any questions or concerns before we begin?

Defining Scholarship

1. How do you define scholarship?

2. How does your definition compare with the definition used on the promotion and tenure committee?

3. What criteria does the promotion and tenure committee use to assess scholarship? What are the most important criteria?

4. What are the most important criteria to assess teaching? Research? Service?
    Probe: What accounts for the similarities or differences?

5. The purpose of my research is to look at how colleges of education are rewarding a specific kind of service which some call outreach, others call faculty professional service. By the term faculty professional service, I mean work done by a faculty member outside the university, based on their scholarly expertise and contributing to the service mission of the institution. An example of professional service would be a faculty member developing a professional development course for special education teachers covering the most current research and practice on developing Individual Educational Plans. By professional service I do not mean serving on a campus committee or chairing an AERA interest group. Do you believe professional service is a form of scholarship? (if no, skip next question) Can you give me examples of the kind of professional service you consider scholarship?

6. Consider two situations. One in which a candidate presented service work which everyone considered scholarship and one in which the candidate presented service work that was not considered scholarship. What was present in the first situation and what was missing from the second?

Procedures

7. This college adopted a policy in _____ on rewarding faculty professional service through the promotion and tenure system. Who developed these procedures and in response to what impetus?
>Probe: Who were the key players in making this happen? (Faculty, Chair, Dean, President, administration, legislature?)
>Probe: What were the critical events, steps, or ideological shifts that influenced the development and implementation of this policy?
>Probe: Were changes made to existing policies? Why?

8. What are the procedures through which service is recorded and reviewed?
>Probes: How are documents collected and analyzed?
>Probes: Are there people on the promotion and tenure committee with expertise in service scholarship?
>Probe: Are teaching, research, and service looked at together or separately?

Outcomes

9. How has the assessment process affected the amount of professional service, kind of professional service, or quality of professional service faculty engage in?

10. Has the assessment process altered the outcomes of the promotion and tenure process? How?
>Probe: What is the impact on the promotion and tenure decision of a candidate who has not done professional service?

11. Has the assessment process affected the way that faculty document service for promotion and tenure?

12. What are the positive and negative outcomes of the new procedures to assess service?

Culture

13. What were the major barriers to integrating professional service into the promotion and tenure system?

14. Rewarding faculty professional service is unusual. What enabled your university to do this?

> Probe: How has the mission of this institution influenced the effort to integrate faculty professional service into the promotion and tenure system?
> Probe: As the policy was developed, what was most helpful?

15. What does the institution do to support faculty professional service? (office space, student assistants, operational support, release time, seed money)

> Probe: Is there any professional development (i.e, workshops, mentoring, discussion groups) in your college for faculty professional service? If not, how do faculty learn new skills, become connected with service projects, etc?

16. How important do you think it is to evaluate faculty professional service as scholarship? Why not just reward service?

17. Do you think it was easier to make the case that it is important to reward service because this is a professional school (like business, journalism, nursing) or was it harder?

18. Are there a group of faculty engaged in service who work together on projects, communicate regularly and support each other? How is this supported by the administration? How do other faculty view their decision to spend time on these activities?

19. Have the new procedures influenced the perceived climate about service as scholarship? For example, would more people at your university today see service as a potential form of scholarship than say five years ago?

Interview Questions for Faculty within the College of Education

Introduction

The purpose of this interview is to better understand the reward system for faculty professional service at_____. I am interviewing faculty who are on the promotion and tenure committee, other faculty within the department, the Department Chair, and the Dean to understand the criteria and procedures for assessing service as scholarship for tenured and tenure track faculty.

I would like to tape record our conversation in order to save me the task of taking notes and to assure the greatest level of accuracy. Is that okay with you? The information you share will be kept strictly confidential, in that no names or departments will be associated with information used in the final report. If, for any reason you would like me to turn off the tape-recorder so that you may go completely "off the record" just indicate your wishes.

As a result of preliminary analysis of interview and survey results, I may need to contact you by phone to either ask additional questions or get clarifications. Do you have any questions or concerns before we begin?

Defining Scholarship

1 How do you define scholarship?

2. How does your definition compare with the definition used on the promotion and tenure committee?

3. What criteria does the promotion and tenure committee use to assess scholarship? What are the most important criteria?

Procedures

4. What are the procedures through which service is recorded and reviewed?
       Probe: How are documents collected and analyzed?

Probe: Are there people on the promotion and tenure committee with expertise in service scholarship?

Probe: Are teaching, research, and service looked at together, or separately?

Outcomes

5. How has the assessment process affected the amount of professional service, kind of professional service, or quality of professional service faculty engage in?

6. Has the assessment process altered the outcomes of the promotion and tenure process? How?

Probe: What is the impact on the promotion and tenure decision of a candidate who has not done professional service?

7. What are the positive and negative outcomes of the new procedures to assess service?

8. Has the new procedure influenced the way that you or other faculty document service for promotion and tenure?

9. Has the presence of an assessment process that rewards service influenced the decisions that you have made about the relative emphasis you place on teaching, research, and service? In your opinion, has it influenced the way other faculty make their choices?

Culture

10. What does the institution do to support faculty professional service? (office space, student assistants, operational support, release time, seed money)

Probe: Is there any professional development (i.e, workshops, mentoring, discussion groups) in your college for faculty professional service? If not, how do faculty learn new skills, become connected with service projects, etc?

11. Are there a group of faculty engaged in service who work together on projects, communicate regularly and support each other? How is this supported by the administration? How do other faculty view their decision to spend time on these activities?

12. Has the process influenced the perceived climate about service as scholarship? For example, would more people at your university today see service as a potential form of scholarship than say five years ago?

Questions for Department Chair, Dean, President, Academic Administrator

Introduction

The purpose of this interview is to better understand the reward system for faculty professional service at_____. I am interviewing faculty who are on the promotion and tenure committee, other faculty within the department, the Department Chair, and the Dean to understand the criteria and procedures for assessing service as scholarship for tenured and tenure track faculty.

I would like to tape record our conversation in order to save me the task of taking notes and to assure the greatest level of accuracy. Is that okay? The information you share will be kept strictly confidential, in that no names or departments will be associated with information used in the final report. If, for any reason you would like me to turn off the tape-recorder so that you may go completely "off the record" just indicate your wishes.

As a result of preliminary analysis of interview and survey results, I may need to contact you by phone to either ask additional questions or get clarifications. Do you have any questions or concerns before we begin?

Procedures

1. This college adopted a policy in _____ on rewarding faculty professional service through the promotion and tenure system. Who developed these procedures and in response to what impetus?

    Probe: Who were the key players in making this happen?
    (Probe): Faculty, Chair, Dean, President, administration, legislature?
    Probe: What were the critical events, steps, or ideological shifts that influenced the development and implementation of this policy?

Defining Scholarship

2. Could you give me an example of the kind of professional service you are trying to reward through this policy?

3. What criteria does the promotion and tenure committee use to assess scholarship? What are the most important criteria?

Outcomes

4. How has the assessment process affected the amount of professional service, kind of professional service, or quality of professional service faculty engage in?

5. How do you think this policy influences Junior. tenure-track faculty behavior?

6. Has the assessment process altered the outcomes of the promotion and tenure process?
> Probe: What is the impact on the promotion and tenure decision of a candidate who has not done professional service?

7. How has the assessment process affected the way that faculty document service for promotion and tenure?

8. What are the positive and negative outcomes of the new procedures to assess service?
> Probe: How have the new policies changed views of scholarship?

9. Has the way you coach Junior faculty about service and promotion and tenure changed over the last few years? If so, how?

10. What role have you played in getting candidates with strong service portfolios through the promotion and tenure process? How recently was that? Were they successful?

Culture

11. What were the major barriers to integrating professional service into the promotion and tenure system?

12. Rewarding faculty professional service is unusual. What enabled (allowed) your university to do this?
> Probe: How has the mission of this institution influenced the effort to integrate faculty professional service into the promotion and tenure system?
> Probe: As the policy was developed, what was most helpful?

13. What does the institution do to support faculty professional service? (office space, student assistants, operational support, release time, seed money)
> Probe: Is there any professional development (i.e, workshops, mentoring, discussion groups) in your college for faculty professional service? If not, how do faculty learn new skills, become connected with service projects, etc?

14. How important do you think it is to evaluate faculty professional service as scholarship? Why not just reward service?

15. Do you think it was easier to make the case that it is important to reward service because this is a professional school (like business, journalism, nursing) or was it harder?

16. Are there a group of faculty engaged in service who work together on projects, communicate regularly and support each other? How is this supported by the administration? How do other faculty view their decision to spend time on these activities?

17. Has the process influenced the perceived climate about service as scholarship? For example, would more people at your university today see service as a potential form of scholarship than say five years ago?

Mid-West State University Process

1988, September $10.2 million grant

1992, January   University committee formed

1995, March   Second committee formed

1996, September   *Indicators* published

1997, September   Provost sends *Indicators* to deans and department
                         chairs

School of Education Process

1982-1988   Dean Schreier works with Holmes group, develops
                         professional development schools.

1988   Dean Schreier acts as dean and associate dean for
                         Lifelong Education, writes a grant to restructure life-
                         long education.

1985-1990   Cohort of 8-10 faculty hired with service roles

1990-1991   Most of 8-10 faculty tenured and promoted

1993   Dean Hennessey arrives and begins making changes
                         in service expectations

1995   Dean Hennessey establishes a two-tiered system for
                       promotion, new informal rules and requirements for
                       service as scholarship

1997-1998   Promotion and Tenure Committee reviews four can-
                       didates that use the *Indicators* to make the case for
                       their service as scholarship.

REFERENCES

Adamay, D. (1994). Sustaining university values while reinventing university commitments to our cities. *Teachers College Record, 95*(3), 324–331.

Ansley, F. & Gaventa, J. (1997, Jan/Feb). Researching for democracy and democratizing research. *Change, 29*(1).

Antonio, A. Astin, H., & Cress, C. (2000). Community service in higher education: A look at the nation's faculty. *The Review of Higher Education.* Summer, 2000. Volume 23. No. 4.

Baldridge, J.V. (1971). *Power and conflict in the university: Research in the sociology of complex organizations.* New York: John Wiley & Sons.

Becher, T. (1989). *Academic tribes and territories: Intellectual inquiry and the culture of disciplines. The society for research into higher education.* Buckingham, England: Open University Press.

Berger, J. & Milem, J. Dey, E.L. (2000) Faculty time allocation: A study of change over 20 years. *Journal of Higher Education.* Vol 71, No 4.

Bergquist, W.H. (1992). *Four cultures of the academy.* San Francisco: Jossey-Bass.

Bernstein, A.B. (1994). *Knowledge utilization universities.* Boston: New England Resource Center for Higher Education.

Birnbaum, R. (1983). *Maintaining diversity in higher education.* San Francisco: Jossey-Bass.

Birnbaum, R. (1988). *How colleges work.* San Francisco: Jossey-Bass.

Blackburn, R.T. & Wylie, N. (1985, March). *Current appointment and tenure practices: Their impact on new faculty carreers.* Paper presented at the annual meeting of the Study for Higher Education, Chicago, IL.

Bledstein, B.J. (1978). *The culture of professionalism.* New York: W.W. Norton & Company.

Boice, R. (1992). Lessons learned about mentoring. In *developing new and junior faculty* (M.D. Sorcinelli & A.E. Austin, eds.). San Francisco: Jossey-Bass.

Bok, D. (1991). Universities and the search for a better society. In J.L. Bess (Ed.), *Foundations of American higher education* (pp. 688–698). Needham Heights, MA: Pearson Custom Publishing.

Bok, D. (1982) *Beyond the ivory tower.* Cambridge, MA. Harvard University Press.

Bolman, L.G. & Deal, T.E. (1991). *Reframing organizations: Artistry, choice and leadership.* San Francisco: Jossey-Bass.

Boyer, E. (1990). *Scholarship reconsidered.* Princeton, NJ: Carnegie Foundation for the Advancement of Teaching.

Boyer, E. (1994, March 9). Creating the new American college. *Chronicle of Higher Education, 40,* A18.

Braskamp, L.A. & Ory, J.C. (1994). *Assessing faculty work: Enhancing individual and institutional performance.* San Francisco: Jossey-Bass.

Bringle, & Hatcher (2000). Institutionalization of service-learning in higher education. *Journal of Higher Education.* Vol 71, No 3.

Brown, R.S. & Kurland, J.E. (1990). Academic tenure and academic freedom. *Law and Contemporary Problems 53,* 325–355.

Campoy, R.W. (1996, March). Teacher education goes to school. *The American School Board Journal,* pp. 32–34.

Carnegie Foundation for the Advancement of Teaching. (1996, September 13). Survey: Faculty attitudes and characteristics: Results of a 1995–1996 survey. *Chronicle of Higher Education, 43,* A12

Carnegie Council on Policy Studies in Higher Education, (1976). *A classification of institutions of higher education* (Rev.ed). Berkeley, CA: University of California Press.

Chait, R. (1995). The future of academic tenure. *Priorities, 3,* 1–11.

Chait, R. (2001). *Questions of Tenure.* Cambridge: Harvard University Press.

Checkoway, B. (1997) Reinventing the research university for public service. *Journal of Planning Literature* No 11. pp 308–319.

Checkoway, B. (1999, July). *Opening plenary session.* Presented at the Strategies for Renewing the Civic Mission of the American Research University, Wingspread Conference, Racine, WI.

Checkoway, B. (2001). Renewing the civic mission of the American research university. *The Journal of Higher Education.* March/April. pp. 125–147.

Chronister, J.L. & Baldwin, J.V. (1999, June). *Non tenure track faculty.* Comments made at Harvard University, Graduate School of Education.

Chronister, J.L. Baldwin, R.G. & Bailey, T.G. (1991, November). *Full-time non-tenure track faculty: Current status, future prospects, remaining research questions.* Paper presented at the annual meeting of the Association for the Study of Higher Education, Boston, MA.

Clark, B.R. (1987). *The academic life.* Princeton, NJ: The Carnegie Foundation for the Advancement of Teaching.

Creamer, E. (1998). *Assessing faculty publication productivity: Issues of equity* (J. Fife, Ed). Washington, DC: Association for the Study of Higher Education.

Crosson, P.H. (1983). *Public service in higher education* (J. Fife, Ed.). Washington, DC: Association for the Study of Higher Education.

Dey, E.L., Milem, J.F., & Berger, J.B. (1997, March) *Changing patterns of publication productivity: accumulative advantage or institutional ismorphism?* Paper presented at the meeting of the American Educational Research Association, Chicago, IL.

Diamond, R.M. & Adam, B.E. (Eds.). (1995). *The disciplines speak.* American Association for Higher Education. Washington, D.C.

DiMaggio, P. & Powell, W. (1983). The iron cage revisited: Institutional isomorphism and collective rationality in organizational fields. *American Sociological Review 48*,147–160.

Driscoll, A., & Lynton, E.A. (1999). *Making outreach visible: A guide to documenting professional service and outreach.* Washington, DC: American Association for Higher Education.

Edgerton, R., Hutchings, P., & Quinlan, K. (1991). *The teaching portfolio: capturing the scholarship in teaching.* Washington, DC: American Association for Higher Education.

Edgerton, R. (1995). Foreword. In E.A. Lynton. *Making the case for professional service.* Washington, DC: American Association for Higher Education.

Elman, S.E. & Smock, E.M. (1985) *Professional service and faculty rewards: toward and integrated structure.* Washington, DC: National Association of State Universities and Land Grant Colleges.

Fairweather, J.S. (1996). *Faculty work and public trust: Restoring the values of teaching and public service in American academic life.* Needham Heights: Alyn & Bacon.

Fairweather, J.S. (1994). Faculty rewards: The comprehensive college and university story. *Metropolitan Universities, 5*(1), 54–61.

Fairweather, J.S. (1993). Faculty reward structures; toward institutional and professional homogenization. *Research in Higher Education, 34*(5), 603–623.

Fairweather, J.S. (1993, July–August) Faculty rewards reconsidered: The nature of trade-offs. *Change, 25*(4), 44–47.

Finkelstein, B. & Efthimiou, H. (1999) In search of status: Teacher education in the United States. In P. Morris & J. Williamson (Eds.), *Teacher education in the Asia-Pacific region : A comparative study.* New York : Garland.

Fisher, C. & Gitelson, R. (1983). A meta-analysis of the correlates of role conflict and ambiguity. *Journal of Applied Pyschology, 68*, 320–333.

Fox, M.F. (1985). Publication, performance, and reward in science and scholarship. In J.C. Smart (Ed.) *Higher education: Handbook of theory and research.* Vol. 1. Ediston, NJ: Agathon Press.

Gamson, Z.F. (1995, January/February). Faculty and service. *Change.*

Gamson, Z.F. & Finnegan, D.E. (1996). Disciplinary adaptions to research culture in comprehensive institutions. *The Review of Higher Education,* (19)2, 141–177.

Gamson, Z. (1997). Higher education and rebuilding civic life. *Change.* No 29. pp. 10–13.

Giles, D. E. & Eyler, J. (1998) A service-learning research agenda for the next five years. In R.A. Rhoads and JPF. Howard (eds.) *Academic service-learning: A pedagogy of action and reflection.* Pp- 73–80. New Directions for Teaching and Learning. San Francisco: Jossey-Bass.

Glassick,C.E, Huber, M.T., & Maeroff, G.I. (1997) *Scholarship Assessed.* San Francisco: Jossey-Bass.

Gmelch, W.H., Lovrich, N.P. & Wilkie, P.K. (1984). Sources of stress in academe: A national perspective. *Research in Higher Education,* 20, 477–490.

Gmelch, W.H., Lovrich, N.P. & Wilkie, P.K. (1986). Dimensions of stress among university faculty: Factor analysis results form a national study. *Research in Higher Education 24,* 266–286.

Gouldner, A.W. (1957). Cosmopolitans and Locals: Toward an Analysis of Latent Social Roles. *Administrative Science Quarterly,* 281–307.

Harkavy, I. & Puckett, J.L (1991). Toward effective university-public school partnerships: An analysis of a contemporary model. *Teachers College Record, 2, 556–583.*

Harkavy, I. & Puckett, J.L. (1994) Lessons from hull house for the contemporary urban university. *Social Service Review, 68, 299–321.*

Hirsch, D. (1996, May). An agenda for involving faculty in service. *AAHE Bulletin. 48(9), 7–9.*

Hollander, E. (1999, July). *Plenary session, action steps for advancing the cause.* Presented at the Strategies for Renewing the Civic Mission of the American Research University, Wingspread Conference, Racine, WI.

Hollander, E. & Hartley, M. (2000) Civic renewal in higher education: The state of the movement and the need for a natural network. In T. Ehrlich (ed), *Higher education and civic responsibility.* Phoenix, AZ Oryz Press.

Jencks, C., & Riesman, D. (1968). *The Academic Revolution.* Chicago: The University of Chicago Press.

Kennedy, D. (1997) *Academic duty.* Cambridge: Harvard University Press.

Kerr, C. (1963). *The uses of the univeristy.* Cambridge, MA: Harvard University Press.

Kerr, C. (1982). Postscript 1982. *Change*, 23–31.

Kirshstein, R. J. (1997, March) *What faculty do? A look at academic work.* Paper presented at the meeting of the American Educational Research Association, Chicago, IL.

Kuhn, T.S. (1970) *The Structure of scientific revolutions* (2nd ed.). Chicago: University of Chicago Press.

Lawson, H.A. (1990) Constraints on the professional service of education faculty. *Journal of Teacher Education 41*(4), 57–70.

Levine, A. (1994) Service on campus. *Change.*

Lincoln, Y.S. & Guba, E.G. (1986). *Naturalist inquiry.* Newbury Park, CA: Sage publications.

Long, J. and Fox, M. (1995). Scientific careers: Universalism and particularism. *Annual Review of Sociology, 21,* 45–71.

Lynton, E. A. (1995). *Making the case for professional service.* Washington, DC: American Association for Higher Education.

Lynton, E. A. (1991). *The Mission of metropolitan universities in the utilization of knowledge: A policy analysis.* Boston: New England Research Center for Higher Education.

Lynton, E.A. (1983). A Crisis of purpose: Reexamining the role of the university.*Change 15,* 18–23, 53.

Lynton, E.A. (1994). Knowledge and scholarship. *Metropolitan Universities 5,*(1) 9–17.

Lynton, E.A. & Elman, S.A. (1987). *New priorities for the university.* San Francisco: Jossey-Bass.

Lynton, E.A. (1998, March). Reversing the telescope. *AAHE Bulletin, 50,* 8–10.

Malone, R. (1999). *Tenure Track Faculty Socialization.* Unpublished doctoral dissertation, University of Maryland, College Park.

Merriam, S.B. (1988). *Case study research in education: A qualitative approach.* San Francisco: Jossey-Bass.

Maryland Higher Education Commission (1994). Documents collected for internal study of faculty workload issue.

Mills, C. W. (1959). *The Sociological Imagination.* New York: Oxford University Press.

National Center for Higher Education Statistics, (1990). *Institutional Policies Regarding Faculty in Higher Education.* Washington, DC: Author.

New England Resource Center for Higher Education (1996). Documents from "Program on Faculty Professional Service and Academic Outreach."

O'Meara, K.A. (1997). *Rewarding faculty professional service.* Boston: New England Research Center for Higher Education.

O'Meara, K.A. (1995). *Community service professionals: An emerging profession.* Masters thesis, The Ohio State University.

Patton, M.Q. (1980). *Qualitative evaluation methods.* Newbury Park, CA: Sage publications.

Peters, S. (1997) Public scholarship and the land-grant idea. *Higher Education Exchange.* Pp. 50–57.

Ramaley, J. (1999, July). *Concluding plenary session: What are the priorities? What are the next steps? What have we learned.* Presented at the Strategies for Renewing the Civic Mission of the American Research University, Wingspread Conference, Racine, WI.

Rice, R.E. (1991). The new American scholar: Scholarship and the purposes of the university. *Metropolitan Universities, 1,* 7–18.

Rice, R.E. (1993). Scholarly work and professional practice. *New directions for teaching and learning, 54,* 71–78.

Rice, R.E. (1996). *Making a place for the new American scholar.* Washington, DC: American Association for Higher Education.

Rice, R.E. (1999). (1999, July). *Roundtable discussion: Strategies and structures for institutional change.* Presented at the Strategies for Renewing the Civic Mission of the American Research University, Wingspread Conference, Racine, WI.

Riley, G & Baldridge, J. V. (1978). *Policy Making and Effective Leadership.* San Francisco: Jossey-Bass.

Rudolph, F. (1962). *The American college and university: A history.* Athens, GA. The University of Georgia Press.

Ryan, D. (1980). Deans as individuals in organizations. In D. Griffith and D. McCarty (Eds.) *The dilemma of the deanship.* Danville, IL. The Interstate Printers and Publishers.

Sandmann, L., Foster-Fishman, P.G., Lloyd, J., Rauhe, W., Rosaen, C. (2000) Managing Critical Tensions: How to Strengthen the Scholarly Component of Outreach. *Change.* January/February. Vol 32. No 1. pp 44–52.

Schein, E.H. (1985). *Organizational culture and leadership: A Dynamic view.* San Francisco: Jossey-Bass.

Schein, E. H. (1992). *Organizational Culture and Leadership.* (2nd ed.). San Francisco: Jossey-Bass.

Schön, D.A. (1983). *The Reflective practitioner: How professionals think in action.* New York: Basic Books.

Schön, D.A. (1995) Knowing in action: The new scholarship requires a new epistemology. *Change.* November/December. Pp. 27–34.

Schramm, W. (1971). *Notes on case studies of instructional media projects.* Working paper. Washington, D.C.: The Academy for Educational Development.

Scott, W.R. (1995). *Institutions and organizations.* Newbury Park, CA: Sage Publications.

Selfin, P. (1991). *The teaching portfolio: A practical guide to improved performance and promotion/tenure decisions.* Boston: Anker.

Senge, P.S. (1990). *The fifth discipline.* New York: Currency Doubleday.

Serow, R.C., Brawner, C.E., & Demery, J. (1999). Instructional reform at research universities: Studying faculty motivation. *Review of Higher Education, 22*(4), 411–423.

Sewell, W.H. (1992). A theory of structure: Duality, agency and transformation. *American Journal of Sociology, 98,*(1), 1–29.

Shulman, L.S. (1993). Teaching as community property. *Change 25, 6–7.*

Siehl, C. (1985). After the founder: An opportunity to manage culture. In P. Frost, L., Moore, M. Louis, C. Lundberg & J. Martin (Eds.) *Organizational Culture.* Newbury Park, CA: Sage Publication. 125–140.

Singleton, S. Burack, C.A., & Hirsch, D. (1997). Faculty Service Enclaves. *AAHE Bulletin,* Vol. 49, No 8.

Singleton, S. Hirsch, D., Burack, C.A. (1997) *Organizational structures for community engagement.* Boston, MA: New England Resource Center for Higher Education.

Solmon, L.C. & Astin, A.W. (1981). Departments without distinguished graduate programs: Reputational ratings in history, economics, english, chemistry, sociology, and biology." *Change* 13(9), 23–28.

Sorcinelli, M.D. (1992). New and junior faculty stress: Research and responses. In M.D. Sorcinelli and A.E. Austin (Eds.). *Developing new and junior faculty: New directions for teaching and learning,* (Vol. 50. pp. 27–37). San Francisco: Jossey-Bass.

Taylor, H.L. (1997) No more ivory towers: Connecting the research university to the community. *Journal of Planning Literature.* No 11. pp. 327–332.

Tierney, W.G. & Bensimon, E.M. (1996). *Promotion and tenure: Community and socialization in academe.* New York: State University of New York Press.

Tierney, W.G. (1999, January). *Faculty of Education in a Period of Systematic Reform.* Paper presented at Faculty Roles and Rewards Annual Conference. San Diego, CA.

Trower, C.A. (1996) *Tenure snapshot.* Washington, DC: American Association of Higher Education.

Tuckman, H.P. (1976). *Publication, teaching, and the academic reward structure.* Lexington, MA: Lexington Books.

U.S. Department of Education. (1993). National Center for Education Statistics, National Study of Postsecondary Faculty, "Faculty survey" and 1988 National Survey of Postsecondary Faculty, "Faculty Survey."

Viechnicki, K.J., Yanity, D. & Olinski, R. (1997, March). *Action research in a school/university partnership.* Paper presented at the meeting of the American Educational Research Association, Chicago, IL.

Veysey, L.R. (1965). *The emergence of the American university.* Chicago: The University of Chicago Press.

Walshok, M. (1999, July). *Concluding plenary session: What are the priorities? What are the next steps? What have we learned.* Presented at the Strategies for Renewing the Civic Mission of the American Research University, Wingspread Conference, Racine, WI.

Walshok, M.L. (1995). *Knowledge without boundaries.* San Francisco: Jossey-Bass.

Ward, K. (1998) Addressing academic culture: Service-learning, organizations and faculty work. In R.A. Rhoads and JPF. Howard (eds.) *Academic service-learning: A pedagogy of action and reflection.* Pp- 73–80. New Directions for Teaching and Learning. San Francisco: Jossey-Bass.

Washington, R.O. (1993, November). *Implementing the urban mission of an urban American university.* Presented at the Fourth Annual Conference of the Alliance of Universities for Democracy, Budapest, Hungary.

Whitt, E.J. (1991). Hit the ground running: Experiences of new faculty in a school of education. *The Review of Higher Education 14,* 177–97.

Wolverton, M., Wolverton, M.L., & Gmelch, W.H. (1999). The impact of role ambiguity on academic deans. *Journal of Higher Education,* 70(1), 80–106.

Wright, C.A., & Wright, S.D. (1987). Young professionals. *Family Relations 36* (2), 204–208.

Yin, R.K. (1994). *Case study research: Design and methods. Applied Social Research Methods Series, Vol. 5.* Newbury Park, CA: Sage Publications.

Young R. B. (1990). *The Invisible Leaders.* Washington, DC: National Association of Student Personnel Administrators.

Index